C000129904

The universe
of risk

FINANCIAL TIMES
Prentice Hall

In an increasingly competitive world, it is quality
of thinking that gives an edge – an idea that opens new
doors, a technique that solves a problem, or an insight
that simply helps make sense of it all.

We work with leading authors in the fields of
management and finance to bring cutting-edge thinking
and best learning practice to a global market.

Under a range of leading imprints, including
Financial Times Prentice Hall, we create world-class
print publications and electronic products giving readers
knowledge and understanding which can then be
applied, whether studying or at work.

To find out more about our business and professional products,
you can visit us at www.financialminds.com

For other Pearson Education publications, visit
www.pearsoned-ema.com

Pearson
Education

The universe
of risk

How top business leaders control risk and achieve success

Pamela Shimell

FINANCIAL TIMES
Prentice Hall

An imprint of **Pearson Education**

London · New York · Toronto · Sydney · Tokyo
Singapore · Hong Kong · Cape Town · New Dehli
Madrid · Paris · Amsterdam · Munich · Milan · Stockholm

PEARSON EDUCATION LIMITED

Head Office:
Edinburgh Gate
Harlow CM20 2JE
Tel: +44 (0)1279 623623
Fax: +44 (0)1279 431059

London Office:
128 Long Acre
London WC2E 9AN
Tel: +44 (0)20 7447 2000
Fax: +44 (0)20 7240 5771
Website: www.financialminds.com

First published in Great Britain in 2002
© Pamela Shimell 2002

The right of Pamela Shimell to be identified as Author
of this Work has been asserted by her in accordance
with the Copyright, Designs and Patents Act 1988.

ISBN 0 273 65642 2

British Library Cataloguing in Publication Data
A CIP catalogue record for this book can be obtained from the British Library

This publication is designed to provide accurate and authoritative information in regard to the
subject matter covered. It is sold with the understanding that neither the author nor the publisher is
engaged in rendering legal, investing, or or any other professional service. If legal advice or other
expert assistance is required, the service of a competent professional person should be sought.

The publisher and contributors make no representation, express or implied, with regard to the
accuracy of the information contained in this book and cannot accept any responsibility or liability
for any errors or omissions that it may contain.

10 9 8 7 6 5 4 3 2 1

Designed by Claire Brodmann Book Design
Typeset by Pantek Arts, Maidstone, Kent.
Printed and bound in Great Britain by Biddles Ltd, Guildford and Kings Lynn.

The Publishers' policy is to use paper manufactured from sustainable forests.

About the author

Pamela Shimell is Managing Consultant at the risk management and strategy consulting firm PRISCONSULT.

She previously worked in Assurance and Business Advisory at Arthur Andersen where she launched a new UK risk management competency, Environmental Risk Consulting. While at Andersen she worked in the UK and world-wide on assignments in teams of up to 44, with professionals from global corporate finance, business risk consulting and assurance, energy and utilities, petroleum products, tax, real estate, Anderson legal and business consulting.

Before that she was managing director of Industry & Environment Associates (IEA), Oxfordshire. She is known for having devised the first comprehensive corporate environment policy for a UK client, and is one of the leading practitioners of stakeholder risk consulting. She has advised clients on staff training, public affairs and crisis management.

She has been a contributor to *Investors Chronicle*; *Thames Valley Business* magazine; *Waste, The Sunday Times Business News* and *The Times*. Previous publications include *A Trouble-Shooter's Guide to Environmental Management Systems* (Kogan Page); *Directors' Environmental Liabilities* (Arthur Andersen client publication, 1999); *Greening the Workplace* (first draft for the Trades Union Congress, 1991); *Corporate Environmental Policy in Practice* (International Journal of Strategic Management, Long-Range Planning, 1991); and *Corporate Environmental Policy* (Institute of Directors Manual, 1991). She has given presentations to many conferences in the UK and mainland Europe, and was featured as one of three significant practitioners in *The Greening of Business*, the BBC TV programme on environmental auditing.

She is married with two sons, Simon, aged 20, who is reading philosophy at the University of Sussex, and Robert, 23, who works in the IS department at Invesco Perpetual, Oxfordshire.

Her specialities in consulting are in business start-ups; managing change; strategy; renewable energy; and environmental, ethical and social risk. She has provided expert advice to three study groups on renewable energy and electricity from renewable sources set up by the European Union's Economic and Social Committee (ECOSOC).

Contents

Preface

By John Richards
Joint Managing Director,
Société Générale Asset Management

This book by Pamela Shimell gives us a variety of perspectives on business risk and what it means to the different players on the stage. She shows that there is a new willingness among companies to incorporate risk assessment and management in the business decision-making process, and this is well covered in Parts I to IV, Corporate commitment, Knowledge management and the New Economy, Key issues and players, and the Universe of risk, as well as in the interviews with British and American-based consultants and business leaders in Part V Corporate survival and the dynamics of change. Management style and decision-making in the 'old' and 'new' economies are discussed in revealing interviews.

As a fund manager, evaluating public companies and managing investments in them on clients' behalf, I am always interested in understanding how management control their business and in the overall structure of corporate governance. It tells you something about the people and the culture of the firm.

> "I am always interested in understanding how management control their business and in the overall structure of corporate governance. It tells you something about the people and the culture of the firm."

Since the adoption of the Combined Code and the Turnbull report, standards of governance have undoubtedly been raised across the board. However, it has not eliminated the prospect of companies going badly wrong because of poor risk control, and in some sense the shock to expectations is all the greater as investors can be falsely comforted by the apparent existence of an adequate governance infrastructure.

Whatever management systems are in place, it is people who run companies. Paradoxically the more clarity and accountability in the management structure, the more authority and discretion a CEO has in the short term. Long term, the consistent shortening of the average tenure of a CEO shows us the other side of the accountability coin.

As managers of institutional or pension fund assets, our clients expect us to be their representatives in ensuring that corporate governance standards are upheld. This role can also stretch to SRI (Socially Responsible Investment) and the environment. Although we embrace this role willingly, I sometimes wonder whether as external observers we are really in a position to make an informed judgement on how risks are managed in a business. We may not have the detailed knowledge of each company's risk management systems that the board and the auditors have. We are reliant on accurate disclosure in accounts and other documents to determine whether there are any obvious gaps. The analysis is not as precise and easily comparable as it is with financial data. Every business is different, and investors can profit by asking management the right questions about their attitude to risk, and how they control it.

What we are most focused on is understanding the risks that can have the biggest impact on shareholder value. These are often factors that management will be coy about in the public arena. For example, for a utility, the management of regulatory risk is key, but this means that a company can be in a permanent state of negotiation, occasionally akin to a game of bluff. This is hardly the stuff of maximum transparency. Equally, to understand the risks of a company missing opportunities or succumbing to threats, we need to have an understanding of how effectively the management team operates and how the individuals relate to each other. These things are a matter of inside knowledge. Businesses run too autocratically are inherently dangerous, but we have to distinguish between strong leadership and tyranny. We also know that, within limits, companies can meet disclosure requirements of an adequate governance structure without necessarily doing so in spirit. Standards are being raised across the board, but the search for exceptional opportunities and dangers continues.

> **Businesses run too autocratically are inherently dangerous, but we have to distinguish between strong leadership and tyranny.**

The New Economy bull market, as we see in the comments of Giorgio Anania, President and CEO of Bookham Technology, was characterized by a 'land grab' mentality. Speed of execution was the priority because 'money was for free'. The subsequent bust has been painful and will no doubt have exposed shortcomings in risk management in many cases.

The key to any boom is how it is financed. In this boom the stock market did the job it is supposed to do in that it was equity finance that supplied most of the fuel for the investment boom and not bank debt. If it had been debt, in many cases we would be looking at quite a significant financial disaster.

Managing the financing risk and allocating the 'free' equity capital was the key decision that determined the establishment and ultimate survival of companies.

For a time the equity market took on the role of a venture capitalist but on a giant scale and without the experience to control the excess or the ability to leave the party.

That the technology and telecoms bubble developed to the extent that it did is a source of embarrassment to many investment professionals. Of course the forces of fear and greed, that so often dominate the direction of a market, played their part. But for a bull market to become a bubble there has to be something systemic that prevents normal countervailing forces from regulating the excess. I would point the finger at the combination of more widespread index-tracking investing, which provides a block of buying power at any price, and the investment processes increasingly adopted by the institutional investors.

> **Of course the forces of fear and greed, that so often dominate the direction of a market, played their part.**

Investment 'risk' to most institutional fund managers is the likelihood that the performance of a security or a portfolio will deviate from that of the relevant benchmark index. The risk that your client's capital may be sharply impaired or enhanced in the short term is not, to many fund managers, a dominant concern. Many fund managers will have explicit or implicit restrictions on the extent to which their portfolios can deviate from the construction of the index. This can result in counter intuitive behaviour and reinforces the 'herd instinct' for which investors are often rightly condemned. The more that a particular sector rises and the more its market capitilization is boosted by IPOs, the more investors will tend to capitulate and buy into it regardless of recent price movements. They do this to control the deviation from the index. Even worse, in their own terms they are *reducing* not *increasing* risk by doing so.

A sector that represents 2 per cent of the index can be ignored. A sector that represents 8 per cent cannot without having a large impact on a portfolio's propensity to track the index. As the IT and telecoms sectors rose in 1999/2000, the shares became more and more expensive, which in turn encouraged more companies to issue shares to capitalize on the rich valuations – thus ballooning the weighting of those sectors in the index. Rather than act as a deterrent, the expensive valuations stimulated more buying, driven by capitulation on the part of institutional investors and the continuing speculative demand from the private investor. This phenomenon of effective forced buying by institutions is, in my view, the key to why the bubble was unchecked. As long as investment risk is so narrowly defined then the suspension of common sense will be a recurring phenomenon.

John Richards is Joint Managing Director, Société Générale Asset Management (SGAM), where he is responsible for strategy and for developing the asset allocation policy for clients' portfolios. A senior UK equity fund manager, he graduated in 1983 from University College, London with an honours degree in economics. Before co-founding SGAM in 1997 he was a director at Mercury Asset Management, where he was a member of the management committee for MAM's world-wide business, and Chairman of the Asset Allocation Group.

Acknowledgements

I t is difficult to know who to mention first in acknowledging all the support, information and inspiration that so many people have provided to make this book a reality.

First, I should like to say a big thank you to John Richards of Société Générale Asset Management, who read the manuscript online and wrote the Preface. He performs a valuable service to the book in adding a new perspective – that of the professional investment manager. He makes some very important points on the realities of corporate governance, on disclosure and on what I call 'director risk', a sub-division of 'people risk'.

Second, there are all the people mentioned in these pages who have shared their management skills and experience. Many of them I did not know before this project started. So a big thanks to them – and I hope we can stay in touch and remain friends.

Third, I owe an enormous debt to my two sons Robert and Simon, who keep me in touch with the New Economy and show me that there are new generations for whom shopping online, mobile phones and using computers are as natural as going to the opera, gardening and drinking malt whisky. I owe a particular debt to Robert who works in the IS department of Invesco Perpetual for helping me out with the graphics.

I have, over the years, learned a great deal from all my consulting clients. Because of them I have developed knowledge, skills and experience which have led me into new areas of business and knowledge. I have always said that I learn as much from clients as I teach them. We are all in the business of sharing.

I felt very comfortable after just one meeting with Laurie Donaldson, Senior Acquisitions Editor at Pearson Education. His soft Scottish humour makes him a joy to work with. Many thanks too to publishers Financial Times Prentice Hall.

August 2001

Executives featured in this book: UK

Name	Position	Organization
David Gamble	Executive Director	AIRMIC
Jon Symonds	Chief Financial Officer	AstraZeneca
Peter Morgan	Chairman	Baltimore Technologies
	Non-executive Director	Oxford Instruments
	Ex-chairman	Pace Technology, NPI, IBM
Philip Thomas	Litigation Lawyer	Bass
Anthony Cherry	Head of Risk Management	Beachcroft Wansbroughs, Solicitors
Dr Giorgio Anania	President & Chief Executive Officer	Bookham Technology
Gareth Hayward	Stockbroker	Charles Stanley Asset Management
Heiko Haasler	Brand Manager	De La Rue
David Thomas	Director	EffiSoft
Richard Pursey	Managing Director	Global Continuity
Allan Leighton	Chief Executive	Going Plural
	Chairman	lastminute.com
	Chairman	bhs
	Chairman	Race for Opportunity
	Non-exec Director	Wilson Connolly Holdings
	Non-exec Director	British Sky Broadcasting (BSkyB)
	Non-exec Director	Leeds United FC owners Leeds Sporting
	Non-exec Director	George Weston
	Non-exec Director	Consignia
	Non-exec Director	Dyson
		ScottishPower
Anthony Lee	Director	KLegal
Leonie Power	Solicitor	KLegal
Peter Morriss	Global Head of Information Risk Management	KPMG
Andrew Steet	Partner, Technology Assurance Services	KPMG
Sir Peter Michael	Founder/shareholder/	Classic FM
	Former trouble-shooter	PM Winery
		Virtual Music Stores
		Global Continuity and others
		Cray Electronics, etc
Peter Keen	Managing Director	Merlin Biosciences
Jonathan Pockson	Chief Financial Officer	Microscience
Stephen Barlow	Group Chief Internal Auditor	Prudential
Richard Gossage	Head of Group Risk	The Royal Bank of Scotland Group
John Richards	Joint Managing Director	Société Générale Asset Management (SGAM)
Adam Turner	Managing Director	Virtual Music Stores

Executives: USA

Name	Position	Organization
Arthur C. Ciccolo	Department Group Manager, Information and Knowledge Management	IBM Research Division, Hawthorne, New York
Susan Rucker	Partner Head of Enterprise Risk Consulting	KPMG New Jersey, USA
Steven A. Ballmer	President and Chief Executive Officer	Microsoft Corporation
Jeffrey S. Raikes	Group Vice-President, Productivity and Business Services	Microsoft Corporation
Beverly J. Hirtle	Vice-President	New York Federal Reserve
Mary Harris	Vice-President	PA Consulting, Washington DC
Brian Fullerton	Global Director of Risk Management	Merrill Lynch Investment Managers Princeton, New Jersey
Lawrence J. Amon	Chief Financial Officer	National Wildlife Federation, Reston, Virginia

Introduction

Risk, recession and the New Economy

Managing business risks in the 21st century New Economy is a very different proposition to managing risk in the closing years of the 20th century.

The New Economy has transformed business. It is powered by technology-dominant professionals. The knowledge often resides with the youngest members of the corporate community.

From 1995 to 2000 the business growth pattern of the TMT (technology, media and telecommunications) sector which started to dominate western economies was like a juggernaut racing at full speed. It was characterized by years of exponential growth such as had never been seen before.

The companies concerned came to dominate economies and stock markets by their rapid growth, profits and asset bases. Then suddenly in 2000/2001 the juggernaut shuddered to a halt. Many CEOs admitted they could no longer predict corporate growth further ahead than the next week. In 2001 John Roth, Nortel Networks' Chief Executive, bluntly told the world: 'It is not possible to provide meaningful guidance for the company's financial performance for the full year 2001.' It was a shock to the markets. Few were prepared for the fact that the Canadian networking equipment-maker could no longer forecast its performance for the rest of the year.

Few were prepared for "the fact that the Canadian networking equipment-maker could no longer forecast its performance for the rest of the year.

By early 2001 Cisco Systems, which in November 2000 was enjoying a growth rate of more than 70 per cent, suffered the 'fastest deceleration that any company had ever experienced', said Michelangelo Volpi, Cisco's Chief Strategy Officer. It was to lay off 8,000 employees immediately, 17 per cent of its payroll. The share price fell by more than 40 per cent in the first quarter of 2001. The US economic downturn would continue for 'at least three more quarters' and possibly longer, said John Chambers, Cisco Chief Executive.

Even Jack Welch of GE admitted: 'I can see GE's visibility for 75–80 per cent of the business clear as a bell…but for the short-cycle businesses, I don't see it.'

If the rise and rise of world stock markets in the closing years of the 20th century was powered by TMT stocks, the lapse into world economic recession and a bear market in 2000/2001 is just a sign that the technology juggernaut has stopped for fuel. It could not continue at the speed it was going without a pit-stop.

The relapse into zero growth (or worse) for much of the technology sector is not a victory for Old Economy companies and values. New technology and values will not go away. The best features of the New Economy are ingrained. Increasingly business is based on an information technology infrastructure: PCs, e-commerce, e-procurement, e-security. Knowledge, and the speed at which it is transmitted, is the new infrastructure of business.

Even the smallest companies today have websites and are internet-focused. E-mails now accomplish a large part of what the fax, the courier, the phone and human relations used to achieve. Although the phone and personal contact will always be vital elements in business success, they are used less in relative terms.

While the world economy and stock markets were in growth mode, risk management was neglected by many companies – although its growth as a board-level 'must-have' is charted in this book. In a recession risk management becomes critical.

Adam Turner, Managing Director of VMS (page 279), Giorgio Anania of Bookham Technology (page 42), and Jonathan Pockson, Chief Financial Officer of Microscience (page 214), talk of what it is like working in companies at the sharp end of technology in the 21st century.

'You have to manage the culture in your organization and resist all the demands for security and stability and all that. Accept that the faster technology gets, the more you have to create an environment and a culture that gets used to change, that is comfortable with change,' says Turner.

'I have never seen anything like the type of phenomenal speed which you have in the fibre-optics industry,' Anania told me. 'It changes all of your conceptions of how you run a business. In 2000 money was for free. Literally you could get a billion dollars by snapping your fingers. So the only thing that mattered was how quickly you could do things.'

> **In 2000 money was for free. Literally you could get a billion dollars by snapping your fingers.**

Pockson says: 'I am an accountant. But I have been in biotech for 10 years and I feel the excitement of bioscience. Although biotech is risky, it is incredibly rewarding. The capital growth the company can generate is incredible.'

These names and companies are new. But established Old Economy executives relish risk-taking. 'The outcome isn't always going to be as you predicted,' says Sir Peter Michael of Classic FM. 'I like doing things that are very, very intriguing. I love the whole challenge of it. I'd like to think that it was calculated. Financial risk is paramount. It normally takes three times as long as you think it will. Once you commit to something you have to be prepared to have deep pockets. What that means is that, in making an investment, pretty roughly you need to think in terms of putting in one third at the start, and have a balance of two thirds left for later.'

'Businesses won't grow without taking risks,' says Allan Leighton, Chief Executive of Going Plural, formerly Chief Executive of ASDA (page 265). 'But you can really mitigate that risk. That's in the planning and the execution. And that's not always to do with time. It's to do with the quality of the planning and the quality of the execution.'

Hans Rausing, who for many years managed the Tetra Pak empire, believes in 'risk minimization through risk maximization. There is no way you can succeed in business by playing safe. It is always less risky to take risks'.

'If you have 100 per cent security, you have 100 per cent inactivity,' says Peter Morriss, KPMG's Global Head of Information Risk Management.

And Microsoft's Bill Gates says, 'To be a market leader you have to have what Jim Collins calls "big hairy audacious goals". You can't look at just the past or current state of the market. You have to look at where it's likely to go, and where it might go under certain circum-

> **To win big, sometimes "you have to take big risks.**

stances, and then navigate your company based on your best predictions. To win big, sometimes you have to take big risks.'

These guys are not playing roulette. Their risk-taking is calculated, knowledge-based and founded on experience.

Many aspects of risk management (people, reputation and ethical risk to name but a few) referred to only briefly in this book could have been dealt with in great detail, and indeed have to be in any corporate assessment and management of risks – as they are during my own consulting activities. Limitations of space, and the publisher's desire not to make this a technical manual, mean that they have not been accorded the detail they require in the real world!

About this book

Whereas in the past risk management was confined to operational functions such as accident and emergency response and financial risk, today the fundamentals of corporate risk management need to be embedded on a global scale. If this is not done reputations and business plans can be blown out of the water.

In Part I Corporate commitment (page 3), I argue that changes in corporate governance company law, pensions reporting and accountancy require board-level corporate commitment to risk management.

In Part II Knowledge management and the New Economy (page 13), I look at IT, IS (information systems), corporate self-knowledge, the external knowledge space and some New Economy companies.

Under Internal Knowledge Management, I suggest that many companies are neglecting the fundamentals of corporate survival. They fail to ask themselves, 'Where is/was the company going – yesterday, today and tomorrow? How will the business world in general look tomorrow? How do we combine robust Old Economy fundamentals with New Economy infrastructure to grow the company? And what are the risks involved?'

Under External Knowledge Management I look at how the internet gives the public, press and media, and investors instant information about corporate performance. Organizations therefore need to manage their external knowledge space to avoid risks to reputation, brand and the bottom line.

While the New Economy brings new growth opportunities, it also brings new risks. I look at some of the legal and financial risks posed by the New Economy.

In Part III Key issues and players (page 73), I show how the financial players are joined by non-financial players as environmental, social and ethical issues have risen up the business agenda. I talk to an American environment consultant, to a wildlife group finance director about Socially Responsible Investment (SRI), and to the head of AIRMIC, the British risk managers' association.

In Part IV The Universe of risk (page 97), I describe the need for an integrated, embedded, enterprise-wide risk management strategy based on a universe of risk model which I have devised, which 'captures' all significant risks. In this section risk and internal audit directors, and risk management and IT risk consultants from leading companies, describe their own risk management models.

Many organizations that do have a formal approach to risk are addressing the issue only superficially, or they are interested only in what risks will be on the horizon in the next 12 months. This is changing fast. It separates the organizations with vision and good management from the rest.

The investment community would also benefit from a more organized and comprehensive approach to risk – both within their own organizations and in terms of the questions they ask of the companies in which they invest their own and their clients' money.

In Part V Corporate survival and the dynamics of change (page 171), I talk to the other company chairmen, CEOs, finance directors, internal auditors and risk directors listed in the Acknowledgements. The Old and New Economy companies featured were chosen to reflect a cross section of profitable, loss-making, established and start-up companies; public and private companies and pre-IPOs; serial entrepreneurs and corporate men; clients, contacts and organizations and people with whom I was not previously acquainted.

We discuss their approach to risk management, and how they are managing the challenges to corporate survival and the dynamics of change.

I set out to write a simple but comprehensive guide to risk management, a 'hot' issue in management today, and to explore how a selection of companies and executives manage risk.

The book is not intended to go into detail but to give a broad brush view of risk management as a professional discipline as it is developing at the start of the 21st century. There are many, excellent books on individual aspects of risk management, particularly financial and operational risks; and on new risk areas such as weather risk and other derivatives. I have not attempted to cover those here.

The views expressed in this book are the opinion of the author who accepts no liability for any actions based on these views taken by readers or others. The author shall, to the extent permitted by law, have no liability, contingent or otherwise, whether caused by the negligence of the author to the reader or to third parties for the accuracy, timeliness, completeness or reliability of the statements in this book, including, but not limited to, inaccuracies or errors in or omissions from quotes and financial or other data.

Nothing set forth should be construed as a recommendation to purchase or sell any product or instrument or to enter into any transaction, or as a representation for any company mentioned in this book. Any discussion of risks does not constitute a complete discussion of the risks of operating any organization but is merely a commentary on the state of the art at the time of writing in August 2001.

PART I

CORPORATE
COMMITMENT

What is risk? 1

Before we look at the drivers for a greater corporate commitment to risk management, it's important to be clear about what we mean by 'risk' and 'risk management'. So let's look at how various organizations and executives define risk.

AIRMIC (the Association of Insurance and Risk Managers) defines business risk as 'the activity of protecting and profiting from corporate resources and assets'.

Ernst & Young defines business risk as 'an event or action that may adversely affect an organization's ability to maximize stakeholder value and to achieve its business objectives. Business risk arises as much from the possibility that opportunities won't be realized as it does from the possibility that threats will materialize'.

KPMG defines it as 'anything that prevents your organization from achieving a corporate objective. Dynamic entities won't avoid risk, but they will identify, measure and manage it on an ongoing basis, helping increase shareholder value'.

■ What is risk management?

The New York Federal Reserve defines consolidated risk management – integrated or enterprise-wide risk management – as 'a co-ordinated process for measuring and managing risk on a firm-wide basis'.

Stephen Barlow, Group Chief Internal Auditor at Prudential, defines risk management as 'the threat that internal and external events will adversely affect our ability to achieve our goals and hence impact value-creation. It may be that something good won't happen, or that something bad will happen. But taking well managed risks is essential for creating value'.

KPMG says it is 'about taking risks knowingly not unwittingly. An effective risk management structure allows an organization to understand the risks in any initiative and take informed decisions on whether and how the risks should be managed. Corporate governance and risk management is about how an organization can better understand its risk to improve its performance and deliver its objectives'.

Ernst & Young believes that 'a critical attribute of a successful business is the effectiveness of its risk management process: the better the process, the more certainty there is of prosperity and potential long-term competitive advantage'.

I like the definition of business management on the website of George Weston Limited, the $22 billion-a-year turnover Canadian food company.

'Tis the set of sails and not the gales, that determines the way they go.'

In other words management is about controlling risks, not being deluged by them. This definition might equally be applied to risk management.

An interesting insight is provided by Maurizi Castelli, head of the Federation of European Risk Management Associations (FERMA) and a senior executive at Pirelli. He says he knows more about the company than most of his colleagues because managing risk gives him 'hands on' experience of such a wide range of operations.

Why is risk moving up the corporate agenda?

The smart companies recognize that risk management is a board-level responsibility. New legal requirements and guidance on corporate governance, financial reporting, pensions and company law make it necessary to manage and report on business risk in a more holistic and accurate manner.

Corporate governance

A major reason why risk is moving up the corporate agenda is the requirements in many countries for better corporate governance. This is loosely defined as the system by which companies are directed and controlled.

These demands have been brought about by criticism of corporate management from a number of quarters, 'interested parties', financial and non-financial stakeholders. Some of these are described in more detail in Part III Key issues and players. The main areas from which this criticism has come are institutional investors, such as pension funds and insurance companies which are taking a more active part in protecting their investments; mass share ownership; environmental, ethical and social groups; and other non-government organizations (NGOs) and focus groups. Press, media and campaign groups have played no small part.

It has also been fuelled by the furore over large pay deals for senior executives. Whenever a company reports poor results or redundancies, this news is now invariably linked to the take-home pay and bonuses of the CEO.

> **" Whenever a company reports poor results or redundancies, this news is now invariably linked to the take-home pay and bonuses of the CEO.**

In the past, even with their fiduciary obligations, some executive directors have taken the short-term, strictly bottom-line, view. Indeed, company law reinforced this tendency. At worst, executive, and non-executive directors, have neglected those fiduciary duties.

The UK's legal requirements and guidance include:

- the Combined Code;

- the Turnbull report;

- FRS12 Provisions, Contingent Liabilities and Contingent Assets;

- new pension fund reporting requirements;

- Modern Company Law, the Final Report of the Company Law Review Steering Group.

In 1998, following the work of the Committee on Corporate Governance, the London Stock Exchange published a new listing rule and related principles of good governance and code of best practice. This Combined Code was effective from 1999.

Directors were required to:

- review the effectiveness of all internal controls, financial and non-financial;

- include a corporate governance compliance report in their annual report and accounts;

- ensure that performance-related remuneration formed a significant proportion of each executive's remuneration package;

- incorporate challenging criteria in incentive schemes;

- name non-executive directors in their annual report;

- ensure that the remuneration committee and the majority of the audit committee were independent non-executive directors.

In 1999 the Institute of Chartered Accountants in England and Wales (ICAEW) issued *Internal Control: Guidance for Directors on the Combined Code,* known as the Turnbull report. This is now regarded as the cornerstone of corporate governance. Turnbull requires embedded risk management to be a critical and integral part of managing the business. It makes identification of non-financial as well as financial risks essential when making provision for threats to a business.

There needs to be identification of corporate governance gaps or risks. There needs to be a new agenda for change. Turnbull focuses on the need for boards explicitly and regularly to monitor not only control failures but also control weaknesses and near-misses. In other words boards must evaluate the overall effectiveness of their entire control framework.

> **" There needs to be identification of corporate governance gaps or risks. There needs to be a new agenda for change.**

When Turnbull was published many companies did not appreciate the implications. Many saw it as a box-ticking exercise. Indeed traditional business risk evaluations within the annual financial audit encourage such box-ticking. This is no longer adequate.

In 1998 the Accounting Standards Board (ASB) published FRS12 Provisions, Contingent Liabilities and Contingent Assets which came into force for accounting periods ending on or after March 1999. This was part of a joint project with the International Accounting Standards Committee which simultaneously published a similar standard, IAS37. This guidance has implications for non-financial as well as financial risk assessment.

In 2000 it became a legal requirement for pension funds to report the basis of their investment criteria and to state whether environmental, social and ethical considerations had been taken into account when decisions were taken on which companies to invest pension funds in.

In 2001 the UK government published Modern Company Law, the Final Report of the Company Law Review Steering Group, making it clear that 'high standards of conduct' and improved corporate governance and reporting would be required to 'give shareholders and others the information they need'.

New reporting requirements for directors of publicly quoted companies will require them to:

- take account of long- as well as short-term consequences of their actions;
- recognize the importance of relations with employees, suppliers, customers and others;
- maintain a reputation for high standards of business conduct;
- be aware of their impact on the community and the environment.

The European Commission in 2001 presented a Green Paper on promoting a European framework for corporate social responsibility whereby companies decide voluntarily to contribute to a better society. The paper, intended as a launch pad for debate, takes up the 'triple bottom line' concept, which sees companies voluntarily take on board social and environmental concerns besides their economic ones.

In line with the Commission's proposal for a sustainable development strategy for Europe, endorsed at the EU's Gothenburg summit in 2001, the paper argues that all three elements can dovetail to create more productive and profitable business. It suggests a link between profitability and best ethical and environmental practice. Conscientious companies not only attract and retain the best workers, it says, but they can also get ahead in the technology game which is vital for that all-important competitive edge.

The paper is a direct contribution to the goal, backed by EU leaders at the 2000 Lisbon summit, of making the EU 'the most competitive and dynamic knowledge-based economy in the world, capable of sustainable economic growth with more and better jobs and greater social cohesion'. Part of this challenge lies in combining business profitability with the twin concepts of sustainability and accountability. It is also about striking the appropriate balance between flexibility and responsibility in creating a business-friendly environment.

High-profile announcements of large-scale redundancies have put the spotlight on the way companies interact with their employees in such situations, and management of change is one of the key aspects of corporate social responsibility that the paper discusses.

The year 2000 saw a high incidence of restructuring, with more mergers and acquisitions than ever before. Studies show, however, that few restructuring operations achieve their goal of reducing costs, increasing productivity and improving quality and customer service, as they are often carried out in a way which damages the morale, creativity and productivity of employees. Responsible downsizing, the paper argues, should seek the involvement and participation of those affected by means of open information and consultation, and should include a plan to safeguard employees' rights and enable them to undergo vocational retraining where necessary.

> **The year 2000 saw a high incidence of restructuring, with more mergers and acquisitions than ever before.**

More generally the debate on corporate social responsibility takes place in the wider framework of the Commission's proposal for a European strategy on sustainable development, broadly endorsed at the Gothenburg summit. The strategy's basic message is that long-term economic growth, social cohesion and environmental protection must go hand in hand.

Corporate social responsibility is also about the relationships companies choose to have beyond their premises – locally, nationally, European and world-wide. Good relations with their local setting are important for companies: they recruit most of their staff from the local labour markets and for most companies the local market is also their main market.

A growing number of companies, the paper notes, are adopting codes of conduct covering working conditions, human rights and environmental aspects, especially in their dealings with subcontractors and suppliers. They do so not only to assume their corporate social responsibility but also to improve their corporate image and reduce the risk of adverse consumer reaction.

Part of this involves adherence to the relevant guidelines from the International Labour Organization (ILO) and Organization for Economic Co-operation and Development (OECD). The paper also makes clear, however, that codes of conduct do not substitute for national and international laws, but can complement them. In addition, their effectiveness depends on proper implementation, which in turn requires greater transparency, improved monitoring and measures to assist companies in voluntary adoption.

A successful commitment to corporate social responsibility means instilling it fully in business culture – from planning, implementation and staff policy to day-to-day decision-making – and being seen to do so. Although many multinational companies do already publish corporate social responsibility reports on environmental or health and safety issues, less attention is paid to areas such as human resource management, staff consultation, child labour and human rights.

> **" A successful commitment to corporate social responsibility means instilling it fully in business culture.**

The paper therefore advocates a more holistic approach. This is in line with the recent invitation by the Commission in its communication on a sustainable development strategy that all publicly quoted companies with at least 500 staff publish annual triple bottom line reports.

In the USA, the Securities and Exchange Commission (SEC) is adopting new rules under regulation FD on selective disclosure and insider trading, to address three issues: selective disclosure by issuers of material non-public information; when insider trading liability arises in connection with a trader's 'use' or 'knowing possession' of material non-public information; and when the breach of a family or other non-business relationship may give rise to liability under the misappropriation theory of insider trading. The rules are designed to promote the full and fair disclosure of information by issuers, and to clarify and enhance existing prohibitions against insider trading.

Regulation FD, which took effect in 2000, is designed to create a level playing field for all investors, large and small. The SEC does not want companies to disclose significant information to the market solely through the conduit of securities analysts. Developments or expectations that arguably are material must be communicated to all investors transparently and simultaneously.

Information which is 'material' for purposes of FD must be disclosed. FD doesn't define materiality. Instead it refers to a common guideline under the federal securities laws – 'information is material if there is a substantial likelihood that a reasonable share-holder would consider it important in making an investment decision, or if it would have significantly altered the total mix of information made available'. Materiality is often assessed with the benefit of knowing in hindsight how the market reacted.

It is interesting that Enron believes that, because it is not a UK listed company, it is not required to comply with the principles of good governance and the code of best practice. However, they informed me in a written answer to my question: 'we comply with the requirements of the SEC in the USA, which is comparable to the principles of good governance and the code of best practice'.

In other countries the effect of Turnbull on stock markets and economies should not be overlooked. Companies doing business in Malaysia, for example, should note that Turnbull has been 'exported'. In a global McKinsey survey in 2000, investors stated they would pay large premiums for companies with effective corporate governance.

> **According to a global McKinsey survey published in 2000, investors stated that they would pay large premiums for companies with effective corporate governance.**

▨ Interfaces with other management systems

In recent years organizations with vision have implemented a plethora of manage-ment initiatives, many of which they audit and report on in their annual report and accounts. It has got to the point where there is considerable duplication.

These management systems, audits and reports may include: financial; risk management; ethical, social, health and safety and environment; quality assurance; and information.

I would suggest that risk management provides an umbrella system into which all these duplicating systems, audits and reporting mechanisms can sit.

▨ Who should be responsible for risk management?

An interesting question is who, within the organization, should be responsible for risk management? New corporate governance and legal requirements together with the interests of non-financial stakeholders dictate that responsibility for risk is a main board (as well as a business unit) function.

In the past, the finance director (FD) or the chief internal auditor had responsibility for auditing risk. But there was also a corporate risk management function, which used to be concerned with insurance but which increasingly is developing sophisticated risk management tools and methodologies. Individual functions, such as IT and the business units themselves, have also managed risk. Thus it is that the executives quoted in later sections of this book come from these functions and from chairman and CEO level.

It does not make sense for risk management to be unco-ordinated. It needs to be integrated and enterprise-wide, as described in Part IV, The Universe of risk (page 97). All functions should be singing to the same tune. This 'tune' needs to be set at the centre, at main board level. In a global company it must be heard in all locations.

■ Checklist for CEOs
Corporate survival – are you addressing the risks?

- Can you truthfully say you are actively managing the fundamentals of corporate survival?

- Do you regularly and consistently re-assess the fundamentals of corporate survival?

- Do you have an embedded, integrated, enterprise-wide risk management system?

- Have you ever been caught out by a focus group campaign?

- Are you spending too much management time fire-fighting?

- Can you accurately quantify *all* your contingent liabilities?

- Do you appreciate the power of external stakeholders to disrupt your business plans?

- Do you manage risk in the same way for all your international operations?

- Is risk management a main board responsibility?

KNOWLEDGE MANAGEMENT AND THE NEW ECONOMY

In this section I look at IT, IS, internal knowledge and external knowledge. I examine some IT financial, security and legal risks and talk to New Economy companies.

IT, IS, internal knowledge and external knowledge

2

I t is my belief that risk management models which do not integrate knowledge management into their risk management process from the start are flawed. If you do not have:

- the knowledge infrastructure – **information technology or IT**;

- knowledge itself, the means to access it – **information systems or IS**; as well as

- self knowledge (where was, is, and should the company be?) – **Internal Knowledge**; and

- the ability to access knowledge and to project the organization to the outside world – **External Knowledge**

– then how can you effectively manage risk?

Microsoft's Bill Gates goes beyond this. In his book *Business @ the Speed of Thought* he writes: 'How you gather, manage and use information will determine whether you win or lose...The 21st century will be about velocity: the speed of business and the speed of change.'

He argues that many organizations, particularly those operating globally, don't have the right data to understand the business. The hard- and soft-ware infrastructure is the great enabler. He calls it the 'digital nervous system': 'An infrastructure designed around information flow will be the killer application for the 21st century,' he writes.

> **'How you gather, manage and use information will determine whether you win or lose...The 21st century will be about velocity: the speed of business and the speed of change.'**

Organizations, whether in the public or private sector, need this digital nervous system to grow and to respond quickly to risks and opportunities.

An organization needs to get this right for all its business functions. The risk management knowledge infrastructure is most effective not as a stand-alone knowledge system but as part of an integrated, enterprise-wide knowledge system.

Traditional risk managers and RM consultants may be surprised to see that knowledge management occupies such a major section – and such an up-front position – in this book. But to me this is absolutely fundamental for the reasons stated above. But also because:

■ If you don't have the right information about all your potential risks, current and upcoming, how on earth can you manage them?

■ If you don't have the capability to access all the information you need in real time, how you can make the right management decisions?

■ If you don't have the right info technology to manage all your corporate systems, how can you establish the right risk management knowledge space?

■ If you are not sharing information across the organization, how can your people be properly informed, and make the right decisions?

■ If you do not know what technology is available, how can you stay a step ahead of your competitors?

> **It is essential that board members understand the driving forces behind this new way of doing business and the all-encompassing change it will bring.**

If the main board does not understand this, then it is taking a risk with the company. This has been recognized by the Institute of Directors (IOD): 'With the advent of e-commerce and e-business no business can afford to offload the responsibility for these areas onto the IT department. It is essential that board members understand the driving forces behind this new way of doing business and the all-encompassing change it will bring.' The IOD suggests that members need to:

■ transform out-of-date IT/IS management practices to ensure that it is the business, not the technology, that is driving the business forward;

■ deal effectively with the practical implications of changing business practices brought about by e-business;

■ develop a business culture that capitalizes on current business strengths but which challenges traditional impediments to thinking 'outside-the-box';

■ provide the board-level leadership to maximize the opportunities and minimize the risks inherent in e-business within the framework of best practice.

1 Information technology (IT)

Organizations need to review their IT…

■ hardware;

■ software: breadth and depth of business information systems software (Are systems developed in-house or bought in?);

■ programming;

■ security;

■ complexity;

■ accessibility;

■ customer friendliness;

■ system age and efficiency;

■ website.

According to OVUM the consulting group specializing in IT, e-commerce and new media, the market for web content knowledge management applications alone will soon be worth more than $3.5 billion. This huge growth will be seen in all market sectors, and represents a major opportunity for systems integrators and solutions providers. The web content management market as a whole will be worth $8 billion by 2004.

Does IT add value to your business?

IT investments are often measured against other revenue-generating investments that are much better understood by the finance division or the board. The question is: does IT improve the productivity of the business sufficient to justify the investment? Or are there financial risks involved in the investment?

Jim Allchin, Group Vice-President, Microsoft Platforms Group, advises that 'to keep a competitive edge, companies must ensure their information technology initiatives help drive business success at the lowest cost possible and with manageable risks'. He suggests a step approach to the balance between evaluating the financial risk and advantage of IT investments:

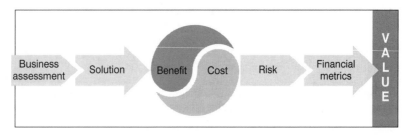

Fig 2.1: Rapid Economic Justification (REJ): focusing on a specific dimension of the economic analysis
Source: Microsoft

Step 1: Understand the business

The business assessment road map, shown below, identifies the key stakeholders, their critical success factors (CSF), the strategy to achieve them, and the key performance indicators (KPI) that determine success.

Stakeholders	CSF	Strategy	KPI	Current	Desired	Process	Owners
CEO							
CFO/VP							
CIO							
IT Stuff							
Resellers							
Suppliers							

Fig 2.2: Business assessment road map
Source: Microsoft

Step 2: Understand the solutions

Next, the project team will work with the owners of the key business processes using flow charts, fishbone graphs and process analysis to identify ways of applying technology solutions to increase alignment with the organization's critical success factors.

Step 3: Understand the cost/benefit equation

This may be in terms of improved reliability and functionality for the company's employees resulting in a 10 per cent cost reduction in system management and support.

Step 4: Understand the risks

Many IT projects successfully build an economic justification identifying benefits and costs, but then fail to live up to the expectations of senior management or stakeholders. Accurately profiling potential risks of an IT investment can help avoid pit-falls by identifying various forms of risk, developing risk mitigation solutions, and adjusting the estimates of benefits and costs accordingly.

Step 5: Understand the financial metrics

Finally, evaluate the impact of the proposed IT investment in financial terms (such as internal rate of return, net present value and payback period).

Proprietary risk management software

A number of companies supply software designed specifically for risk management. This generally allows users to:

■ collect and store data in a consolidated logical framework;

■ conduct analysis upon the data;

■ communicate the results of the analysis effectively.

Existing data sources such as internal and external systems and spreadsheets are pulled into one database. It avoids the traditional problem of having periodically to collate dispersed data in order to see the big picture.

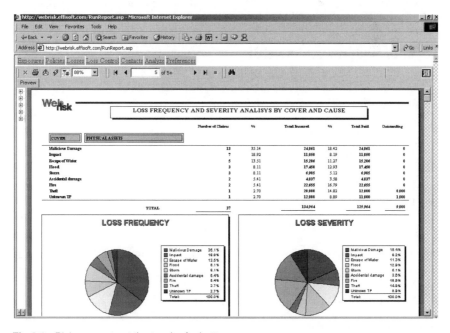

Fig 2.3: Risk exposure at the touch of a button

Source: Effisoft

I asked David Thomas, Director of Effisoft Ltd, how such a system works in practice.

'Take a food and drinks retailer operating in 200 countries. The risk manager (RM) decides that for safety reasons a certain ingredient should no longer be used in each of the 12,000 stores. The RM inputs the required instruction into the RMIS and within seconds the message is distributed throughout the world.

'The instruction is automatically translated into the appropriate language for each store. Thereafter the RMIS provides the RM with a real-time report as to precisely which stores have read and acted upon the instruction. At any given point in time the RM can inform the board as to what percentage of stores have complied.

'Another example may be a global car manufacturer who detects a potential defect in a component used in most production plants throughout the world. To help evaluate the financial risk, the RM requests confirmation from each plant, via the RMIS, as to the cost of replacing all components used in the last 12 months.

> **" The responses feed directly into a database in which the RM can carry out cost-benefit analysis of taking various measures.**

'The responses from around the globe are automatically converted from local currency into sterling, saving effort and time as against manual conversion. The responses feed directly into a database in which the RM can carry out cost-benefit analysis of taking various measures.'

2 Information systems (IS)

Organizations need to review their information system infrastructure, by asking:

- How adequate is internet/e-mail management?
- How often is the IS updated?
- Is the IS adequate on a real-time basis?
- What are the principal assumptions?
- How is the IS used by the owners of risks?
- Is the risk management IS system active or passive?
- Who is ultimately responsible for the IS integrity, timeliness, distribution?
- Accuracy of information?
- Timeliness of information?
- Sources of knowledge?
- Access to knowledge?

Knowledge management is only as good as the knowledge management technology (IT), the systems (IS) and the frequency with which the IT and IS are updated. Increasingly the intranet plays a major part in keeping employees world-wide updated daily.

Information requirements should be defined and updated as necessary. Significant IS needs will relate to:

■ financial transactions;

■ commercial transactions;

■ copyright issues;

■ operational guidelines and results;

■ legal requirements;

■ reputational risk issues;

■ financial reporting guidelines;

■ environment, health and safety and ethical reporting guidelines;

■ bases for judgements and decisions;

■ in-house tools and methodologies for decision-making;

■ external drivers – real-world issues;

■ internal drivers – corporate aims, targets and objectives;

■ energy-trading;

■ procurement;

■ suppliers.

A significant developing area is the management of all this content. Content management was estimated to be worth US$250 million in 1999 when 16 per cent of companies surveyed purchased CM products. This leaves 84 per cent of companies which are increasingly web-enabled and which will require ever better CM products.

3 Internal knowledge management

Internal knowledge management starts back at the ranch. In fact, much of it is so basic that it tends to be forgotten.

Know the organization (yesterday, today and tomorrow)

The first fundamental of risk management is to know the organization (see page 99). Obvious though this may seem, it often fails to be formally addressed. But it is fundamental because, as the organization changes (or fails to change), the risk management issues change. The key questions an organization must ask itself are:

- Where was, is and will the business be going, yesterday, today and tomorrow?
- Have there been significant changes within the business since the last risk audit?
- Does the business outsource or subcontract any of its functions or operations?
- Is all outsourcing and subcontracting audited in the risk management system?
- How has this affected risk exposure?
- How is shareholder value created?
- What are the risks to shareholder value?
- What key risk-potential areas are not being addressed?
- How will change management affect business risks?
- Who are the non-financial stakeholders?
- Is business strategy high- or low-risk?
- Is risk management strategy high- or low-risk?
- Is the organization characterized by a number of decentralized, autonomous companies, product and service lines?
- Does this complexity enable consistent risk management?
- Is the e-mail system optimal or are there associated risks which need to be managed?

Internal knowledge management, of course, also means the organization's intranet. The risks are of unauthorised access; inability access; and responsibility for keeping the system updated in real time.

4 External knowledge management

By external knowledge management I mean the knowledge going out of the organization to any interested parties.

Internet and extranet traffic

Increasingly the media for this information flow are dominated by the internet with e-mails, e-commerce and e-procurement being the major transactions. Internet and e-commerce, particularly the company website, play a major part in keeping employees world-wide updated daily.

There is the risk that the company may be the victim of 'dumps' on its websites of other, often misleading, information. Such corporate data may appear on press or media, commercial or campaign group websites. It ranges from the flattering through the informative to the hostile and inaccurate. The company should have a risk management policy for this aspect of its knowledge management.

Risks associated with e-business

An e-commerce survey among British companies conducted by *e.business review* at the end of 2000, with Actionline Research, NOP and BMC Software, found that:

- there were lots of organizations still at a very early stage of development;

- companies were worried about being left behind;

- there was a great appetite for information from all types of sources;

- technology was changing so fast it was hard to keep pace with what was going on;

- there was a shortage of people with experience of development and implementation;

- strategy and action were slow to develop;

- there were significant distinctions between small and large companies, and manufacturing and service sectors;

- many companies were already reviewing their early efforts and questioning whether the costs justified the financial and operational risks.

Also highlighted was the fact that, of those organizations interviewed, less than half (46 per cent) were involved in or were planning e-business/commerce. Of these,

- 25 per cent were involved only in e-business (35 per cent planning);

- 67 per cent carried out e-business/e-commerce from the same department;

- 33 per cent have separate infrastructures (50 per cent in larger companies);

- 55 per cent said they had an e-strategy (39 per cent in small (50–99 employee) companies, 76 per cent in larger (500-plus) firms);

- 66 per cent of companies said IT managers were involved in strategy formation;

- 72 per cent said business managers were involved.

What sort of activity was taking place?

- 21 per cent had a knowledge management system.

- 25 per cent used e-procurement.

- 3 per cent belonged to an exchange.

- Only 9 per cent were considering joining one.

- 84 per cent had a website, with 66 per cent using it for marketing and 2 per cent for taking orders.

- 5 per cent believed e-business activities were fully integrated.

The findings indicated the existence of both a knowledge gap and a risk awareness gap.

Downside risks of e-commerce and the dot coms

There are many risks which must be identified and evaluated. In many organizations, e-business is being established without reference to corporate risk managers.

There is a limited understanding of the risks and limitations. Some risk managers openly question the relevance of e-business to their organization. Customers are likely to use websites to search for products and services, but may still purchase or procure by more traditional methods such as purchase invoice, telephone, mail order or high street shopping.

In many cases the courier service is a weak link in the chain. E-commerce offers round the clock availability, and the expectation is that delivery will be perhaps within a day or a week. This is not always achieved, and corporate reputation is damaged.

The uncertain economic outlook and a softening in advertising revenues have put some e-commerce sites at risk. Many are not expected to show a return on investments for three years or more from start-up.

> **" The uncertain economic outlook and a softening in advertising revenues have put some e-commerce sites at risk.**

PSINet, the largest independent US internet service provider, faced bankruptcy in 2001. The Virginia-based operator, which has web-hosting sites world-wide, revealed losses of $3.7 billion and went into default on a number of loans from equipment vendors. PSINet had been seen as one of the brightest stars in the internet boom, specializing in providing high-speed internet access and a host of other added-value services.

It fuelled its growth overseas through a string of acquisitions through the late 1990s. But those acquisitions left executives struggling to integrate management teams across Europe and Asia.

Lufthansa and Nike, meanwhile, blamed internet expenses for a poorer than expected first quarter in 2001. Profits at Lufthansa fell to €5 million ($4.51 million) in Q1 2000 from €99 million the year before – very wide of expectations. Other casualties include Framtidsfabriken (Framfab, the future factory) once Europe's largest internet consultancy. Jonas Birgersson, CEO, said not leaving the CEO post sooner was one of his two big strategic mistakes. His skills are in the earlier stages of a company's development, he said. His other big mistake was not realizing the effect that the dot com 'meltdown' would have on his company. A third mistake in 2000 was allowing employee numbers to spiral from 700 to 3,000 in just nine months.

One way of gaining knowledge management expertise is to buy it in. However, some traditional companies, in high street retailing for example, which have gone down that route have regretted it when they have witnessed the costs involved.

Competitor risk is enhanced by internet trading because it is so easy to compare prices over the net. This applies both to Old and New Economy e-business. Price competition for the more simple internet services have increased and Sweden's internet consultancies have been ill-equipped to provide more complex services being demanded by large corporate customers.

Upside risks

In the medium term, given a prudent investment spend at the start, the upside should outweigh the downside. The question is – will revenue increase before the dot coms and e-commerce sites run out of cash?

The e-Bay site runs itself with buyers and sellers paying it between 7 per cent and 18 per cent of the sale price for bringing them together in an auction.

Amazon is getting over the financial risk of setting up warehouses to store products.

And, in the short term, when it works e-commerce is amazingly efficient for both purchaser and vendor. It could be much faster than telephone, mail order or call centre procurement. It could replace a call centre of several hundred people with a website maintenance team of just two or three.

Many New Economy companies will go on to thrive and prosper in an age when consumers will increasingly use the internet and buy from it. As with any company, it is important to look at fundamentals. The questions to ask are:

- Is the company well run?

- Does it have a mix of Old and New Economy executives, skills and expertise?

- Does the company make a profit?

- Is it likely to become profitable in the near-term (12–24 months)?

- What is the cost of sales?

- What is EBTDA?

- What is the price-earnings (P/E) ratio?

- Does it have a sound business plan?

- How does it manage risk?

Legal risks associated with knowledge management

There are a number of legal risks associated with knowledge management. 'It is important that the boards of directors of all companies take a robust approach to risk management and particularly in relation to IT-related risks,' say Leonie Power and Anthony Lee of KLegal, associated UK law firm of KPMG. In a paper written for clients, which they have allowed me to quote from, they advise that 'investors have demonstrated particular concern in relation to IT-related risks'. For example, governance-related questions that have been asked at general meetings include:

- Computers are used extensively within the company's processes. How is data protected by these systems?

- How does the board ensure effective control over outsourced operations?

'Another important reason for taking IT-related risks seriously relates to directors' duties in the context of wider company law,' they say. 'Under English company law a director owes a duty of skill and care to the company of which he is an officer. Traditionally the test applied by the courts in this context was a subjective one and the relevant question was whether the director exhibited a degree of skill which could be expected of a person having his knowledge and experience.

'The test subsequently introduced was whether the conduct of the director was what may reasonably be expected of that director given his particular knowledge, skill and experience. The consequence of the current position is that any director with specific IT skill or who exercises an IT-based function is likely to be held to a higher standard of care than a director without that relevant knowledge or experience. Even if directors do not have specialized IT knowledge they must ensure that proper control and risk management systems are in place with regard to IT-related risks, including legal risks. In this regard there is a perception that the Turnbull report is likely to indicate best practice in the area of risk management.'

" Any director with specific IT skill or who exercises an IT-based function is likely to be held to a higher standard of care than a director without that relevant knowledge or experience.

They note that IT is a substantive area of risk. Turning to the banking sector they note that there is increased pressure on financial institutions to keep pace with technology and to embrace e-commerce: 'Internet banking is the challenge facing such institutions and success demands that the banking business be transformed around an e-enabled set of systems. It is essential also that such institutions keep abreast of cutting-edge technology in relation to front-end, mid-tier and back-office systems (eg trading and settlement systems, mortgage systems and arrangements in relation to applications service provision) in order to be able to deliver a seamless service to customers. Pressure is being exerted to be in a position to deliver real-time prices and straight-through processing. In general, companies are facing the ever-increasing challenge of integration and are under increased pressure to focus on performance and scalability.

'In practical governance terms, it is important that directors agree an effective IT procurement strategy including flexibility in relation to modifying business processes to handle package functionality and minimize the problems attendant with using and supporting heavily modified or bespoke products. IT directors should ensure that there is an effective approach to project management of systems implementations and take into account change management implications, including aligning the use of technology to the HR processes of the business and ensuring that use of the systems in question generates outputs which comply with the relevant regulatory and legal regimes (eg in relation to billing systems). Given that front-end systems are now being used as active channels to market within an e-enabled supply chain, additional change management implications need to be taken into account including regulatory and content risk. For example, an IT director who leads or participates in any initiative to sell products and services online should ensure that a process is in place to keep track of and handle developments in business and legal practice (eg distance selling and data protection laws).'

Adequate disaster recovery measures are increasingly dependent on IT systems.

Power and Lee continue: 'Legal risk management in the context of information systems should focus both on internal risks as well as on risks to third parties, including suppliers, partners and customers. Legal and commercial risks should be identified methodically as part of the company's overall business and IT strategy and appropriate policies and processes implemented in relation to such risks. Both in-house counsel and legal advisers to IT directors can play an essential role in ensuring that effective corporate governance standards are adopted by a company in the IT context.'

Legal and commercial risks arising in the context of systems procurement include: pricing and payment structures, project management (including commitment by key individuals), clarity of deliverables, warranties and indemnities (including EMU compliance), flexibility of use (including rights to outsource), termination and exit strategy, maintenance (including meaningful service levels), escrow arrangements and limits of liability/consequential loss. Legal risks associated with the deployment of web-based systems include regulatory controls, intellectual property rights/content, encryption and digital signatures, privacy, data protection and disclaimers.

The authors warn that it is important that identification and prioritization of legal risk takes place as early as possible. In relation to a company's approach to procurement of IT, risk management processes should ensure that risks are identified before or at the tenders stage. A risk analysis can be undertaken with respect to any proposed contractual documentation where suppliers' standard terms are used as a starting point to colour the approach to short-listing and final selection and assess whether bids are competitive. It is essential that appropriate dispute avoidance and resolution mechanisms are put in place, the authors warn.

" It is essential that appropriate dispute avoidance and resolution mechanisms are put in place.

They add that: 'An essential element of any procurement process is the implementation of appropriate negotiating strategies for use by IT directors and in-house counsel. One possibility is the use of procurement templates which would require that certain concessions could be made only with the authorization of particular people. In the case of negotiations based on supplier terms, IT directors should focus on developing a process to limit risks. For example, in relation to the procurement of low-cost technology which would not necessarily merit a full-scale negotiation, thought could be given to generating a standard side letter to prevail over supplier terms which would address key areas of concern which might otherwise be governed by unacceptable supplier terms.'

Contract 'tool kits' can be developed to ensure that significant legal risks are identified and assessed and to maximize negotiation strength. 'There should be a clear understanding by management as to what legal risks are acceptable to the board,' say the authors, so the board must be kept in the loop.

An obvious approach is to have the organization's standard contractual template on the knowledge management system.

There are also HR risks. Unscrupulous employees, or ex-employees, have been known to hack into their employer's HR IS system. The authors suggest that one possibility is monitoring employees' use of systems such as HR, giving due regard to any legal issues such as those arising in the context of the Regulation of Investigatory Powers Act, 2000, and the human rights issues in relation to monitoring employee e-mail and web access.

The authors conclude that, 'It is important that any systems of legal risk management in relation to the acquisition, implementation and ongoing use of systems add value in relation to the process in question, addresses the issue of managing relationships and expectations once the system goes live and contemplates the change management implications of the company's IT strategy (eg re-engineering sales order and purchase order processing in the context of e-business and seeking advice in relation to data protection and distance selling implications). If a new IT system fundamentally alters the manner in which personal data is processed, it is critical that the legal risks flowing from data protection legislation and regulation are considered and addressed. In the context of implementation and support once the system has gone live, a key component of any risk management process is relationship management as well as dispute avoidance and resolution which enables companies to handle relationships with IT suppliers. As regards adequate disaster recovery measures, it is essential that the relevant definitions in any disaster recovery contract are 'watertight' and that appropriate service levels are agreed.

'The damage caused by unmanaged IT risk is likely to be exceedingly far-reaching, affecting reputation, goodwill and employee motivation as well as giving rise to financial loss and invoking regulatory censure. An essential element to any risk management approach, especially in the context of the scramble into e-business, is to implement an effective corporate communications and affairs strategy to ensure that difficult situations are appropriately handled.

> **'The damage caused by unmanaged IT risk is likely to be exceedingly far-reaching, affecting reputation, goodwill and employee motivation.**

'A recent case in point is that of an internet banking service, problems with which were exacerbated by the fact that the bank's headquarters had not been immediately notified of such problems once they had been brought to the attention of the bank's call centre. Essential to every company's reputation is to ensure that, if something does go wrong, there are appropriate procedures in place to deal with the consequences.'

3

Data-mining with rich search tools

By Arthur C. Ciccolo, Group Manager,
Information and Knowledge Management,
IBM Research Division

Art Ciccolo has line management responsibility for IBM's Information and Knowledge Management Research. The department he manages does fundamental and applied research in many areas of natural language processing (NLP), including advanced search and information retrieval, text analysis, machine translation and document generation. In addition the department applies Human Computer Interaction (HCI) and User Experience skills to a range of applications from web navigation and search to collaboration systems in the retail, distribution, manufacturing and process sectors. He specializes in the areas of knowledge and unstructured information management. His responsibility is to research the art of the possible – and develop potentialities with customers.

I put it to Art that employees who are charged with managing the risks in their own area of responsibility need to be able to access all the risk management intelligence in their organization through a knowledge management system. So RM needs to go digital.

I agree with you. I'd like to extend that view a bit. A lot of the data-mining techniques that have been employed, vehicles particularly for financial hedging and for evaluating financial hedges, are tools that need to be provided with online access. These analytical techniques deal with structured, numerical data.

I want to extend that and move away from the numeric viewpoint, saying how do I justify this? Part of risk management is very specifically risk avoidance. If you are able to detect threats early on then you can implement a strategy for dealing with them. It may be much different from managing the consequence of the threat after it has been realized.

Where am I going? Under a lot of the work we are doing, we deal in knowledge management but we deal in unstructured information management as well. If you say: what's un-structured? It's the stuff that you don't find in typical relational databases. It's image, it's audio, it's video. But most importantly it's text. Most of the information that is out there today is still in text form. It's natural language expressed as text.

We have focused a lot of our energy on natural language processing, approaching it in a number of ways including machine learning systems where basically the machine learns to recognize language as patterns in a very rich statistical sense.

We also have a number of folks who are traditional linguists who are approaching the processing and under-

> **Most of the information that is out there today is still in text form.**

standing of text by a machine to exploit knowledge of grammars and syntax and coupling them with statistical approaches. Finally, we're bringing in a lot of the AI of the past and having explicit knowledge and representation and inferencing systems such that you can have symbolic processing of language.

Now how does this relate back to risk analysis? I'll give you an example of the type of system that we have built and successfully demo'd. If you look at a typically large commercial organization that employs a call centre where you may have thousands of people located, anywhere in the world, answering customer enquiries. They may be providing company or product information. Quite often they are used for problem resolution. If you look at the transcriptions logs. A customer is sitting at the end of the phone and the customer is calling up with a problem. Typically, the company representative is feeding in free-form text. Horrible! The abbreviations, the grammar is horrible! But they are capturing the essence of the conversation. The customer could also be 'conversing' over the web, typing in the text.

Corporations of the size of IBM would generate gigabytes of text from our 'call centres' in a short period of time. So what's interesting here? Well, having tools that process natural language that can 'mine' that text, can look for themes or topics within it. That can follow topics across protracted periods of time.

That might be how a risk was managed?

I'll take that to the next level where we are at. We are focusing in this case on incipient problem detection: being able to find the first instances of a problem. There are obvious legal implications. First, a company may like to deter-

> **I want to be able to detect at a very low level when I first start seeing complaints.**

mine, among all of this chatter that's going on, all of this 'noise', can we find a low-level signal that says, 'I have a problem with this product.' I may have thousands of people calling in, or typing in. They may have hundreds of things to say about the particular product. I want to be able to detect at a very low level when I first start seeing complaints. I have to do this exclusively dealing with the semantics of what's going on. I have to get beyond the syntax. I have to be able to recognize that people are expressing emotion. Are there key words they are using?

Like 'angry'? Or 'tomorrow'? Or 'didn't work'?

That's the sort of thing we're doing very successfully with a customer we're working with. We employ this on our own websites, by the way. We look at what people are saying about our PC products. We find trends, we find the onsets of problems very well.

That's the risk avoidance issue because if you can detect the onset of a problem early on, you can deal with it effectively. The other part of it is if you have failed to detect it but you are going in *post facto*.

> **" I have to be able to recognize that people are expressing emotion.**

In 'mining' the information, you may be able to find early instances of a problem and just how you responded on it and that may serve in further litigation, or avoiding future litigation. Being able to provide that first evidence satisfactorily.

The risk avoidance is one thing. Trying to also employ natural language technology in discovery of potential partners or interested parties who might want to hitch our particular opportunity with doing something we could also envisage, we are going well beyond traditional modes of how a search is done on the web to auditing search capability with natural language assistance. So that rather than typing in some key words and hoping that you may find some results, you are able to converse with the search engine in a much richer way. By trying to determine the intention of the enquiry and position the results of the search such that they are more relevant to the enquiry.

The other thing we do is question and answering. You are probably familiar with the search engine *Ask Jeeves*, where you have limited capability to ask the question and then it brings back a list of documents or web pages that may contain the answer.

What we are working on is a much richer way of doing this where, in response to a well-formed question, it comes back with an answer and tells you the document the answer is in, linking the location of information or location of resources on the world wide web much more effective and relevant to the person doing the enquiry.

The extension of this is we start to look at what we call dynamic e-business. A lot of companies will be providing services that will be delivered directly over the web. In many cases these will be financial services or they will be described in stylized form – something we call UDDI which is the first activity to allow people to describe services and 'post' them in a directory which is queriable over the internet. We are building intelligence into computer systems, so individual user interaction is easier and more productive and new capabilities are enabled for e-commerce. The types of technologies that the group works on are most likely to be useful for IBM middleware products including *Lotus Discovery Server, WebSphere* and the *Enterprise Information Portal*.

Embedded in these decisions is natural text. Again we envision not having people have to search and find these things but have software agents able to search and find what you are looking for. That capability may be a partner that offers financial risk instruments. It may be a partner who would absorb part of a risk associated with whether you, as a manufacturer, could satisfy a customer demand in a particular period of time. Again connecting businesses either by having people search in a very rich way to find potential partners or to have machines find other machines that act as surrogates for the people who are hedging to manage risks.

How quickly is e-business growing?

It's growing very quickly. In my personal opinion, what happened with the dot com mania is an aberration. A lot of people driving IPOs made a lot of money. It created an illusion of a new world that wasn't quite grounded in reality. The reality is that business-to-business e-commerce is significant. It's significant because it saves money. It enables companies to do things that either they weren't able to do in the past; or to be able to do it in economically attractive ways. Purchasing is one example: e-marketplaces are growing rapidly both for purchasing of commodities and provisioning of services. We are beginning to see marketplaces growing and bringing partners together such that deals can be made and groupings of companies responding to opportunities. The business-to-consumer piece is still growing despite all the bad press of the dot coms that weren't offering real value. Almost every major retailer now is doing a reasonable amount of their sales over the web.

> **The reality is that "business-to-business e-commerce is significant. It's significant because it saves money."**

People still fear lack of security over the web.

Security is not really what my group does. The product groups have a good understanding of this. Security ranges from encryption to very sophisticated means of determining that there has been intrusion, monitoring sites and dealing with attacks. While you're implementing security and providing the high quality of isolation that you need, you still have to provide the ability to connect easily. One aspect that is coming to the fore is privacy as more information that relates to individuals becomes available on the web. Security is growing hand-in-hand with not just how you protect the information from malicious destruction but how you ensure that access to it is provided in an appropriate way.

The degree of sophistication of the algorithms is high.

What does the future look like? What are you working on right now?

We're working on increasing the ability of computer systems to interact with people using natural language. Trans-lingual search, real-time translation. As you clearly recognize, as more activity goes online and globalization progresses, your partners may be in New Delhi, Beijing, Paris and Buenos Aires. Not everyone speaks English. Legal documents of necessity may be in the local language. How you deal with the multi-lingual problem and how readily and accurately you can do translations is becoming an interesting problem. We're working in machine translation for a handful of languages. What needs to be done is for us to increase accuracy and scale. Until we can translate 30 or 40 languages with equal accuracy we are not going to have the impact. That's our focus.

Sharing information between countries is a means whereby the risk management framework is set at the centre but managed by individual business units. Online systems facilitate this.

You're absolutely right. There are lots of pieces in this. If you look at the way information is used today you have these news feeds that are just dumping gigabytes of information of all sorts. How do you process that? How do you tap into a continuous stream of news data on a world-wide basis? How do you identify themes and track trends? If you share information with your partners it may not be just on a historical perspective of how things were done. Even if that were the case, you may want to look, say, at how something evolved in the environment. What was being reported? Where? When? What were the indicators that something was happening? What was reported and when?

> **People who have the greatest interests in this are the intelligence community. The CIA and FBI have sponsored most of the research. They want to know every time Saddam Hussein is mentioned anywhere in the world.**

People who have the greatest interests in this are the intelligence community. The CIA and FBI have sponsored most of the research. They want to know every time Saddam Hussein is mentioned anywhere in the world. A company managing risk in volatile areas of the world will also want to be trying to understand discontention, what government actions are being precipitated, what is the climate as perceived by citizens that are being interviewed, what financial measures are being implemented? A lot of what we focus on is locating information through search or categorization of information.

Content management is an important part of knowledge management.

Once you have provided the structure and the categorization, how do you maintain the currency of that information when a site has 28 million pages with a lot of duplicate or similar information across a site that large? That tends to be a structure problem.

Every company has a website. They are going to want more and more value out of that site. Around 75 per cent of companies say they want to publish content to site directly.

Absolutely. Those are the trends we are seeing as well. The trick is how to integrate legacy info in documents in all sorts of documents including pdf and Image. How to integrate stuff with what you're newly publishing and get it seamlessly integrated with structured, relational databases, IMS flat files and so on so that you are able to access the breadth of the information you have. But do it in a consistent way and do it in an integrated way. A lot of our research is addressing how to provide the systems to do that.

What about analysis of that information?

These are the tools for data-mining, feature-extraction, topic-detection, summarization. Pan-path orbit as well.

In financial risk management people are used to thinking about how they generate black shoals models to evaluate a particular real financial option and how you cut data to do that. All of that is relevant. But it's moving on to how you bring unstructured information in the management of risk.

Data-mining

Knowledge Discovery and Data-mining (KDD) is an interdisciplinary area focusing on methodologies for extracting useful knowledge from data. The ongoing rapid growth of online data due to the internet and the widespread use of databases have created an immense need for KDD methodologies. The challenge of extracting knowledge from data draws on research in statistics, databases, pattern recognition, machine learning, data visualization, optimization and high-performance computing, to deliver advanced business intelligence and web discovery solutions.

Breakthroughs in
IT productivity

**By Steven A. Ballmer, President and Chief
Executive Officer and Jeff Raikes, Group Vice-
President, Productivity and Business Services,
*Microsoft Corporation***

S teve Ballmer is Chief Executive Officer of Microsoft, the world's leading manufacturer of software for personal and business computing. Ballmer joined
Microsoft in 1980 and was the first business manager hired by Bill Gates.

Although Microsoft will provide some important customer services, the company's
success will depend on thousands of new and current partners creating innovative customer solutions on the platform. Ballmer understands that Microsoft must be part of
a community of partners, each providing a special focus and added value. He is telling
a financial analysts' meeting in July 2001 about breakthroughs in software productivity. He and Jeff Raikes, Group Vice-President of Productivity and Business Services,
answered some questions I posed about IT security and risk management.

**"" Making productivity
simple, enabling
collaboration for
everyone, being a
platform for business
solutions – that really
resonated with a lot of
customers.**

Productivity is essentially where we
interact with risk management as you
are defining it, in our ability to help
people gather, analyze, collaborate on
and share information through all
levels of a company.

Making productivity simple, enabling
collaboration for everyone, being a platform for business solutions – that really
resonated with a lot of customers. Adding value may be in terms of optimizing the
time for their users. It may be the way in which the software is more accessible. It may
be the way in which they can encourage collaboration through the organization.

2001 will be the year of productivity. I'd like to share with you some of the key
advances that will happen for knowledge workers. I want to look to the future at
things that will impact on productivity.

Office XP is what will make 2001 the year of productivity. We also recently introduced the new version of Microsoft Visio, Visio 2002; Microsoft MapPoint, which helps people visualize business information in a visual context, in the context of maps and geography. We can use intelligence to go out and look at the network and automatically produce network diagrams, to produce exchange messaging infrastructure diagrams, so that people can really understand what they have in the IT professional area. We recently announced Microsoft Data Analyzer, where we show the opportunity of linking productivity tools with business applications and business intelligence. We are now extending into the workgroup area for project management with a new release of Microsoft Project in 2001.

This productivity software can really have a big impact on our business, and give us the opportunity to shift our sales focus on solutions, the context for working with our customers on our products and our technologies in the context of the solutions that they want to apply within their organization. We're also digging in and making sure that the corporate intranet solution, project analysis and collaboration solutions are things that we can build around our productivity software so that customers see Office XP and the complete productivity experience in the context of the solutions that they want for their organization.

> **Our technologies are now becoming fundamental to collaboration, especially because of the shift to using web technologies as a part of the collaboration approach.**

As we look forward in fiscal year 2002, we have the opportunity to sell Office and the complete productivity experience in the context of solutions. We've invested quite a bit in that particular area and have been working with some great partners.

We can build on the SharePoint technologies that we've introduced with Office XP and with SharePoint Portal Server. Our technologies are now becoming fundamental to collaboration, especially because of the shift to using web technologies as a part of the collaboration approach.

What is your positioning on Office XP?

Making productivity simple, enabling collaboration for everyone and being a platform for business solutions.

What's the must-have feature that makes people go for an upgrade?

There is no answer to that question. When we hear from customers, some say the 'smart tags' capability. It may be Task Panes. It may be crash recovery features. It may be in terms of optimizing the time for their users. It may be the way in which the software is more accessible. It may be SharePoint Team Services to enable collaboration.

It's a very rich release. One of the things that we did with the launch is that we had a solutions challenge. We worked with partners from around the world and, in particular, in the United States we had a contest where we showed off the best solutions built on Office XP.

This was really the best launch that we've ever had. We had more than 200,000 people attending our launch events, and that's part of what created the excitement that leads to the customer momentum that you see here.

The early studies both within what we call REJ or rapid economic justification accounts (see page 18), as well as third-party analysis, show that a productivity improvement for common tasks was typically in the range of 10 to 44 per cent.

I wanted to cite a particular pharmaceutical company that saw a 25 per cent reduction in their help desk calls and also saw an 18 per cent reduction in the costs associated with building, testing and maintaining the desktop image.

We have a major pizza company that is using MapPoint as a way for them to evaluate their business and help make sure that their locations are associated with where they see their next major business growth opportunity.

A major IT risk is security of data; real-time updating; and content management. The question is: what are you doing to improve the security of your software? You may like to talk about a computer virus?

Multifaceted answer for this one. First, realistically no system is perfectly secure. If you are running a computer and it is connected to other computers then you face some level of risk. At the same time, there are increasing numbers of attacks.

Second, we are consistently improving the design of our systems to improve security during production. Third, we maintain staff dedicated to finding issues and working with others to resolve them quickly.

Fourth, we make a large and significant effort to educate customers on risks and alert them to the fixes. That is why we were part of the effort, along with the government, to alert people to the virus. Part of the reason why you may hear about Microsoft security issues is that we do a lot to make sure people know and help themselves through good security hygiene. It's a fallacy to think (not sure that you do) that other systems are more secure.

"" Part of the reason why you may hear about Microsoft security issues is that we do a lot to make sure people know and help themselves through good security hygiene.

Fifth, every company needs to ensure that they have good security measures in place and consistently educate users on how to protect themselves and the company's assets.

The Linux phenomenon **5**

T he USA's National Security Agency (NSA) has long been involved with the computer security research community in investigating a wide range of computer security topics including operating system security.

Recognizing the critical role of operating system security mechanisms in supporting security for critical and sensitive applications, NSA researchers have been investigating an operating system architecture that can provide the necessary security functionality in a manner that can meet the security needs of a wide range of computing environments. In 2001, NSA announced that it had developed, and was making available to the public, a prototype version of a security-enhanced Linux system.

The prototype includes enhancements to Linux that provide new, stronger protection against tampering and bypassing of application security mechanisms and greater limits on the damage that can be caused by malicious or flawed applications. The security mechanisms implemented in the system provide flexible support for a wide range of security policies.

The access controls are a combination of type enforcement and role-based access control. The specific policy enforced by the kernel is dictated by security policy configuration files which include type enforcement and role-based access control components. This release includes a set of sample security policy configuration files designed to meet common, general-purpose security goals. The President's National Co-ordinator for Security, Infrastructure Protection and Counter-Terrorism, and the President's Information Technology Advisory Committee, have both called for an increase in the federal government's role as both user and contributor to open source software.

'Open source software plays an increasingly important role in federal IT systems. I'm delighted the NSA's security experts are making this valuable contribution to the open source community,' said Jeffery Hunker, Senior Director for Critical Infrastructure with the White House National Security Council. Since this system is a prototype, there is still much work to be done to develop a complete security solution.

Anyone interested in experimenting with the system or getting more information about it, can visit the project website at *www.nsa.gov/selinux*. This site contains the source to the system as well as some technical documentation about it.

NSA is presenting this system under the terms of the general public licence with the intention to work with the Linux community to refine these enhancements for eventual inclusion into Linux. The system is not intended to be a complete security solution for Linux, nor does it correct any flaws that may currently exist in Linux. The Information Assurance Research Office of the NSA is responsible for conducting research and advance development of technologies needed to enable the NSA to provide the solutions, products and services to achieve information assurance for information infrastructures critical to US national security interests. The security-enhanced Linux prototype was developed in conjunction with research partners from NAI Labs, Secure Computing Corporation (SCC) and MITRE Corporation. Researchers at the NSA implemented the security architecture in the major subsystems of the Linux kernel with some refinements provided by NAI Labs. SCC, MITRE and NAI Labs also assisted the NSA in developing application security policies and enhanced utilities for the system.

Linux is a registered trademark of Linus Torvalds. Incredibly, for a software system which is for free, the Linux phenomenon is a threat to the Windows business. Some people say there's a threat because of that to the Office business.

'There's no company called Linux, there's barely a Linux road map,' says Steve Ballmer of Microsoft, giving a mocking testimony to the David competitor to Microsoft's Goliath. 'It has the characteristics of communism that people love so very, very much about it. That is, it's free. And I'm not trying to make fun of it, because it's a real competitive issue. Today, I would say we still don't see a lot of Linux competition in most quarters on the desktop, and we see a lot of Linux competition in some server markets. And we could either say, hey, Linux is going to roll over the world, but I don't see that happening. That's not what's going on right now.

> **'There's no company called Linux, there's barely a Linux road map.'**

'I actually think there's an opportunity for us to go back into some of the ISP markets and ASP markets where Linux has been historically strong and start to compete more successfully. Not on price, not on the free nature of our stuff, but as we get better development tools, as we make it easier for people to debug their software, as we have sort of a development approach that facilitates the applications that ISPs have been writing, I think we have a real opportunity to push back into some of the markets that have been real Linux strongholds. But Linux has too, with its free price point, and the fact that it runs on the same hardware we do, so we have no hardware advantage versus Linux, which we do tend to have with some of our other competitors, it certainly is something very, very much on our radar screen.'

Since he released the first versions of Linux on the internet in 1991, designer Linus Torvalds has led an ad-hoc international team of computer professionals – effectively all re-designing his system and sharing information for free. The Linux operating system is on the processors of 8 million computers world-wide, and the number is growing. It competes with UNIX, Windows NT and other commercial operating systems, particularly for home use by students and hackers but also by engineers and scientists.

Linus Torvalds works in Silicon Valley where there is a Silicon Valley computer society Linux users special interest group, and a monthly magazine, the *Linux Journal*.

At a UNIX convention in Anaheim, James Gosling, inventor of Java, gave the keynote address, but when it was time for Linus to give his presentation on the future of UNIX, the audience had to be moved to a larger venue.

Torvalds was a student in the computer science department at the University of Helsinki when he used UNIX and wanted to run it on his home computer. However, at the time the software cost $5,000 and it only ran on $10,000 workstations. He devised his own UNIX clone, one that would bring all the hacking power of UNIX to a desktop PC. By early 1991 he had created an operating system that worked directly with the processor and called it Freax, a play on 'free UNIX' or hacker 'freaks'. The application site manager re-named it Linux, after the label Torvalds had put there for his personal use. In 1991, Torvalds released Linux .02, the first functional Linux operating system. He thought it would be taken up by shade-tree programmers who were then using a UNIX clone called Minix to play with their Intels.

UNIX couldn't run on PCs. Linux made an impact at universities, where it did anything UNIX did but on a $1,000 desktop PC. Anyone can download it off the internet for programming or hacking or to convert a desktop PC into a web server.

This was the start of a worldwide virtual collaboration. Torvalds distributed the Linux kernel with source code, and programmers all over the world picked it up and ran with it. Soon he was receiving 'patches' of programming to improve the core from all over the world. Programmers exchanged lines of code, reported bugs and ported the kernel to other computer platforms. Universities began to use Linux to teach programming courses, and numerous businesses began running Linux on their servers.

> **This was the start of a "worldwide virtual collaboration. Torvalds distributed the Linux kernel with source code, and programmers all over the world picked it up and ran with it."**

6

Business at the speed of light

By Dr Giorgio Anania, President and CEO,
Bookham Technology

Giorgio Anania greets me in his minimalist office at Milton Business Park near Oxford and makes me a cup of espresso in less time than it takes to ask 'Would you like an espresso?'

Bookham Technology's President and Chief Executive Officer joined the company in 1998. It raised £119 million in two share offerings, in April and September 2000. At one point the shares, originally priced at £4, had surged to £53.

Bookham's product is revolutionary fibre-optic technology. It manufactures on a single chip what competitors can only achieve with hundreds of different components. But its main market is the telecommunications industry. And that suffered convulsions in 2000/2001, just as Bookham was on the up cycle of exponential growth, having increased revenues to £26 million, up 642 per cent in 2000.

By the summer of 2001 the shares had plummeted to £1.52.

It takes management with balls to weather the crisis that deepened through 2001. The guy with a Masters degree in physics from Oxford and a PhD in plasma physics from Princeton University, New York, who has run American and French companies and provided strategy consulting for Booz Allen, told me what it was like to be managing a high-risk telecoms start-up in 2001.

I have never seen anything like the type of phenomenal speed which you have in the fibre-optics industry. It changes all of your conceptions of how you run a business.

In 2000, money was for free. Literally you could get a billion dollars by snapping your fingers. So the only thing that mattered was how quickly you could do things.

How quickly you could use that money?

Yes. If you could save days it didn't matter if you spent a thousand dollars or a million dollars. Money was no object because money was free. The only thing that mattered was moving faster than the next company – at any cost. That changes your traditional business thinking. Like you do your plan, your profitability analyses, your risk management scenarios. But the biggest risk was being a little slower than someone else. It re-defined the rules.

Our biggest risk was not going for it. There is no slow revolution. You either do it. Or you don't do it.

And it's very costly to do it?

It's costly – and there's no half way – you can't do it at half the speed. Our business only starts making sense above the $200 million/$300 million a year to-get-going-in-it sales level. Really you need to be over $1 billion for the model to start making sense. We spend ten times what we should on research and development. Not 50 per cent more but 1,000 per cent. Because you either go for it. Or you don't go for it. So risk is basic to the whole mandate of the company. Having said that, you put it behind you. You don't think about it.

> **We spend ten times what** " **we should on research and development. Not 50 per cent more but 1,000 per cent.**

The biggest risk elements are:

- Have you picked the right platform (the right technology)? Have you perhaps forgotten that there's another technology that will be able to do some of the things, the same things, for a particular product area?

- Have you picked the right products? If you've picked a product that plays strongly to your technology, and to no-one else's, you will win very big. But if you get one or two products wrong, and you can't afford to do ten just because there's not enough team, then you may have lost a couple of years. A couple of years means you may have lost the whole thing.

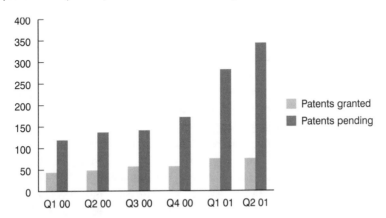

Fig 6.1: Bookham patents growth

- Intellectual capital is a major asset/risk
- Investment in R&D leads to a continuous new product stream
- In Q1 2001 extended product lines and design-in activities progressed in all areas

So what keeps me awake at night is: have we chosen the right opportunity that will take us along the road where we can achieve the maximum possible speed?

And there's a big time lag between designing the product and the customer actually taking delivery and paying you for it?

Yes. You are often developing a design with the customer. Many times they will delay the purchase order. It's a market that moves at the speed of light! But there's a two-year lag before it starts to be profitable. We work for nine months, for example, with a major customer on a major design-in. You work with them on project specifications for a future platform.

So suppose Nortel, which is the number one fibre optics equipment company in the world – they have 50 per cent of all the fibre optics in the world – suppose they want to do a particular feature on a new generation of product. They come out and they talk to us about the specifications of these components that need to go in.

So we take six to eight months to devise a product that works for them and then build the prototype. They test it. They tell us, 'There are a few things that need to be changed.' You change those. Your spec improves. They say, 'Okay that's fine! We like that.' Then they tell you this platform will go commercial in 12 months. So you have been nine months working with them. Then there's a 12 month gap. Then they'll be buying a few here and there to do a couple of tests. Not much. And the business starts 12 months later. In that time they try and sell it to their customers. There is an initial risk because their customers may not want that system. So you're taking all those risks. Plus it ends up being a year and a half or two years.

How do you sell this concept of longevity to your investors?

This is perfectly well understood by the American analysts. They know us, they know comparable companies and they know our customers. In Europe it's been a lot harder to communicate because the players are not here. Most of the analysts aren't familiar with this market. The place where it's happening in our market is in North America.

We are in a very lucky position because we have an extremely sexy story. It's a high-risk story. But it's the sexiest story in fibre-optics!

Very challenging. High-risk. We are lucky enough because our story is so compelling that we made strong progress from a small base in 2000. The financial markets were extremely receptive to our story. So we were able to get a lot of finance. Which is good because our platform is capital intensive.

We are not going for a little play. We are going for a big play. It needs big money or you don't do it. So we are in the lucky situation where you have a unique technology platform that is proving to be as good as we always hoped it would be.

> **" We are not going for a little play. We are going for a big play. It needs big money or you don't do it.**

Your strength is that you are the only company in the world commercially using silicon to manufacture integrated optical components in high volume for internet traffic?
You looked set to capture a significant share of the world's fibre-optic component market.

What we have is a revolutionary technology. It's micro-engineering. What we have to do now is we are constantly re-structuring and increasing our product line to cope with the fluctuations in market demand.

We are a leading provider of integrated components for dense wavelength division multiplexing (DWDM), integrating numerous optical functions into one of the leading communications platforms.

The number of products is increasing so Bookham is now offering Arrayed Waveguide Grating (AWG) multiplexers and demultiplexers; Multi-channel Electronic Variable Optical Attenuators (EVOAs); Optical Channel Monitors (OCMs); and Mux-VOA (40-channel AWG and 40 integrated VOAs).

This has transformed the economics of communication. It significantly reduces the cost, time and complexity of designing and manufacturing fibre-optic components by making it possible to integrate multiple optical functions on a single silicon chip.

It also offers higher performance through the combination of many optical functions on a single chip; reduced losses in optical power that generally occur when light is processed; compact size; lower costs and reliability because we are integrating all components and functions on a single chip.

Today every time you send a duplex, demultiplexer, channel of light you do it with one component. If you are doing it to 40 different colours of light you need 40 different components. That may be 500 or 600 parts. In our case we print maybe 100 of those things on a chip. It's like electronics: 40 years ago you'd have tubes and various components; today you've got 100 million transistors. We have something that can make a big impact.

> **Although we are losing money in 2001, we have the technology and we have the cash flow to push it forward. If it takes us a year, we can support strong spending for a year. If it takes two years, we can support it for two years.**

Although we are losing money in 2001, we have the technology and we have the cash flow to push it forward. If it takes us a year, we can support strong spending for a year. If it takes two years, we can support it for two years.

Shareholders understand and the board understands that this is a high-risk-high-reward game. You either play this game or you don't get into this game. I believe our shareholders and our board understand it well. I would say the American shareholders might understand it better than the general UK public. But generally speaking, the main players understand well what we're trying to do.

You got a lot of stick from British analysts when you went for your second placement in August 2000, investors became nervous and the shares fell by 5 per cent.

What we did was we accelerated our development. We dramatically boosted R&D. We dramatically boosted the infrastructure. We started a £150 million capital expansion plan which would enable us to double every quarter. That is an incredible amount of money.

To double what every quarter?

The idea was to double the business every 90 days.

The revenue?

Mmm.

Every 90 days?

We did in 2000.

In the year 2000, if you take away some R&D payments, we grew by almost 70 per cent in revenue terms every quarter. And in shipments we doubled every quarter.

Imagine, every 90 days we are doing twice as many things. We are going from 200 people to 400, to 600, to 800 to 1000 between 30 December 1999 and 30 December 2000. Like clockwork. This is something you have to have lived to figure out what it feels like! A five times increase in people over one year. Which means, if I hadn't talked to people since the last quarterly announcement, half the people in the company would never have seen or heard me. That's a shock because you come back from being a small family and then you find the company is twice as big as when you last pulled everybody together. Which means for a while there is a lot of chaos.

But now the market is contracting again?

By 2001, the market had slowed. Near-term visibility in our marketplace remains poor but we think revenue for the second quarter of 2001 will be between 45 per cent and 55 per cent down on the previous quarter.

The biggest risk today would be the failure to work differently to match your business to the market which is on its head.

We now have to focus on profitability and a different set of imperatives. It is a reaction to the very quickly changing market. I have never in my life seen an industry that goes through these types of rapid transitions.

What we have done is we have changed tactics. There's a certain humility in making some of those trade-offs. You must have done it in a small company before you understand that you are both fragile but also you're on to something that has a 'use by date'. It's a trade-off you have to have learned how to make.

> **What we have done is we have changed tactics. There's a certain humility in making some of those trade-offs.**

Two years ago we were thinking that we would be making one of our products, a transceiver in millions and millions of identical parts. Like the motor industry. They now have common chassis, common engines and so on, but they change small details so as to be able to offer a range of apparently very different models.

We are undertaking a similar restructuring. We are moving our manufacturing from one that's product-specific and hard-wired to cells that handle four, five, six different types of products.

Similarly we have to be prepared for our manufacturing headcount to go up and down steeply because, if you can't estimate sales, well maybe you have to have labour policies in place and expectations that allow you to cope with that. We need to lose around a further 100 jobs, about 12 per cent of our current workforce.

So when the telecoms sector dive-bombed, you changed tactics?

Exactly. You cannot eliminate variability so you have to plan for it. That's how we are increasingly managing our manufacturing and people risks.

You find an opportunity at Nortel. You go for it. You find an opportunity at Siemens, a smaller player but still big enough for someone like Bookham and you go for it. Over three years you expand the product line and you expand your customer segment within each customer line.

Let me see if I've got this right. There is strategy and there is tactics. When the market goes pear-shaped you have to let go of the strategy for a moment and concentrate on the tactics of supplying what the market wants at a particular time. You have to let go of the strategy while you pay attention to the cash flow. Is that right?

That's one detail. You might do particular business deals that might not be exactly what you want but they move you along the road along which you need to move.

In a small company you have to have a fine balance of strategy and tactics. Knowing where to go for the tactical deal. Knowing when to swerve a bit to the left. To do a bit of a slowdown.

We make short-term product decisions. Every product is pretty much customized to a customer. We pick which product/customer combinations we will go with. Every day of the week. You may lose six months. It's not a case of filling out a box or identifying a risk element.

If we pick the wrong product we could lose it. If we pick areas that do not play optimally to our technology, and give the opportunity for other companies to quickly come in and match us, then we have lost it. If we pick customer design-ins then for some reason the customer ends up not doing well and we have made a guess on the wrong customer, then we have lost it. Those are the three main risk elements. If we make mistakes there, too bad!

It's all very well having the technology. But if it is not commercially focused you can go badly wrong. There's a parallel here with the biotech companies. They are also working on discovery science. But the discoveries need to beat the market, to work and be commercial. So the challenge is to get your researchers commercially focused as well as scientifically focused, isn't it?

I wouldn't put it that way. We have researchers and engineers. Clearly the engineering management needs to have precise targets of what we expect the output to be. An engineer has a particular task and tries to innovate when doing that, which we encourage at every level. Whether he is commercially focused or not is not relevant as long as he is innovating and producing what he's asked. The hard commercial choices are made at vice-president level. Those people definitely need to be commercially oriented.

We are not talking about a university environment where people do blue-sky research. In a company like ours you have very short-term objectives. There is a buzz over in the engineering group. People are not going off and doing blue-sky research. You don't forget that you have something due on Thursday!

Is it all directed at particular customers or to customers you have in mind?

There are various levels. Nearest to the market we have got people working on a particular product opportunity, say, a Lucent package multiplexer with this particular characteristic. So there's nothing at all vague about it. There are deadlines.

You have a contract which you are fulfilling?

We have decided we will provide a part to this customer. We think the customer will then decide to design-in. We have made a product decision. It is handed down to the engineering group with particular engineering, cost and time targets. They have to deliver against that.

Taking a step back, there are some people who work on broad technology elements. Like how do we improve the packaging of these products? How do we improve some characteristics of our chips? That's not product-driven, it is specifications-driven. It has a longer timeframe but it's under pressure as well.

We have some products that go out in eight days. We have some people who work on technology platforms that will feed products over the next 6 months, 12 months, 18 months. Then we have people who are given longer-term concepts to resolve, which might be two years out but these are specific concepts they need to resolve.

If we look at your customers, they are changing. In 2000 Nortel was the largest customer, accounting for 51 per cent of sales. I think Marconi Communications accounted for 26 per cent of revenue; and Lucent, for 10 per cent. You've gradually been building the customer base to, what, over 130?

Every quarter the customer base changes significantly. In the first quarter of 2001 Nortel had dropped to 35 per cent; Marconi was 27 per cent. Number of customers is not a revealing parameter. Three companies in fibre-optic systems are 70 per cent of the world market; five account for 90 per cent of the world. If you have 100 extra customers, it doesn't change much. What really matters is how deep you go in those five companies. Bookham could grow 100-fold selling only to Nortel which is the largest player with half the market. There is also Alcatel in France, Marconi in the UK and companies like Huawei in China.

People forget that there are now more phone lines in China than in Europe. Economic development in China has tripled in the last three or four years.

People forget that there are now more phone lines in China than in Europe. Economic development in China has tripled in the last three or four years.

So China is the growth market of the future? It is also a source of cheap labour. Practically all optical components made by your competitors are manufactured in China.

We are probably one of the few companies that hasn't got a factory in China. And there is a good reason why we haven't. Our technology does not depend on cheap labour. Most optical components are made by hand, assembling hundreds of parts. Companies start doing it in California and end up doing it in China. They have to bring the price down.

That's yesterday's solution?

Bookham's solution is to bring the price down, not by labour cost reductions but by printing a thousand functions at one go on a wafer.

On our latest chip we take a multiplexer with 40 channels which replaces 400 bits and pieces if you were to do it *not* on a chip. Then we take 40 integrated variable optical attenuators and we put all of that on a single chip. Now, even assuming that you had Bookham's multiplexer instead of the 400 bits and pieces, but you had 40 different attenuators inside each separate package, you would need 80 bits of fibre, 80 metres of fibre to connect the multiplexer to each one of the 40 attenuators and 165 precision fibre connections of a millionth of a metre.

Now if you had 80 metres of fibre and 165 connections, that's hours and hours of work and you'd better do it in China! In the case of Bookham, we print all of that on the same chip and completely eliminate all of that. That is what's so significant about our technology. This is the Mux-VOA module which Lucent is employing in its next-generation optical networking systems.

If you look at Bookham in two years, I would expect us to have even more products and a lot more different design-ins. Big players – Lucent, Nortel, Marconi, Fujitsu – should still be three quarters of our sales because they are three quarters of the market. In a sense that risk you can never get rid of because that's the market. Those are the players. With Nortel in future we may have ten products specified instead of a single product.

If you have a single product and something happens to a particular line, you are clearly at high risk. But there's no way round that. You've got to get started. When you get started you get started with one. Then you have two and so forth. Are we at risk with small numbers of customers? Absolutely. Will that risk reduce as we develop more customers and more products? Absolutely and it will take the time-frame of the design-ins which is three years or more.

Are you looking for long-term strategic development including alliances with key industry players?

This industry is a small world. There's a new concept – co-opetition.

Co-opetition?

Co-opetition is a mixture of co-operation and competition. What it says is that in an industry that is moving at the speed of light, at any one moment no-one has everything and there isn't the time to develop it.

So you may be running along when an opportunity comes out. Another company also wants to go after it. That's your competitor but neither of you can actually do that particular product by themselves. So you quickly put together something that allows both of you to address that new business. You may be competing against your strongest competitor but it may be your strongest ally in that particular product area. Of course all these links happen at all levels. Everyone knows everyone else. Ten years ago this industry was 100 people.

> **You may be competing against your strongest competitor but it may be your strongest ally in that particular product area.**

> **Everyone knows everyone else. Ten years ago this industry was 100 people.**

The industry is also consolidating. People end up together. You've got alliances, competition, it changes like a Viennese waltz or an American country dance where you switch partners.

It happens in computers, with Compaq and IBM forging alliances with competitors and customers.

In our industry the product life cycle is so short that they get made and undone faster. A lot of alliances in other high-tech industries have often come about because the capital investment required to get into that area is a big risk that needs to be shared. The semi-conductor area, a new fab (wafer fabrication facility) might be $1 billion or $2 billion. Most companies don't want to put that type of investment on the table so you have alliances.

Our industry is not driven by capital investment. It is driven by time. You do not have a year and a half to develop that competency. If someone has it, you go and speak to him next week and try to get going on a product that may be ready in six months.

Am I right in thinking that most of your wafer fab is manufactured in the USA? Most of your A&T (assembly and test) is manufactured in the UK?

Today all the manufacturing is in the UK.

Didn't you acquire a turnkey facility in Columbia, Maryland, which is predicted to result in cash flow savings of $45 million (£30 million) over the next three years?

We were building a facility from scratch in Swindon for a cost of £150 million and then were able to find a facility in the USA for less than $10 million that was ready-made so we saved £100 million by acquiring the American facility and getting it 18 months sooner.

We are preparing to transfer the very complex process over from the UK to the USA. This will take several months of fine-tuning but we will be in the position to manufacture in the USA by the end of 2001.

We've multiplied our production capacity significantly during 2000/2001. Gradually we will start ramping up the US facility. Right now the facility in the USA is ready 18 months before we need it. We have the luxury of being able to do it at our own pace. If we need capacity sooner, we can turn on the fab quickly. It can turn on a dime.

I guess you are in the same situation as companies like Nortel and Cisco? They suffered in 2000/2001 because their production and inventory levels were high at a time when sales failed to materialize?

Our inventory levels are lower than any of our competitors. In 2000 they grew from £5.3 million ($7.9 million) to £7 million.

When will you become profitable?

The Bookham model, which is a high-technology investment model, starts making money when we are beyond high-£30 million per quarter. That's roughly break-even point for Bookham. Without saying anything that's a forward statement, which legally I'm not allowed to do, when we get to that level of sales, that's the natural point at which we start seeing bottom-line profitability.

First quarter, sales 2001 were £11.6 million. The industry is in a tight reduction period with practically all companies shrinking by about 40 per cent. Sales are likely to come down for Bookham as they have for everyone else. This information has been in the public domain since the first quarter of 2001.

An industry that has been growing 70 per cent per quarter is now shrinking by half in 90 days. Nortel with 5,000 people has lost 61 per cent of its business in 90 days. When people say 'high-risk technology company' they always like the up-slope! There's a down-slope as well

An industry that has been "" growing 70 per cent per quarter is now shrinking by half in 90 days.

51

and you need to be able to do both. In mid-2001 the industry experienced the deepest contraction it had ever seen. But the data indicate growth of 100 per cent next year.

You have to get your arms around 50 per cent shrinkage overall and then be ready for 100 per cent growth after that.

Many TMT CEOs are saying they couldn't predict a quarter, let alone a year, ahead.

To the extent that you can, your business processes need to be built to cope with that.

How long can Bookham remain independent?

We are in a fast-moving area. If there is a rationalization, presumably it will be part of something bigger. If it added value there would be synergy for shareholders and synergy for the employees. If we can grow as fast by ourselves, that would not be necessary. We have one technology platform which we think is phenomenal and which we are pushing forward as fast as we can. We do not need someone else to push it forward fast. But if being involved with someone else would enable us to push it forward faster then that would be good for the technology platform and good for the shareholders because extra value would be created by the acceleration. If that were the case, there would be nothing wrong with it. It would be natural dynamics.

How do you think high-tech start-ups, like Bookham, are coping with the fundamentals of risk?

As I said, you need to be very tactical in what you do. One of the big problems in Europe, for starters, is not that the scientists are not good. They are excellent. But management and financial analysts are not so used to start-ups. In the USA, there are people who have done every single job four times before. In Europe you have typically experienced managers from large companies which you bring in.

It is a different game. You do not do the business plan in the same way. Success in a start-up is eight parts opportunity and two parts strategy.

Why do you think there are so many more people with start-up experience in the USA? Is it the entrepreneurial climate? Or the investment climate? Or what?

Europe has relatively few people who have done three or four start-ups, you know. Who have made those mistakes.

At the beginning I think it was a lot to do with the university climate in California. Maybe some feeling that the Europeans were extremely rigid and conservative 20 or 30 years ago. Once it gets going it feeds on itself. In California you are not taking a risk by jumping on a start-up. If it doesn't work, you jump on to the next one. There's always start-ups. And there's always people who rotate around from one to another.

All used to failure? Or used to success?

Failure can be an extremely valuable experience. It develops your business sense in an enormous way. As long as you make it out to the other side somehow. You may not become a millionaire but you attack the next one and the next one and every time you are a lot stronger. When you go to California, there is an enormous depth of people who have done that now for a generation. They now have that in the way they behave.

The same thing happens in pockets for example in Italy where people have this entrepreneurial culture which is not technology but which grows inside the family or whole villages, where people all jump into particular industries and are very competitive. Michael Porter in his book *The Competitive Advantage of Nations* studied those types of events. His conclusion is that you need to be highly concentrated and then the systems feed on themselves. Europe never did that. I'm at my fourth start-up…

Tell me how you made the transition from plasma physics to a high-tech start-up.

The day I finished my PhD I threw everything away and started at the bottom in consulting with the biggest strategy company at the time, Booz Allen, in New York City. The first day on the job we were told that we had six weeks to completely re-organize one of America's largest finance companies. Go and analyze what makes them tick, what works, what doesn't, we were told.

I think I learned more in my first six weeks as a strategy consultant than in the four years of my PhD. That learning curve did not slow down. You learn to find commonalities of problems across industries. You work in chemicals, telecoms, aerospace, cars, finance, computers, electronics and animal nutrition. You get more out of a year of that type of experience than in five or ten years in one company.

> **Most people burn out in a couple of years. I kept that up for five years. I was the first person without an MBA that they promoted internally.**

Most people burn out in a couple of years. I kept that up for five years. I was the first person without an MBA that they promoted internally.

In 1989 you launched one of America's two first DSL (the technology to provide high bandwidth to the home) companies, which you created and brought to the commercial stage. There you specialized in the telecoms sector, growing the business to more than $100 million in three years. You were involved in Raychem Corporation's telecom start-up.

After about 15 years in the USA you returned to consulting with OC&C Strategy Consulting, a McKinsey/Booz Allen spin-off in Paris. But you'd been there and done that so you soon moved on.

Yes. It was *deja vu*. Once you've taken a business from one person to 50, 60, 70 that turned into a £200 million business, you have this feeling that you can do anything in the world. You never get that bug out of your system.

I found this company in the south of France with extremely good polymer technology – but no business skills. I joined as number two with the promise of rapidly becoming number one. The company was doing optical polymers for optical telecom networks. The market was not ready. We took the polymer technology and turned it into a drug-delivery and pharmaceutical company. Flamel was one of the first-ever French companies floated on NASDAQ in 1996.

You also need people on the board who have been through hyper-growth businesses or businesses like the one you have chosen to be in. In our case it is a hyper-growth, high-technology business.

■ Analysis

This was a most interesting discussion on many different levels.

1 Anania brings experience of two different business cultures – the USA and Europe. And they are *very* different. He talks about the Americans' greater exposure to start-ups, what makes them so experienced and robust in how they deal with crises, picking themselves up and starting all over again. How decisions made in a start-up are light years away from anything that 'corporate man or woman' has to deal with. It's survival that is at stake! It explains why Bookham's management is held in high regard by city analysts.

2 Bookham Technology is interesting because it is 'bricks and mortar' as well as 'clicks and mortar'. The 'bricks' in this case are fibre optics manufacture.

3 Bookham, which was floated only in April 2000, was always regarded as a long-term punt because of the ambitious nature of its science. It was on track to achieve its business plan until recession struck the telecoms sector in 2000/2001. It is lucky to have Anania who, apart from having been involved in company start-ups and turn-rounds, is a physicist, with degrees from Oxford and Princeton, and has been in strategy consulting.

When it came to the stock market the position was clearly explained. It needed investment and it needed it fast to enter a high-tech sector.

4 Bookham's biggest risk is that it has paid the price of investing at a mind-blowing rate in a high-tech sector – in terms of R&D, factory space, equipment and highly qualified staff. The resulting high cash burn has lengthened the timescale to profitability at the very time when its customer base is suffering from a market slowdown. The risk is that the cash will run out before it turns profitable. Bookham, belatedly, responded to the risk by cutting staff.

5 As with Baltimore, its lowest risk option is probably a takeover by a cash-rich multinational which can use Bookham's technology and benefit from the

excellence of its staff. The huge growth in specialist optical components has made the sector an appetizing target for hungry tech giants looking to move into new sectors. The largest shareholders are Andrew Rickman, who founded the company (22 per cent); Scientific-Atlanta Strategic Investments (3 per cent); Cisco Systems (4 per cent); and 3i Group (4 per cent).

Acquiring high-tech start-up companies and thereby getting hold of the latest products across markets that drive the internet was what enabled Cisco to stay ahead of competitors. But many multinationals are tightening their belts due to a slowdown in speculative investment by their customers.

Bookham may make a better fit for Intel, which has purchased three small optical component firms – Cognet, nSerial (for $68 million) and LightLogic (for $400 million). It has expertise in growing from a highly specialized technology base. It is already an investor in Bookham and a price tag of around $900 million should not be a problem.

While there is no growth it has to be a cash-rich company that embarks on new acquisitions – or one that is willing to take a speculative risk. Those rich enough to speculate on the future stand to profit from it. Microsoft perhaps.

6 The upside is that its management has balls. As New Economy shares started to plummet in June 2000, *The Times* Business section said, 'Top management inspires confidence'. *The Sunday Times* Business section described Bookham as having 'an exceptional product, which if exploited fully will make Bookham a substantial global firm'.

The Times' Tempus column said in August 2000 that 'its optical microprocessor technology does look very good and its broadband internet marketplace is fantastically promising. Bookham's manufacturing skill appears every bit as valuable as the ability to design end product. Top management inspires confidence. It is scary stuff and it could go horribly wrong. But it is worth betting it will continue to go very right.'

> **Top management inspires "" confidence. It is scary stuff and it could go horribly wrong. But it is worth betting it will continue to go very right.'**

Investors Chronicle took a more sanguine view in May 2001, commenting that Bookham's technological superiority should be moving it into the 35 to 45 per cent net margin phase: 'Except it isn't (with) losses widening, Bookham is currently valued at around £468 million, a staggering 18 times trailing sales'. But

◼ Analysis

it liked the restructuring and noted that, 'DWDM component sales now account for around two thirds of quarterly sales, and have been growing at a rapid rate' (166 per cent in the first quarter of 2001). At that rate it could reach the magic £30 million sales and break-even by 2003. The writer concluded that the share price was fairly valued in mid-2001.

7 On the corporate governance side there are three worrying aspects. The first is that there is no internal audit function. This is a weakness in the financial management of the company and must be remedied.

Second, it is questionable whether a non-executive officer of the company, Lori Holland, who, by definition, is legally bound by fiduciary responsibilities to question anything with financial implications for the shareholders, should also be acting as a consultant, and therefore benefiting financially and being involved in executive decisions.

Third, the executive and non-executive directors have impeccable skills and experience. But it is worrying that they are either academics – who may have a propensity for research-based as opposed to commercial decision-making – or full-time non-execs. Two are over 73 years of age. It would boost confidence if non-executives from successful FTSE 100 and NASDAQ companies were appointed.

8 Analysts said the company's strong cash position – enough to last about another nine quarters at its present burn rate – should see it through the slowdown, while its investment in research and development would allow it to benefit when the upturn came.

Bookham reported a pre-tax loss of £13.4 million in the second quarter of 2001, compared with the £8.2 million loss the previous year. After exceptional items, including larger-than-expected charges of £31 million, the company's pre-tax loss came in at £44.6 million, compared with £11.7 million in the first three months.

Turnover increased 27 per cent on the year to £5.9 million, but had slipped about 50 per cent from the £11.6 million recorded in the first three months of the year.

Revenues from customers Nortel and Marconi fell but Nortel, which earlier had reported a $19.4 billion second-quarter net loss, continued to be its largest customer, accounting for 70 per cent of Bookham's revenues during the quarter, compared with 36 per cent in the previous three months. However, that was set to fall. Analysts commented that the company was managing the downturn well. It had cash of £215 million at the end of the second quarter of 2001.

New Economy risks 7

By Peter Morgan, Chairman, *Baltimore Technologies*

I first met Peter Morgan in 1997 when he asked me to be 'expert' to his 'rapporteur' on a European Commission Economic and Social Committee (ECOSOC) study group on renewable energy. His special skill in electricity supply came from his chairmanship of South Wales Electricity (SWALEC). He also chaired the mutual pension fund NPI before it was sold off. His 'main job' – before he went plural – was at IBM which he joined after Cambridge. At IBM he rose to be a director of the French company before holding a similar post in the UK. He is now involved at chairman or director level in various IT start-ups including Baltimore Technologies, Oxford Instruments and IDP. He is, inter alia, an underwriting member at Lloyd's of London; a director of the Association of Lloyd's Members; a Liveryman of the Worshipful Company of Information Technologists; and Vice-President of the London Welsh Male Voice Choir.

We have worked on several ECOSOC study groups together and spent many hours discussing strategy while travelling between London and Brussels, in restaurants and hotels. Peter is an absolute sucker for punishment and even writes reports on the flight back from Brussels.

Like other successful businessmen I know, he also has a healthy appetite for having fun. There is always the talk of the latest meal he has enjoyed in a Michelin-starred Italian restaurant, that cruise, or journey in the Middle East with his wife. And, of course, Peter will never agree to an EC meeting which coincides with the hospitality evening which opens the Chelsea Flower Show. 'The other European countries just don't understand this is a priority!' he once told me.

He turned digital TV box manufacturer Pace Technology round. I remember him telling me he was buying a lot of shares in Pace where he had been appointed chairman following its stock market flotation, when they were trading at around 50p; within a year or so they were selling for more than 500p.

But probably his greatest challenge has been his involvement with the New Economy start-ups in the UK and France, to which he was appointed because of his IT and 'Old Economy' values.

> **I watch, for example, what's happening to Marks and Spencer in France – not with disbelief because I've worked in that country. I know that politics are involved in all this stuff.**

Any company is vulnerable. I've always believed that…I watch, for example, what's happening to Marks and Spencer in France – not with disbelief because I've worked in that country. I know that politics are involved in all this stuff.

What is also true is that change is endemic to business. If you look at the top 1,000 companies in Britain in 1980 and the top 1,000 today, you will see that they are quite different. If you look at the FTSE 100 today, it is different from what it was a year ago.

In my experience the company that is succeeding today is very vulnerable: the changes that led it to succeed yesterday are actually a recipe for failure tomorrow. Most companies in the end can't deal with new generations of risk. They are generally the risks that arise because the world is full of change. Companies don't move fast enough; don't recognize the changes that will defeat them.

This is what I feel. Companies have to ask the What if…question. Where were we yesterday, where are we today and where do we want to be tomorrow?

I think people have different views of why they were there, where they went, what they meant to do.

Do you think there is a difference between public companies on the one hand and start-ups or those which are owner-managed on the other?

There are still many owner-proprietors today. What is clear to me is that, in many companies, there is a massive change that takes place when the founders go. Broadly speaking, whatever the company, the founders had a vision. They were able to carry this through even in the most difficult circumstances. For example, when Hanson was at the helm his company did all right. Afterwards I felt there was not the same sense of what they should be doing. Tomkins without Greg Hutchings is another example. The strategy that worked yesterday was not perceived to be right today.

Or perhaps they got out at the right time? Company history is full of wonder boys who achieved something then got out just before the company collapsed back into debt, isn't it?

In very big companies the CEOs who are brought in become stewards of something that they didn't think of. They have a different basis on which they make decisions to go forward. By and large people from founder companies are working to a set of principles and if they succeed then patently they are using successful principles. How do the principles get picked up and carried forward by the next generation?

We've been through the 19th–20th centuries when you had the owner-proprietor, sharply focused on profit. In recent times the CEOs of certain large public companies have acted as if they were proprietors.

Yes! Look at the American IT industry!

Now we are entering into a new ball-game. We are getting further and further away from that scenario...

No we're not! We've got as many owner-managers around today – Gates, Larry Ellison, Michael Dell... These are the industries of the 21st century, founded by individuals who you could argue were as successful as Rockefeller and the people who did the 19th and early 20th century businesses. What you have is a life cycle of companies and they start off privately, then they acquire some capital; and they go to the stock market, then the founder continues to be a significant shareholder.

You have to recognize that for any company, at each stage of its development, the person who founded it and brought it to that stage may not have the capacity to take it forward. So it is a unique set of companies who (a) manage to go forward and survive and don't fail and (b) the same guy who through it all manages to take it forward and still be at the helm when it becomes a public company. In my experience that was Watsons at IBM. But when that first-generation family goes, then you are in the hands of professional managers and the stock market. Then it becomes much more challenging to give it that inspiration that came from the guy that took it all the way.

> **If you look at the value of the stock market today and ask, when were the companies founded? I think you will find that, in the last 25 years, half the value of the stock market was created.**

If you look at the value of the stock market today and ask, when were the companies founded? I think you will find that, in the past 25 years, half the value of the stock market was created.

You can't talk about the whole face of industry being in the same phase. It is always in multiple phases.

Certainly the value put on TMT shares in recent years led them to dominate. Why do you think a lot of dot coms were not cash flow- and profit-oriented? Why have so many of their stock market values been decimated over the past 18 months?

I think there are probably a couple of factors. I think that, up to a point in time, no stock exchange would float a company that did not have a multi-year track record. One of the things that changed was that stock markets were prepared to float companies that did not make profits. Historically they would not have been allowed to float.

Second, you had an investment bubble where investors were prepared to put money into revenue growth rates as opposed to profit growth rates. The assumption being of course that a profit would follow. The assumption being that the business models were inherently profitable. But that the investment in marketing to get enough reach, and then products to get enough capacity, had to be done first.

Certainly in the case of Zergo and Baltimore, Zergo (which had been taken over to form the core of Baltimore) was profitable. When we went to the London Stock Market we set out to raise finance to grow the company much faster than we could otherwise achieve.

In the USA the capital markets are way ahead of Europe. The huge growth in the market value of technology shares was achieved by a major redirection of investment. The vast growth of venture capital funds is another example of this focus. An EU capital market does not yet exist in this way. The euro is a vital precursor but equity and venture capital markets remain underdeveloped for this purpose.

The NASDAQ system has fallen down, hasn't it? Because despite its requirement for disclosure of risk, these companies floated, prices rocketed, there was major, major selling. Then cash flow evaporated and profits failed to materialize.

When we made an application for the offering of shares in Baltimore Technologies plc on the NASDAQ, part of our offer document had to be an assessment of the risks involved. We wrote that the 'offering involves a high degree of risk. You should carefully consider the risks and uncertainties and other information in this prospectus'. But many investors were so eager to get a slice of the action that share prices, in Baltimore and other start-ups, became grossly inflated. Despite warnings by analysts and in the financial press, the shares soared for several months. Take the case of Cisco. There's nothing wrong with Cisco's business except the shares became too expensive. There's something new in as much as it may now have competition. It may have grown faster than any company but fundamentally Cisco hasn't changed that much.

I think if you look at it there are two issues affecting NASDAQ. One is that companies were launched at multiples of their profitability or potential profitability. It was assumed that they could achieve profitability. The ones that were making profits, their prices were based on P/E ratios that had no historic foundation. Literally they were unlikely ever to return money to their shareholders. It was a huge bubble.

At one stage in 2000 Amazon could have bought Wal-Mart. Now Wal-Mart, who might benefit from Amazon's e-commerce expertise, shows no interest in Amazon. In March 2000 the bricks-and-mortar companies could have been bought out. Now it is the New Economy companies who are desperate to find buyers. But Old Economy companies are saying 'no thank you!' to unprofitable start-ups.

AOL Time Warner!

But it's about who your customers are too. The US economy's in recession. It is not a broad-based recession – yet. A large part of the American economy consists of TMT companies. These are the ones in recession. They are shedding hundreds of thousands of jobs. The knock-on effects on the US and world economy are going to be huge when they work through. Many jobs and much spending power, many companies and national economies outside TMT will fall by the wayside.

Technology companies are certainly on a different cycle. If you take just one example. You have the people who make the equipment that makes semi-conductors. You have the people who make semi-conductors. You have the people who use semi-conductors and the people who make PC peripherals – printers, consumables, system software and the media producers, wired telecoms networks, the people who make wireless systems. Then you have the pure internet operators – and the companies that supply them. You are not dealing with a homogeneous market.

I agree. It's actually misleading to talk about the 'New Economy' as a homogeneous sector. There are hugely successful, established companies like Microsoft. There are more recent start-ups who have gone bust, have a cash burn and borrowing legacy that will probably never enable them to make a profit. And there are others who are doing the 'Old Economy' stuff of cutting cost and cutting staff until they can turn themselves round.

The New Economy is hugely important. It has enabled a new paradigm – as our ECOSOC study group made clear (*Employment, Economic Reform and Social Cohesion – Towards a Europe of Innovation and Knowledge*, CES 244/000 E/o, March 2000). This refers to 'a new paradigm: that of the economy of innovation and knowledge, which is becoming the main source of wealth...In conventional use the term new paradigm means growth without inflation, and is used in the context of US monetary management. In practice this means higher levels of employment without inflation, as can be demonstrated by the lower US levels of unemployment.'

> **The New Economy is "" hugely important. It has enabled a new paradigm of the economy of innovation and knowledge, which is becoming the main source of wealth.**

Growth is being enabled by:

1   the dynamic IT sector or, more correctly, the information society technologies (IST);

2   information-based industries such as media and finance;

3   the progressive transformation of traditional asset-based industries;

4   the explosion of venture capital;

5 the proliferation of new enterprises, many exploiting new technologies;

6 sustainable development imperatives.

There are risks in not appreciating that the goal posts have changed.

Yes, there are many changes which pose risks for companies which do not recognize them and revise their strategies accordingly. Hall, in his book *Soul of Enterprise* (1993), called it the Old and New Soul of the Enterprise.

In the Old Economy profit was the priority; in the New Economy customer service dominates and customers who used to be at arm's length are drawn into a partnership. In the Old Economy assets were tangible; in the New Economy people are recognized as assets. In the Old Economy thinkers are separated from doers; in the New Economy they are one and the same. The Old Economy was dominated by hierarchy; in the New Economy teamwork is the buzzword. The Old Economy was dominated by measurement, financial control and economies of scale; in the New Economy performance indicators relate to sustainable development as well as turnover and profit; and time is even more of the essence than before.

Management risks and opportunities also change, as Cannon noted in *Welcome to the Revolution* (1996). There are people risks in the change from reliance on lifetime employment to lifelong employability. There is the change from concentration on downside risks to maximizing opportunities for change. The narrow view of shareholders is being replaced by wider stakeholder consensus. The Old Economy concentrated reward in the hands of a few; the New Economy distributes profits among other stakeholders, including employee share options. The New Economy takes the holistic, integrated view. It creates its own rules.

In the Old Economy there was individual accountability. New Economy companies have a no-blame culture: risks are managed by teams and there is team accountability.

But you have to remember that:

- certain Old Economy values prevail;

- the customer of the New Economy is the Old Economy;

- customers create jobs.

Companies who are good at managing their people risks see innovation as a social process exploiting the knowledge, skills and creativity of their people. New forms of working, such as teaming, often across functions or 'competencies' make it possible to utilize all the available knowledge and skills. This broadens the scope for action and decision-making, turning the risk of being left behind by competitors (often start-up companies) into opportunities for increased competitiveness, productivity and better working conditions, consultation and participation.

In ECOSOC we pointed out that the rapid pace of structural change opens up risks and opportunities:

- Labour-intensive activities are replaced by capital-intensive activities.

- Durability of knowledge is shorter.

- New forms of working require greater social skills (emotional intelligence).

- There must be more job mobility and 'export' of knowledge.

- There are more short-term, casual and self-employment contracts.

What has happened in the USA?

First, there is an economic downturn across the whole economy. The B2C bubble has burst. That means a lot of customers for PCs, servers and switching equipment are no longer there. Worse than that, the stuff's all second-hand on the market. The third thing is that, in fact, there's a change taking place in the shape of the industry. There will be a decline in demand for PCs as such. They will be replaced by telecoms, personal assistants, set-top boxes and other stuff coming forward.

But we don't know if some of this third-generation telecoms technology is deliverable? Whether it will work? Whether it will sell? What the radiation risks are for users?

If you are manufacturing or selling PCs you may identify a downside risk here. The same goes for manufacturers of semi-conductors etc. So it is generally considered that there will be a shift in the industry. Some companies are in distress. It's not because NASDAQ's gone to hell but because their marketplace risks from new products are changing. Going back to what we said before about constant change.

> **Some companies are in "" distress. It's not because NASDAQ's gone to hell but because their marketplace risks from new products are changing.**

Also, companies like Cisco in the USA and Marconi in the UK have got rid of tens of thousands of people and that will depress consumer demand?

Until recently US employment was going up all the time. It may have just turned. It's still marginal. There was a huge demand. They were importing skilled workers from all round the world. That was the point about the US economy.

What's happening in e-commerce? A lot of corporate risk managers I talk to see the risks but don't appreciate the opportunities for their companies. Some companies are finding that their forays in dot com-land have huge supply-side costs for little marketing value. (See pages 17–20 and 23–5.)

Within many industries, say, the pharmaceutical industry, which is not an industry of which I have any experience, there is scope for a B2B exchange that they should be party to. I can envisage a pharmacy.com which presumably will sell things that people are too embarrassed to go into chemist shops to buy.

The one is not a substitute for the other. It's rather like a businessman spending a night in a hotel. Some people will just go to the mini-bar in their room and watch TV and other people will go down to the bar and talk to whoever is sitting next to them. Those two aspects of people's behaviour you can see in Amazon.com. Some people will read about a book, buy it on Amazon. Other people will want to go to Waterstones and browse. Barnes & Noble's big selling point is coffee so that you can not just browse but be comfortable in the sofas drinking coffee.

My thinking about *clicks versus bricks* comes from listening to the chairman of NASDAQ in 1986 at a financial services conference in London. It was a time when the Big Bang was just about to happen, about three months away, and everybody wondered whether the Stock Exchange floor would survive. I was surprised that the SE floor did close down. I guess it was the scale of the thing, the volume that there is in London. Friends of mine who operate in that area say how difficult it is now to form a consensus on anything in London because there is no place where people can meet and talk. That meeting and talking is important in human affairs.

For quite a while the meeting and talking has been replaced by automatic trade triggers.

But Wall Street's still a floor. NASDAQ's not. NASDAQ is automatic.

That's one reason for the extremes, the volatility in the markets.

Yes. Wall Street suffers less violent swings than NASDAQ.

So NASDAQ's system of flagging up risks has failed. It did not stop the dot com bubble. It had an in-built failure?

It's not just that. I think the dominance of e-commerce has been over-hyped. There are the two sides of human nature: the hermit and the gregarious side. Both come into play. Nerds. Sad, grey people sitting at screens all hours of the day and night. That's one dimension but I don't think you can polarize people into these camps. People fall into both camps. People fall into camps depending on their mood. The internet is for hermits. Busy people who have no time or inclination to shop. The amazing thing about the internet world is that you are talking about a rapid rate of change. You have the marketplace changing at breakneck speed.

The strength of western economies, as against eastern command economies, has always been that the market will decide what will succeed. Lots of different stuff can succeed. Everything that happens in the western world is determined by what people will and won't buy.

The other thing that was characteristic was that venture capitalists were prepared to invest money – and they are now finding out what works. The companies that went to the wall, what they were doing didn't work.

I read that the cost of training a venture capitalist is £50 million – because that's the average amount each one loses while he or she is learning the job.

The dot com bubble is probably the biggest single period of testing in the market that we have ever seen. Most intense. Quite extraordinary. Everybody is now gathering breath.

> **The dot com bubble is "probably the biggest single period of testing in the market that we have ever seen. Most intense. Quite extraordinary. Everybody is now gathering breath."**

What happens now?

The tendency in the TMT industries is for the stock market value of companies where they are making profits to return to the norm. Online retailers are saying they will be profitable on an EBITDA (earnings before interest, tax, depreciation and amortization) basis, not on a normal profit basis. All of these companies have huge goodwill. Until they write off their investments they are not going to make money on a net basis. But if they make money at an EBITDA level, which is where the cash is, they will have money in the bank. The problem is that not many companies have a year's money in the bank.

Almost any company can get to profitability in a year if they refine their business model, do the business and cut their costs according to the revenues.

I think that's a tall order. Particularly with the USA in recession and the rest of the world likely to follow. Looking back, were the risks too great?

You have to define who is taking the risks. A normal NASDAQ prospectus explains to potential investors that there is no certainty that the products will work, that customers will buy the products, that there won't be competitors they haven't thought of, and, and, and…

Clearly in many cases that set of risks *all* came about. But those risks are there when the investors take the risks. They are not hidden from them. It may be that investors are not prepared to believe, rather as sometimes too much money may be paid for a company. They may have been not only blind to valuations. They may have been blind to the risks. The risks were there. Going back to what I said about the rate of growth in the market over the last two years, we were clearly in a period of experimentation. By definition if product one works and succeeds in the market, by definition products two, three, four and five come along.

The thing that worries me about many New Economy start-ups is that there is frequently no comprehensive, structured risk management, no corporate governance structure in place. To me there can be no strategic planning without business risk planning. If you don't have inte-grated risk management across all operations and locations up-front you can't do strategic planning, can you? Mark H. McCormack writes in What You'll Never Learn on the Internet: *'If someone showed me a five-year plan, I'd toss out the pages detailing years three, four and five as pure fantasy. If I were a business school professor, I'd tell my students, "Anyone who thinks he or she can evaluate business conditions five years from now flunks".'*

You have to make a strategic plan on the overall dimensions of the business, products, markets, competitors, geography and if cash is available to you, etc. You make an assessment when you make a plan of the scale of risk you're taking on. You presumably make a plan in which the risks in all of these areas are deemed to be acceptable.

All technology businesses appear to move to the right: products come late, customer take-up comes late, etc. You have to factor that in when you make the plan. You say, well, I can stand a six- to nine-month slippage if it happens. Otherwise you just wouldn't go down that road.

So normal risk is there but you make assumptions about risk areas identified. You are much more concerned about trying to execute professionally and get things done in the right way. You know, business is a risk. Companies fail. The formula for yesterday's success is the prescription for tomorrow's failure, market forces being what they are.

> **When you make a strategic plan it is important you are not overwhelmed by the risk that's involved. You have to focus on the positive.**

When you make a strategic plan it is important you are not overwhelmed by the risk that's involved. You have to focus on the positive. It is the art of the possible. Can we afford slippages? Are there any economies we can make? And so on.

Is it more difficult today to run a successful business?

I don't suppose it's any more difficult to run a business making bricks. Or a business making beer, although there have been a lot of changes in the beer industry. The point about technology is that you are always breaking new ground. I suppose the thing about the past few years is that we have built companies round new products whereas perhaps the products tended to be just a margin of an old product effort – as opposed to building new business round ideas. We had the technologists leaving the big companies because they had a big idea, getting venture capitalists to support them, building a business round an idea. Not every idea works. The ones that worked have made fortunes.

Bill Gates, Larry Ellison – they are the Brunels of today.

More the Rockefeller and Carnegie I think.

How have you at Baltimore Technologies addressed business risk?

In our London SE and our NASDAQ prospectuses and our most recent reports, we produced comprehensive schedules of the risk factors in our environment. Our risk management processes are targeted at mitigating those risks that we identified. Turnbull requires that, if the risk factors change, this is brought back to the board regularly. These become the ongoing subject of boardroom discussion.

In the old days it was possible that the audit committee only looked at who stole the petty cash. Between one strategic plan and another, risks may not have been given the priority they are now afforded.

Offering of shares in Baltimore Technologies plc
Application for quotation of ADSs on NASDAQ

Risk factors

This offering involves a high degree of risk. You should carefully consider the risks and uncertainties and other information in this prospectus.

Risks relating to our business and operations

1   We are in the process of changing our business model from providing hardware-based information security products and services to licensing software-based electronic security solutions: the investment required to effect this change will result in significant losses for the foreseeable future.

2   We have a limited operating history under our new business model and you may have difficulty evaluating our business and operating results.

3   Fluctuations in our operating results may cause our share price to be volatile.

4   Our recent growth has placed a significant strain on our management, systems and resources, and we may experience similar difficulties managing our future growth.

5   We may be unable to successfully implement our acquisition growth strategy which may be required in order to remain competitive.

6 We have a history of losses and anticipate future losses which could adversely affect the value of our shares and ADSs.

7 Our ability to sell our products depends on widespread adoption of public key cryptography which has not been and may never be widely adopted.

8 Our products which are based on public key cryptography security may become obsolete.

9 Some of our competitors have more resources and are more established than we are, especially in North America, which may harm our ability to expand into this market.

10 We depend on the services of our senior management and other key personnel whose knowledge of our business and technical expertise would be extremely difficult to replace.

11 Unless we establish and maintain relationships with strategic partners which successfully market our products, we will have to devote substantially more resources to the distribution, sale and marketing of our products.

12 The lengthy sales and implementation cycles of our large and complex electronic security solutions may cause our operating results to fluctuate.

13 Our electronic security products are complex and may contain unknown defects which could harm our reputation, result in product liability litigation or decrease market acceptance of our products.

14 Because our products could interfere with the operations of our customers' other software applications, we may be subject to potential product liability and warranty claims by these customers, which may be costly and may not be adequately covered by insurance.

15 Government regulation and other requirements may restrict the ability to sell our products.

16 Our intellectual property could be used by others without our consent because our ability to protect our intellectual property is limited.

17 Some of our products use intellectual property licensed from third parties; the loss of our rights to use this licensed technology could harm our ability to market these products.

18 We currently do not have intellectual property rights to sell our full product line in the United States and we may not be able to successfully penetrate the US market as a result.

19 Our products may infringe the intellectual property rights of others, and resulting claims against us could be costly and require us to enter into disadvantageous licence or royalty agreements.

20 Our year 2000 compliance efforts could be costly and time consuming and our business could suffer if we or our customers do not adequately address year 2000 risks.

Analysis

Baltimore Technologies is a New Economy company, one of many start-ups, specializing in e-security, a highly competitive growing market. Just how quickly, or, more likely, slowly, that market develops will have a major effect on the profitability and share price, not to mention the survival, of the company.

Morgan is an Old Economy executive who knows the sector well. As Chairman of Baltimore Technologies there were limits to how much he was prepared to comment. In 2000 revenue was up 219 per cent from £23 million to £74 million. Loss before EBITDA was up from £20 million to £25 million.

With the boom then crash in IT shares during 2000 and 2001 Baltimore has been to heaven and back. The exponential rise in its share price led to its bumping in and out of the FTSE 100. It was once valued at £7 billion – in the second quarter of 2001, that was down to £250 million. The reasons are obvious:

- The plunge in IT stocks.
- Corporate takeovers, which if delayed might have been carried out much more cheaply.
- The recession in the USA.
- Deferment of customer orders, leading to a 17 per cent drop in revenues.
- £73 million of reported losses in the first quarter of 2001.
- Cash burn of £8 million a month by the summer of 2001.

Baltimore's annual report records that, in 2000, as part of its strategy to 'become the leader in e-security', Baltimore acquired five businesses:

1 Cyber Trust Solutions Inc, acquired from GTE Corporation. This 'added e-security hosting capabilities and strengthened our presence in the US market'.

◼ Analysis

2 Network Solutions Japan, a majority stake.

3 The above consolidated the operations of Cyber Trust Japan into a new company, Baltimore Technologies Japan.

4 Content Technologies Holdings Ltd, an acquisition of 'the global leaders in content security and developers of the MIMEsweeper product suite'.

5 Nevex Software Technologies Inc. The acquisition of this Toronto-based company provided 'entry into the fast-growing market for access and authorization management systems'.

Like many New Economy companies, it has not been around long enough to have a track record. It had a share price hyped on the promise and on the business plan to deliver profitability by 2002. That forecast was deferred in the second quarter of 2000 to a profit forecast for 2003.

Cost-cutting measures to save more than £30 million a year are promised. Eighteen per cent of the workforce – 250 jobs – was cut in May 2001. With shares down from 901p to 28p or less in 2001, Baltimore is a member of the '90 per cent club' – companies whose share price plummeted more than 90 per cent in a year. But, as *Investors Chronicle* pointed out, markets swing wildly – both on the way up and on the way down.

Baltimore has had a difficult six months in which it has issued two profit warnings, lost a number of top executives and undertaken a major restructuring. Its first-quarter 2001 results showed that the slowdown in IT spending was taking its toll on the company. Revenues fell 17 per cent quarter-on-quarter and gross margins were under pressure.

Management's answer has been the combination of a cost-cutting programme and a revised marketing strategy. As well as deciding to shed 250 staff as part of a rationalization of recent acquisitions aimed at generating £30 million – £35 million in annual savings, Baltimore said that its new marketing focus would be on PKI software which helps authenticate web-based transactions.

> **While welcoming the plan, analysts remained concerned at the cash burn.**

While welcoming the plan, analysts remained concerned at the cash burn which was around £8 million a month during the quarter, and with net cash of £84 million Baltimore may need more finds to see it through to forecast profitability in 2003.

Analysis

The company has a clear grasp of yesterday, today, tomorrow issues, but a weakness is the absence of a comprehensive, structured risk management system. Describing how the company is meeting new corporate governance requirements in the European Union and the USA should be another priority. Shareholders may well demand such changes if they are to stay with the shares and the management.

The company was predicted to have a year's cash in hand. With US, EU and other world economies in recession, the sales curve is drooping and the money is going to run out sooner – unless drastic cost-cutting measures are implemented.

Many of the risks identified in the placement documents are specific to the security products which the company is in business to manufacture. But companies such as Computacenter, which supplies computers and related software, found that, even before the public offering, the service offering quickly became not only the fastest growing part of their business but also produced higher margins. In fact, in the fiscal year 1997–98 consulting and other services for hardware information security products accounted for 57 per cent of Baltimore's revenues. The decision to go out of consulting is therefore one which Baltimore could usefully rethink.

Many users will be looking at how best to integrate security products into their IT systems – and which security products to use in what is a competitive market. This is not addressed in the prospectus which states that the company 'changed our strategic objective to that of becoming an international provider of software-based electronic security solutions and we reduced emphasis on consulting services'.

Another risk which Baltimore needs to define and manage is people risk. Having lost a chairman and a chief executive in less than a year, this is clearly an area for attention.

PART III

KEY ISSUES AND PLAYERS

have already flagged up the legislation and guidance which is propelling a more comprehensive form of risk management up to the boardroom. I also mentioned the non-financial risks that publicly quoted companies are now required to take into account in the management of their organizations.

Some of the key issues – environmental, legal, reputational and corporate branding – are covered in Part IV The Universe of risk (page 97). The internal players will be shareholders and employees. External stakeholders include the press and media, as well as environmental, ethical, human and animal rights and social pressure groups, organizations and focus groups.

In this section I talk to some of the players who have also been instrumental in getting companies to address both financial and non-financial risks. But first a vignette from Ancient Rome which shows that stakeholder risk is nothing new.

In 1986 I was in Philadelphia consulting on a project managed by Penn Phoenix Inc for the city to reuse incineration ash in construction projects. I had the good fortune to meet a Mr Gardner Cox, now sadly deceased.

> **The Roman Senate in 165 BC had approved plans for an overhead viaduct to carry water from the Sabine Hills to Rome. It was to be 55.9 miles long. The 'Greens' of Rome were having none of it!**

Gardner, a Latin scholar, was an executive director with the Penjerdel business forum.

He drew my attention to a contemporary account of opposition to a project in Ancient Rome. The Roman Senate in 165 BC had approved plans for an overhead viaduct to carry water from the Sabine Hills to Rome. This was a major construction project for the time. It was to be 55.9 miles long and would involve the drainage of marshland – always a sensitive environmental issue! But the 'Greens' of Rome were having none of it! They opposed the planning consent on ten counts:

1 Overhead sections of the aquaduct would be unsightly and destroy a scenic vista enjoyed by many.

2 The project would lead to uncontrolled and undesirable growth on the hills in question. The Pontine Marshes were treasured by Roman environmentalists as a priceless treasure to be held in trust for future generations. They should not be drained and despoiled.

3 Shadows cast by the overhead segment would harm the olive groves and vineyards.

4 Quarrying would scar the terrain.

5 Some 800 to 1,000 donkey-drivers who provided water would be deprived of their livelihood.

6 Public fountains and baths, prominent among the benefits which the aquaduct would provide, were not necessary.

7 Many of the wisest scholars of the time believed that periodic bathing at altitudes of 100 metres might be harmful to human health. Long-term cumulative effects were predicted and more research was thought necessary.

8 The plan gave insufficient consideration to the flow of non-drinkable water.

9 Underground aquaducts were easier to maintain. The only problems so far encountered had been the intrusion of tree roots and the build-up of lime deposits.

10 An overhead aquaduct would be extremely vulnerable and would certainly be interfered with by the enemies of Rome in the event of siege.

However, the outcome of an inquiry was that the project went ahead, the marshes were drained and the aquaduct was commissioned in 144 BC.

The role of the corporate risk manager is changing

8

By David Gamble, Executive Director, *AIRMIC*

A IRMIC (the Association of Insurance and Risk Managers) is the leading UK organization representing the views and interests of risk and insurance managers in the private sector. It has more than 160 corporate members, and around 900 individual members, many of whom represent top-ranking FTSE 250 companies as well as the areas of higher education, charities and NHS Trusts. AIRMIC members control risk premium well in excess of £2 billion. AIRMIC is dedicated to raising the profile and standards of risk management.

I asked David Gamble what was new in risk management. How was it developing as a professional service?

It's becoming clearer and clearer with the advent of Turnbull and other new corporate governance requirements that there is a need to demonstrate good corporate governance to shareholders and customers. This is the driver for various trends which AIRMIC has identified. There is also a recognition by the (UK) government of the importance of managing risk – in government business as well as in corporations.

As part of the strategic planning of the organization the risk management process should closely follow the strategic planning process: define objectives; evaluate key internal and external opportunities and threats; develop strategies to maximize opportunities and minimize threats; monitor, review and adapt.

Two surveys we conducted in 2000 showed that:

- 80 per cent of UK risk managers expect to increase self-insurance and risk retention measures within their risk management programmes in the future;

- service levels from insurers have fallen in the past two years, and less than a third of risk managers expect things to improve;

- there is a move towards increased use of external consultants and a growing trend in favour of fee-based contracts and payments;

- the risk manager's role is expanding, and this is reflected in the increased number of risk assessment initiatives being undertaken by organizations. More than 80 per cent of risk managers reported increased activity, and even more expected the number of such initiatives to grow in the future;

- more than a quarter of those responding agree that there has been an increase in the number of innovative products offered by service providers (major brokers, consultants and insurers) – but, tellingly, 50 per cent of risk managers are expecting and hoping for even more innovation. They are questioning the value of consultants who undertake only high-level risk management audits. Faced with a market offering poorer service and signs that premiums are set to rise, decision-makers within companies are looking elsewhere to resolve their risk concerns – and increasingly turning to their in-house risk management functions, supported by external broking and consultancy services, for solutions. Our research shows that more than 65 per cent of our members are reporting significant growth in the scope and nature of their work-role, with very, very few (3 per cent) expecting their responsibilities to reduce in the future.

> **There is no one single person or group which has the 'ownership' of risk within an organization.**

There is no one single person or group which has the 'ownership' of risk within an organization. But risk management should be a central part of any organization's strategic management. It is the process whereby organizations methodically address the uncertainties attaching to their activities with the goal of achieving sustained optimization of the risk/reward relationship.

The board, led by the CEO, have the ultimate responsibility for risk, but they need to be more 'hands on' than they may have been in the past. The board have responsibility for the corporate governance of the organization and for creating the environment and the structures for risk management.

We recognize internal auditors, chartered accountants, and a whole range of operational managers who have an important role to play in managing risk.

We see our role as leading risk management as far as we are able. We recognize that we all have an extremely important role to play. As has the investment community because they should be asking the really important corporate governance questions of the board.

The board and particularly the CEO are clearly the key officers of any organization. They need to look to the risk community, to consultants, the accountants that they are reporting the risk in a transparent way.

We are currently working on a British Standard for risk management. We hope that one of the key things that will come out of that will be more attention being paid to the upsides as well as the downsides of risk.

The upside is that there is a potential for good risk management to release cash flow, minimize outflow?

Yes. Our members don't want to be seen as merely the people who say, 'No'. They want to be seen as people who manage for a positive outcome. The work that AIRMIC and the Association of Local Authority Risk Managers (ALARM) have been doing with British Standards has given us a better understanding of the upside of risk – and its importance for corporate risk managers in gaining 'buy-in' for what they do. Compared with ten years ago, far more attention is being paid to upsides.

How do you define 'upside' and 'downside'?

Upsides are the positive outcomes from good risk management. A course of action which has uncertainties can be managed for positive results. These may include achieving sales or making more sales than expected. The sales mentality is interesting. Sales managers cannot admit to doubts about the company's products or services. In general, they don't manage for the downside. Downsides are the negative outcomes we have focused on in the past – catastrophic losses arising from floods, earthquakes, fires and so on. But loss of markets can be equally catastrophic.

> **The sales mentality is interesting. Sales managers cannot admit to doubts about the company's products or services. In general, they don't manage for the downside.**

An interesting area is that on the one hand you have people who go for zero risk. On the other, people who say they go for maximum risk. I'm not sure there is necessarily much difference between these two approaches so long as managers do the fundamental research before evaluating and managing the risk?

I think it is very interesting the same companies who have been making things happen are those who have really researched the 'market' and how this positive message has affected people. I would say that market research and test marketing are clearly important tools of upside risk management.

Techniques for identifying downside risk include threat analysis, fault tree analysis, failure mode and effect analysis.

They can benefit from data management and tools such as graphical summary of the data, statistical inference, measures of central tendency and dispersion, dependency modelling, SWOT analysis, event analysis, BPEST (business, political, economic, social, technological) analysis, real option modelling, and probability analysis.

The public sector is less used to taking risks. The National Audit Office guide, *Supporting Innovation: Managing Risk in Government*, is an attempt to make civil servants risk-aware but not risk-averse. Civil servants and government view and manage risk in a different way to the private sector.

This fits neatly into knowledge management because would you not agree that the first fundamental of risk management is this up-front research, and internal knowledge management, knowledge of their own company?

I think that is important and also that in managing disasters the better you are prepared at doing that when disaster never strikes in the manner for which you have prepared.

To what extent can risk managers anticipate the risks posed by terrorist acts? The G8 summits are taxing for risk managers in cities like Seattle, London and Genoa where world leaders meet.

Well, some companies know they are more likely to be targeted. If you are aware that you may be affected you need to have in-depth understanding of these events. The most you can do is protect your properties and your customers in any way that you can. These events certainly put risk managers into overdrive. It is basically a logistical operation. Risk management isn't a single decision. It is a pre-planned logistical response for each stage in the crisis.

If people are absolutely hell-bent on the destruction of your organization, the way to manage this risk is to reach out to them.

Who are your members?

We've got 900 members. Our main members are private sector including 75 of the FTSE top 100 companies; around 25 of the largest European and American companies with operations in the UK; around 20 local authorities; 30 universities; 25 charities; and a few from the NHS and the police.

What are the current causes of concern?

Our risk surveys show that reputation risk comes high on most companies' agendas.

Operational risk will always be an important area for management and for reducing the costs of failure by positive risk management. At one company I worked for, which was in the print finishing business, we were constantly having fires at the head of the binding machines. Because of deadline pressures the line managers wouldn't stop the machines to investigate the problem.

> **Our risk surveys show that reputation risk comes high on most companies' agendas.**

I came in and said why are we having these fires? Eventually, after discussions with the suppliers, installers, the maintenance and operations people, we found that an extraction pipe that had been installed had too small a diameter. When we replaced it with a wide diameter pipe, the cutting head no longer overheated so we didn't have any more fires.

Who picks up something like this if there is no formal risk management responsibility? It probably gets absorbed in costs. Eventually it shows on the bottom line – although management probably doesn't recognize it as a cost resulting from the absence of good risk management.

When I was working in Japan I found that the Japanese approach to control management involves as many people as possible. They plan any project in great detail. The whole process means it takes a long time to reach the decision-making stage. But once they've got to that decision point the implementation of the decision is very quick and they usually have considered just about everything and get the right result.

The other interesting thing in my experience was the way the Japanese start work on projects before contracts are signed.

That's a big risk. You may not win the contract.

No. It's a question of finalizing details. You get to a point where you recognize that it's all going ahead and you get on with it. Otherwise you fall behind schedule. You can understand why the Japanese find it difficult when we hold back and then they take us to court when a project is not commissioned on time. On one occasion they had a particular date when they wanted a construction project to finish and so we went ahead with the piling before we had signed the contract. That is an example of taking a calculated risk.

That's an interesting example of how every situation is fraught with risk. But it's not a case of no risk or a lot of risk. Everything is relative.

Zero risk doesn't exist. One course of action has x risks; an alternative course of action has a y risk factor. It is all about relative risk and the balance of risks.

You both took a punt on whether the other was trustworthy?

That's right. It's a question of business integrity.

How does AIRMIC take forward its understanding of all the upcoming risks in what is now a dynamic business environment?

We have a number of Special Interest Groups (SIGs) which study the most topical or important upcoming risks. We have SIGs for captives, e-commerce, environment, international, integrated risk management, liability, property, travel industry, contractors financial institutions, and retailing.

We develop methodologies. One was the Y2K Contingency Planning. The purpose of that report was to provide a checklist that could be used to evaluate existing contingency plans. It covered top-down commitment, project scoping, and risk assessment (business impact, threats, opportunities and risks).

We have developed a package on sickness absence management. This gives a detailed model of just how much sickness absence is costing. How big can the problem be? In one company's case, it was estimated that sickness absence was costing over £200 million. It's also important to send a message to everybody. It's like stress, to treat the individual you have to manage the whole situation.

> **" How big can the problem be? In one company's case, it was estimated that sickness absence was costing over £200 million.**

In 2001 we revised our *Guide to Developing a Risk Management Process*. This warns: 'The ability of your organization and its people to adapt to change will determine how far you innovate the management of risk and how fast you can change your risk management systems... Prioritizing what can be accomplished over what time scale is likely to enable success in the long term at a rate of evolution possible for your organization to follow.'

The e-commerce SIG is developing *Guidelines for Internet Operations*. Your IS is your corporate memory. That's a very interesting example of the upside and downside of risk. If you can get it right and implement it correctly you end up with a significant advantage over your competitors. Another great advantage is that the knowledge system is there for anyone who has access to it. It doesn't walk out the door when a person leaves the company.

Electronic communication has its drawbacks. I want to have a face-to-face meeting with someone to talk something through and he keeps saying, 'I'm too busy. Send me an e-mail.' You can't actually steer people by e-mail. It doesn't have the same immediacy. It's not interactive in the same way.

Risk is often coupled with uncertainty?

A course of action can have uncertainties – like sales, even more sales than you expected. It could have downside risks. Everyone knows that sales people do not consider the downside risks at all. They will assume that everything is going to be absolutely wonderful.

Executive travel carries risk. A common occurrence is that many companies will fly their executives in to a meeting on separate planes in case of accident and then put them all in the same bus going up a winding, single-track mountain road.

I once offered a client of mine a trip in a hot air balloon for Christmas. I said, 'You may wish to check your corporate insurance cover on this.' He came back and said he'd better not go, which was a shame! I gave him a food and wine hamper instead – good but infinitely more boring! You can practise too much risk avoidance. It can spoil all the fun. Business should be fun.

Yes. My deputy chairman told me about a colleague of his who was going on an outward-bound holiday which involved things like bungee jumping. He asked: 'Are we covered for this?' The deputy chairman said: 'No. But have a good time!'

> **I once offered a client of mine a trip in a hot air balloon for Christmas. I said, 'You may wish to check your corporate insurance cover on this.' He came back and said he'd better not go. I gave him a food and wine hamper instead.**

9

Addressing focus group concerns

By Mary Harris, Vice-President, *PA Consulting*, Washington DC

I've known Mary Harris since 1985 when she contacted me from Philadelphia to ask if I would work with her on an environmental mediation project for an American client having a spot of bother in Europe. I'd previously met her business partner Joel Epstein when he came across to the UK to learn about WARMER, the energy-from-waste campaign that I was advising at the time.

A lot of what I have learned about addressing environmental issues comes directly from Mary. It's not just that the Americans were streets ahead of the UK on this for many years. It is her whole outgoing manner which wins people over. The rule of thumb where community dialogue is concerned is: 'Would I buy a second-hand car from this guy?' Mary certainly passes that test.

While I was able to help her out with European contacts and legislation, she was the one who added to my instinctive knowledge on how to address public perception issues at a time when nobody else in the UK had the skills, experience or inclination to assign any importance to focus groups.

Mary was formerly executive director of the Pennsylvania Environmental Quality Board. She is a graduate of University of Pennsylvania's Wharton School of Finance and Commerce. A native of the Jersey shore and Philadelphia, her passions are boats, water and birds. Her commitment to volunteerism and fund-raising have given her the opportunity to contribute to many successful public and private organizations. In addition to the National Wildlife Federation, these include: the US Business Council for International Economic Development, Pennsylvania Power & Light Company (Chair, Public Advisory Council), the Linda Creed Foundation (breast cancer awareness), and the Dauphin County (Pennsylvania) Drug and Alcohol Council.

When I was in Washington DC with her in June 2001 she drove me down Route 66 to a meeting at the National Wildlife Federation, of which she is a director and a trustee. I managed to tape this conversation:

Mary, you gained an MBA at Wharton in Finance and Accounting. But you immediately turned down numerous job offers. Why was that?

I decided at the time that, rather than going into banking which is really what I had focused on, that I'd start my own business. I had worked in government for about seven years but I decided that really the thing that got me up in the morning was large infrastructure projects and the risks associated with them. So I began a firm called Public Management Consultants Inc. And really that was to help clients balance the risk of managing public interests in building large infrastructure projects. We worked for builders of power plants, transmission lines, sewage systems, and waste disposal facilities, landfills in particular.

That pretty much became my career for nine or ten years until I sold the company to RCG Hagler Bailly. I guess it was in 1989. I had just won a very large contract to assess the risks associated with the siting of a low-level radioactive waste disposal facility in the mid-Atlantic region of the United States. I really felt it was time to associate with a much larger firm. It gave us a much broader national capability. Then, in 2000, Hagler Bailly was taken over by the UK consulting group PA Consulting.

Initially you specialized in environmental issues and addressing public concerns, didn't you?

Huh! Mainly it was taking the public point of view into consideration. Probably one of the largest risks associated with building a major facility is the risk that you could never realize it. One of the biggest risks there was was that the public opposition, and particularly local opposition in the community, would be so large that it would be impossible for a project to go forward.

> **One of the biggest "risks was that the public opposition in the community, would be so large that it would be impossible for a project to go forward."**

Do you think that this has got worse over the past 20 years?

No actually, I think it's got better. I think the real failures in taking projects forward have now caused them to take all this into consideration very early in the planning process. I think the best companies do several things. First of all, they analyze the community itself to determine whether or not their project is consistent with the values in the area or in the region where they're going to locate. Then of course there's the environmental impact. Will they be able to develop and operate the project? Not only are they consistent with the public's aesthetic and the environmental values but where they can handily meet all the regulatory requirements for that region.

In the early 1980s issues such as wetland protection and species protection were just beginning to become engrained in the public consciousness and engrained in the corporate consciousness. You've seen the development of Environmental Impact Statements, making sure that you can meet air and water regulations. I think that the public in general and local communities on particular projects put companies in touch with what they really expect which is a much, much broader interpretation of environmental impacts and the risks that they are willing to take.

Of course there was a huge concern in the United States, and I suspect it was everywhere, about the potential for hazardous chemicals such as dioxins and liquid discharges and wastes from industrial facilities. The first things that were demanded were risk assessments. How much risk did emissions from this plant pose. It was common in the USA for regulations to be based on risk-based standards. The issue was to ensure that the risk was as low as possible. For example, emissions from power plants revolved around public health issues and the ability for individuals to live in the plume of these emissions for 70 years without harmful effects such as a cancer or a pulmonary complication.

There was a huge proliferation of toxicologists, epidemiologists working in the service of the Environmental Protection Agency and within companies, estimating what the public health risk was. Often it was required for developers, whether it was a power plant, a hazardous waste disposal facility or even a common garbage landfill, to perform a risk assessment and to provide that to the public before they could proceed.

What advice do you give your clients?

'Tell it again and again and again' is important. But companies are really missing something if they don't follow the other side of that. So then we have a third thing, which is 'Listen hard, listen well and make sure that you respond appropriately' because companies typically know what they need to know to move their project forward. But there is always another point of view.

They may not understand completely how they'll change a community or the public perceptions of risk that exist in an area. The public is looking at a very different kind of risk. They are concerned about health, wildlife and habitat. They are particularly concerned about property values – like, what's the risk that my property will be devalued by this industrial development? What's the risk to the health of my children? What's the risk to being able to live a full and healthy life? They really are coming at the risk question from two very, very, very different paradigms.

I think it's three-dimensional. I always describe it as a Rubic's cube: even if you look at the two sides and all the risks that they both identify, when you try and put a monetary value on those risks, the two sides will value them differently, depending where they are coming from.

Putting a monetary value on natural resources or public health has been a rather controversial area. That's one of the areas that our firm got involved with very early on: the valuation of public benefits. For example, when Hagler Bailly was famous for quantifying in monetary terms either the benefits of increasing environmental standards or the damages caused by environmental degradation – and this would include the mortality and morbidity – we got into some difficult calculations. You know, what is the value of a life? What is the cost of illness? We even had a case with the Four Corners Power Plant out by the Grand Canyon in Colorado. To value the damage caused by the air pollution by the power plant. As it turned out, a certain percentage of the

> **We got into some difficult** "" **calculations. You know, what is the value of a life? What is the cost of illness?**

time, the haze was so great that travellers to this scenic wonder could not see the canyon. The costs included how much money people had spent to get there, how many people travelled there to see this view which was obscured, how many days they were prevented from seeing anything. The courts considered it all carefully. They felt that the damages were great and that it was important to preserve the visibility of the canyon. Visibility was a resource that had to be preserved. Environmental standards should be established to preserve that public benefit. So it goes beyond public health risk to the aesthetic resource, the quality of life.

You're heavily involved now with the National Wildlife Federation. They're very keen to ensure the purity of water and habitats. They undertake lobbying if they feel that air, water or wildlife are at risk.

Yes. The National Wildlife Federation was started back in 1936. Interestingly enough NWF was begun by a political cartoonist. The man was a journalist for a popular newspaper which often ran environment-oriented stories. There was no lobbying organization for the sportsman. At that time they were not environmentalists. The term did not even exist. The concept was to preserve the wild spaces and preserve places for animals and nature in the United States. Their mission was very much one of education. Their focus was to give people enough information about habitat protection to enable them to provide a voice.

It spilled over. Today it is a national network of like-minded state and territorial groups, seeking balanced, common-sense solutions to environmental problems that work for wildlife and people. It is a 'big tent' organization uniting people from all places, walks of life and political persuasions on the common ground of restoring and protecting wildlife and wild places. Representatives of 46 state and territorial affiliates meet annually to set NWF's conservation agenda.

It is the nation's largest member-supported conservation group, uniting individuals, organizations, businesses and government to protect wildlife, wild places and the environment. It engages with governments as well as developers.

In June 2001 it was pleased at its success at lobbying Congress to pass the most comprehensive conservation funding legislation in history. The Conservation and Reinvestment Act (CARA) would provide long-term conservation investments for states and local communities. CARA should be a hand-in-glove fit for the Bush administration. It does not require a dime in new taxes. More than 220 members of the 435-member House have become CARA co-sponsors.

NWF is fighting the entrenched interests of those who do not want to give the states an assured source of conservation funding. We also know that no conservation legisla-

" We also know that no conservation legislation in recent history has gained such a broad base of support at the grassroots, among state and community leaders and in the Congress itself.

tion in recent history has gained such a broad base of support at the grassroots, among state and community leaders and in the Congress itself. CARA would use a portion of current offshore oil and gas drilling lease revenue to provide just over $3 billion in annual conservation investments through the year 2015. A substantial majority of the funds would flow directly to the states and local communities to provide reliable investments for wildlife management, open space, parks, ball fields, environmental restoration and historic preservation.

Like me, you started out with waste disposal clients. But we both increasingly got involved with energy matters.

Hagler Bailly is probably best known as an energy analyst. It works in 170 countries and really has a very deep and broad energy capability. It's interesting now that many consulting firms are moving away from the generalist management consulting model to the industry-specific specialist groups, that's something we had all along.

How do you rate energy risks on the radar screen of a company's business risks?

I would define energy risk as not being able to get the power and heat that you want at the price that you want. Is that really a financial risk? Is it an operational risk? It depends. For a very energy-intensive industry like aluminium, this is a heartland issue. If 14 per cent of your costs come from energy consumption…Other organizations may have small energy costs as a percentage of total operational costs but may be highly dependent on the quality or the phasing of that energy supply.

" In the United States and most industrialized countries, most of the risk is associated with the cost of energy.

In the United States and most industrialized countries, most of the risk is associated with the cost of energy. When you move outside the United States to the developing world or the transitional economies, there you are really talking about the availability of energy and the ability to get energy to the places that need it, to provide it 24x7. This still doesn't exist in a lot of places.

What's your 'take' on the reasons behind the 2001 energy crisis in California?

That's an example of a well-conceived policy very poorly implemented.

You're talking about deregulation?

Yes.

Socially responsible investment

10

By Larry Amon, Chief Financial Officer, *National Wildlife Federation*

L arry Amon is excited. 'One of our large-format films, *Dolphins*, was nominated in 2001 for an Academy Award in the documentary category. We didn't win an Oscar but it was an honour to be nominated.'

Larry is Senior Vice-President for Finance and Administration and Chief Financial Officer of the National Wildlife Federation.

Dolphins is narrated by Pierce Brosnan and features songs and music by Sting, including an original song he wrote for the film. It is one of the National Wildlife Federation's giant screen films and has proved a big box office success, grossing more than $37 million world-wide since its March 2000 release. In making films that are compelling and beautiful, we can educate and inspire people to take action to protect wildlife and wild places. We've made a number of large screen films: *Whales, Bears, Tigers, Wolves.*

Like Dances with Wolves – but not the same director?

Yes, agrees National Wildlife Federation's Mary Harris. But in this case the wolves are the stars.

I am visiting Larry and Mary at NWF's new headquarters in Reston, Virginia. Although the NWF is a not-for-profit organization, it has considerable muscle power. The annual budget is around $125 million and it has 600 staff across the USA. It is affiliated to 46 local state conservation organizations across the country which are financially and legally independent of it but work very closely with it.

The numbers are mind-blowing compared with what UK conservation groups work on!

Larry: My favourite line that my WWF UK colleagues use is in the UK we run organizations on the smell of a rag! The whole idea of endowment, invested reserves, a rainy day fund or something to help fund current operations is a foreign concept to them. We are lucky to have these reserves at NWF.

Mary: We have a rag room! If we need a rag, we pull it out.

Larry: We are always in a growth mode. We are always looking for new revenue areas. We have just bought a new internet company called eNature.com. We already have access through direct mail membership to the 3 million to 5 million people in the USA who are direct mail responsive and actively identify themselves as conservationists. They give to a number of other organizations as well and that's a fairly stable cash flow for us. What we don't have access to are an additional 30 million to 45 million people who are gardeners, anglers, outdoors people. They like nature but they have not yet identified themselves as conservationists or environmentalists, but eNature.com is going to provide them with a range of information on the natural world and species. We have a database of field information on birds, butterflies, insects and reptiles. If you put your zip code in, it will tell you all the wildlife that is in your backyard or your neighbourhood. A big part of our work is getting people to take action. They go out, they experience the natural world, they become activists and hopefully they join us.

> **A big part of our work is getting people to take action. They go out, they experience the natural world, they become activists and hopefully they join us.**

What are your major financial risks?

We need to ensure a constant inflow of revenue. We manage that risk by having a diversity of revenue sources. We manage our risk so we are not dependent on any one of them. They include membership subscriptions, bequests and planned giving, the merchandise catalogue, the kids' publications, restricted grants from foundations, corporations and major donors, and cause marketing arrangements with corporations that sponsor programmes or enter into licensing arrangements with us to distribute our educational materials with their products. What's really important is that we understand each of these 'business lines' so that we can monitor and make sure that they are 'profitable'.

How do you address corporate governance issues?

We take corporate governance issues seriously. This is evident in our 'green screen' investment strategy and our 'green' building.

National Wildlife Federation's aim is to raise awareness of conservation and environmental protection. It was therefore considered appropriate that, in managing its affairs, it should put its money where its mouth is. There is a certain amount of the revenue that comes in that we keep as operating cash to pay the bills each week. The rest is managed by a separate corporation with a separate board of trustees which look after our investments. We use outside money managers. We have a diversified portfolio. We have growth, value and domestic equity funds. We have an international money manager. We have a fixed income bond manager. We also use an outside consultant to help monitor results.

Mary: The outside money managers really do the investing. We try to meet the targets that the trustees have set. We basically establish what the portfolio allocation will be, how we will allocate incoming assets, what's most appropriate for the Federation, and how we think we are going to be drawing on the funds over the next five years. We use a consultant to help us evaluate the performance of our investment managers annually against various investment performance indices. We need to know that they are performing in the top percentile.

Larry: There's a lot of similarity between our investment policy and that of a conventional pension plan. We have a lot of the same investment goals. We are responding to the risks of market fluctuations and long-term gains and losses. We talk about it at board level in terms of what the real objectives of the endowment are. Not only do we want to draw out annually a certain percentage to help fund the operations but we're looking for long-term growth maximization in those funds.

What are your investment criteria?

We set two sets of criteria – financial and environmental. We invest in equities and bonds. Other than the building, which is owned by the Federation, we don't have any real estate or venture capital investments. In 1998 NWF's board of directors commissioned its finance committee to study how the NWF could 'green' its investment strategy.

The corporate governance issues start with the fact that you have fiduciary responsibilities to maximize the returns on your investments. At the same time you have a conservation mission that you are meant to be fulfilling. You have in some ways a fiduciary responsibility there as well. You wouldn't want to be spending money on something that wasn't reinforcing that mission.

> **We set two sets of "criteria – financial and environmental.**

Mary: The role and main risk of the board members is fiduciary responsibility. It means that when we accept money from anyone for the purposes for which our organization was founded, there are two items of value for the donor: one is the item they are getting such as a subscription to one of the kids' magazines; the other is the cause-related benefit of their dollars which we are investing for the future. We should be clear that the funds are supporting our mission, and not going to something that is off-mission.

It is important, number one, to preserve that capital. When we talk about bequeathals, this money was donated for this mission. Like doctors, we must do no harm. The second is to grow that capital and make sure the Federation can benefit from it. Really we want to make sure that the way the money is invested is not working at cross purposes with the mission of the organization. The 'green screen' helps to set our investment criteria.

We do not tell our investment managers that they are prohibited from making investments in certain companies. They understand the green screen criteria and they have the company scores. By telling them to hang on to the good portfolio score and improve it over time, they are free to work within that framework.

But after the fact, you know, we are looking at our performance in the marketplace – but against a 'green' standard. What matters is how we walk the walk.

The challenge with boards of organizations is that the fiduciary and mission responsibilities are often seen as conflicting. If we invest in certain companies we may not be maximizing our returns. Are we going to get ourselves in trouble?

Many people on our board come from the commercial world where there isn't this conflict, so they are often reluctant to take a 'green screen' or social approach. In the past, what we have seen is *exclusionary* screens, where you say you can't invest in certain companies or industry sectors. When you do that, you could be cutting into the ability of your money managers to earn returns for you – or to meet the index benchmarks you are holding them to. What we have done is not to exclude companies but look for those that are best-in-class. In a nutshell we defined the goals as:

- The screen should reflect NWF's mission and objectives.

- It should not materially affect the portfolio's financial performance.

- It should require minimum staff time to implement.

- It should be reasonably priced.

The investment strategy is based on:

- a best-in-class evaluation of individual companies;

- a scorecard evaluation of the entire portfolio;

- use of an outside professional research firm for evaluation and scoring.

> **" You ask, what are they doing? How are they managing their environmental risks? We create a score card.**

The *best-in-class* methodology evaluates a company's environmental performance relative to other companies in its industry. Only if the potential investment return is equal does environmental policy become the deciding factor.

You ask, what are they doing? How are they responding to outside pressures? How are they managing their environmental risks? How effective are they at it? If they have environmental problems, how do they deal with them? Who are the most progressive in each industry sector? We create a score card.

The *scorecard methodology* rates the portfolio's environmental performance, and this is monitored for changes over time. This combined best-in-class/scorecard approach provides the portfolio managers with the flexibility to invest in any or all profitable industries and to use the same performance benchmarks as without a screen.

We use an *outside research firm* based in Toronto, New York and London which minimizes the NWF staff time required for green screening. Based on the proposals received from six research firms, as well as in-depth analysis of the methods they use to evaluate the environmental performance of companies, the NWF committee that looked at this concluded that Innovest Strategic Value Advisors would be the most appropriate firm for evaluation and scoring.

They have a model that combines up to 60 environmental risk criteria with a financial analysis to produce a score. You can figure out which company is the best in a particular industry sector. The AAA (outperform) is better than a CCC (underperform). We only focus on the US equity market. That's where you can get a lot of information right now on these risk management factors.

We only rate companies that are in 'impact-ful' industries – those that are involved with natural resources, chemicals, energy. There are service industries and others where there is not a lot of environmental impact and we are not spending a lot of our resources analyzing them.

We add up the scores of the companies we've invested in. That tells us how well we're doing – or not. Second, it gives us a benchmark. If the portfolio gets a good score, we want to hang on to that good score or improve it in time.

Innovest then also scores companies that we have *not* invested in but are in the investment universe of our money managers. Between the two US equity money managers there are 300 to 400 companies in their investment universe.

We haven't got as far as saying if we end up with any bad performers in our portfolio, get rid of them right now. But if we get any CCCs, we will get rid of those over time. We're pushing our money managers in that direction. I think this has two valuable effects. One is that it aligns our investment management with our mission.

The second thing it does which is very effective is that it is starting to educate the money management world about Socially Responsible Investment (SRI). When they get other clients coming to them indicating an interest in the stuff, they are ready. They understand the issues. They are more receptive. We thus leverage our values into the financial services world.

Do commercial organizations ever ask to see your methodology?

Yep. We have just put this system together in the past two years. We really wanted to get some history with it. Innovest is interested in going public with this. There are a number of mutual funds and investment managers who provide SRI screens and criteria for investing using exclusionary screens. But I haven't seen this combination of scorecard, best-in-class and improvement over time anywhere else.

Larry, as he walks outside: Let me show you another way in which we are being faithful to our mission. We moved into this building in 2001. We used tax-exempt financing to purchase the building. We had moved some of our operations to our field offices over the years, meaning we were left with too much space and were paying too much rent at our headquarters. Constructing a facility of the right size and with the right features helped us to reduce our occupancy costs by $1 million a year. We have 6½ acres here, right next to a 400-acre park. The idea is that we're trying to set an example of an environmentally friendly building that's state-of-the-shelf. The stuff we used doesn't cost any more money but it's 'green'. Other businesses can look to NWF as a prime example of how to be both environmentally sensitive and fiscally responsible. Striking that balance is what we call common-sense conservation.

> **Striking that balance is what we call common-sense conservation.**

The ways in which we are doing that are, first of all, we're going to have the most beautiful parking lot in Virginia. It's going to be a backyard wildlife habitat demonstration. The meadows and trees will provide a habitat and food for wildlife to live and to raise their young. We have a specific demonstration project out back.

The run-off from the parking lot, rainwater and flood water go into bio-retention ponds where they are cleaned of pollutants from the parking lot and toxins in the rain. These drain into the creeks that go through the woods behind us and into the Potomac River and finally the Chesapeake Bay. The water will leave the site cleaner than when it came on. Landscape architects incorporated flowering and fruit-bearing plants for wildlife food, ponds for water and logs and brush piles for shelter.

Solar panels heat water for the showers in the building. The building is long and narrow. This is the south side where we have this wire trellis. Virginia creeper and other deciduous vines such as trumpet vine and honeysuckle have been planted to provide solar protection in the summer when it gets to 80 or 90 degrees here. In the winter, the leaves will fall off and we'll get the exposure that we need for heat. The east and west sides where the sun is low in the sky don't have any windows. It's energy efficient.

Is the screen an original idea? It's a couple of metres forward from the building?

One and a half metres. They still allow views and natural light which is maximized in this building. The only place I've seen it is at the Finnish Embassy in downtown DC on Massachusetts Avenue. They've had theirs up for five years. It takes about three years for the vines to cover it. We are only using native plants on the site. We have about 18 different vines. If we've had to destroy some of the site with asphalt, we're putting it back by going vertical here! The flowers will provide for insects and birds.

There's a house finch's nest already up there. There's the bird, *Carpodacus Mexicanus*. The bird is endemic to western North America and has extended its range prolifically over the past 20 years to be essentially ubiquitous throughout the USA. This is a male with a bright red breast.

Between the building and the parking lot you have a wild flower meadow?

It needs some work. It will be mowed periodically so the flowers can come up. We're starting work on a pond in front of the building including a couple of cascades and a bridge to demonstrate what people can do with water in their backyards.

Inside it's 100 per cent open plan. We're all in work stations. It was important for all of us to look out into the natural environment of woods and trees and natural light. That's another advantage of the long, narrow building design. Inside there are delightful sculptures of eagles and dragonflies on screens. We don't have windows that open because that's not energy efficient. But we do have balconies so people can step outside if they want to get some fresh air.

The carpet is non-gassing. There can be a lot of toxics in the glue in normal carpets which give off fumes; and they are often treated with chemicals. This is made from some natural and some recycled materials.

The floor in the library is bamboo, which is as hard as hardwoods. It's no more expensive and no trees were cut down. It's a grass. There's an abundance of bamboo. Our doors and building accents are constructed from wood certified by the Forest Stewardship Council.

Did NWF start as a lobbying organization or an educational organization?

Part of our mission has always been to influence policy. We focus on educating our leaders and representatives. It is the USA's largest private, non-profit conservation education and advocacy organization. It is the USA's largest member-supported conservation group, uniting individuals, organizations, businesses and government to protect wildlife, wild places and the environment.

> **Part of our mission has always been to influence policy. We focus on educating our leaders and representatives.**

The mission is to educate, inspire and assist individuals and organizations of diverse cultures to conserve wildlife and other natural resources and to protect the Earth's environment in order to achieve a peaceful, equitable and sustainable future.

Have you considered using eNature for statistics gathering? There's a parallel in the IT field. Linux, the IT software operating system, has the whole world to help develop the system. Will you engage people so they feed in the wildlife they see in their backyards? The potential for interactive information building is huge once you are online with an active system.

Exactly. One of our programs is the backyard wildlife habitat program. We certify people who make their backyards habitable for wildlife. We've been going out and gathering information from them. ENature will do exactly that. First of all we'll have access. Through eNewsletters we'll talk about conservation issues. We'll link them to nwf.org.

I'd like to ask you about how your advocacy works. How do you work with organizations such as government and EPA? I know you have lobbyists on Capitol Hill. You have been active on the Clean Air Act, in the Clean The Rain Campaign, Conservation and Reinvestment Act and on health-related issues such as mercury, dioxins and lead?

Mary: Every year our affiliates come together. They guide the direction of policy. It's a very grass roots-led organization.

Larry: That's exactly right. The resolutions that the affiliates vote on at each year's AGM become part of the NWF's portfolio. The policies can come either from affiliates or from affiliates and staff working together. Or the staff may make proposals. But grass roots advocacy is what NWF brings to the table in terms of the environmental and conservation movement. Whether it's Everglades Funding or Clean The Rain, our lobbyists on the Hill have our grass roots right behind them! They act as the voice of that constituency.

Mary: It's a very interesting model of governance. But a very powerful one to have affiliate organizations in every state that are robust in their own right coming and making the policy and electing directors.

PART IV

THE UNIVERSE
OF RISK

The risk model **11**

In this section I describe the need for an integrated, embedded, enterprise-wide risk management strategy based on a universe of risk model, which I have devised, which 'captures' all significant risks. The models and checklists are simple enough to be self-explanatory. I talk to risk and internal audit directors from banking, investment management and insurance about their risk management philosophy and models.

Corporate commitment	Knowledge management	Key issues and players	UOR tools and methodologies	The dynamics of change
Corporate governance issues	IT IS Internal KM External KM Security E-commerce Legal aspects	Financial Environment Ethical Political Social	Risk definition Risk classification Methodologies Risk mapping Risk ownership	Corporate survival Upcoming risks The new dynamics

Fig 11.1: The universe of risk

Where were we? (Alice in Wonderland)

- Where are we now?
- What are we doing?
- Why are we in this?

- Where do we want to be?
- What risks can we manage?
- Where is the world going?

Where should we be?

YESTERDAY **TODAY** **TOMORROW**

Fig 11.2: Yesterday, today and tomorrow
Copyright: Prisconsult 2000

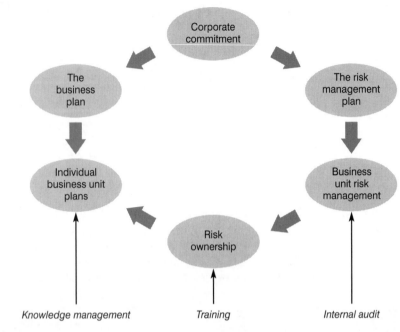

Knowledge management   Training   Internal audit

Fig 11.3:   Intergrating risk management into the business plan

Copyright: Prisconsult 2000

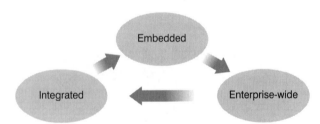

Fig 11.4:   Risk management: embedded, integrated and enterprise-wide

Copyright: Prisconsult 2000

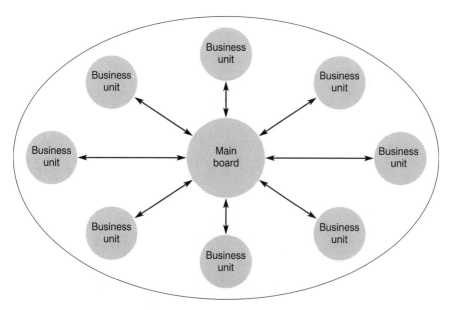

Fig 11.5: Business unit reporting in embedded risk management
Copyright: Prisconsult 2000

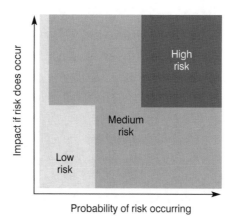

Fig 11.6: Risk map
Copyright: Prisconsult 2000

Fig 11.7:   Strategy and execution – Old Economy   Copyright: Prisconsult 2000

Fig 11.8:   Strategy and execution – Old Economy   Copyright: Prisconsult 2000

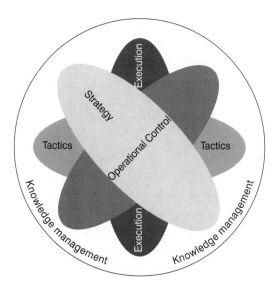

Fig 11.9: Strategy and execution – New Economy

Copyright: Prisconsult 2000

Risk assessment and management

Risk management is the overall process which defines the strategy to identify and manage risk. The three important aspects of the universe of risk model are that it should be:

■ **integrated**. The risk management strategy should leave nothing to chance. There is a universe of risk model which 'captures' all significant risks and identifies, analyzes, prioritizes and manages those risks.

■ **embedded**. The scope of risk is potentially so wide that this is not something that can or should be managed by a small team – whether that team is at the top of the corporate ladder or elsewhere. It certainly can no longer be the exclusive preserve of the insurance manager. By 'embedded' we mean that every person working for the organization knows the risk management system, the model, the hoops that they have to go through in everything they do – monthly management meetings at business unit level, board meetings, new project analysis, or ordinary, everyday operations.

■ **enterprise-wide**. In a global economy, enterprise-wide risk management must be established to ensure consistent embedding of the integrated strategy across all locations, operating units and countries where the organization does business.

A consistent framework for evaluating risk and return is a useful tool in identifying merger and acquisition opportunities. Integrated risk management systems can help organizations understand the risk/return trade-offs between products, services, customers and markets.

The risk map (see Fig 11.6) is based on the principal assumptions: objective, non-objective, internal, external, verifiable, non-verifiable, likely, unlikely, predictable, unpredictable. It assesses levels of risk for various operations and strategies.

Corporate positioning: yesterday, today and tomorrow (see Fig 11.2): internal knowledge management involves exploring where the organization was, is and wants to be. The company that does not change does not grow. Heraclitus, the philosopher of flux, sought to prove that everything was in perpetual motion through his river paradox. Although a river may look much the same as it did yesterday, 'one cannot step in the same river twice', he said.

Peter Keen, Managing Director, Merlin Biosciences, notes: 'You have to work hard to keep on top of it. The business models change. I think it's fair to say that, if you're doing what you were doing two years ago, then you're probably doing it wrong.'

Global Continuity's Richard Pursey is clear about the stages his business has gone through as it has reinvented itself several times to keep abreast of market demands. 'The business has changed as the market has changed,' he says.

Oil company Shell has a group called the game-changer panel, with $20 million venture capital to back unconventional new business ideas from within the company. Diageo, the food and drinks conglomerate, has scrapped budgets in an attempt to free staff to react more quickly to their markets.

> **The race goes to the swift, but the race also goes to the sure footed.**

John Harvey-Jones in *Making It Happen – Reflections on Leadership*, writes, 'Industry and business are essentially a race where unless we are out in front someone else will be. The race goes to the swift, but the race also goes to the sure footed and it is the achievement of a balance between these two characteristics, plus the right choice between the new trail and the well-proven road, that lead to success.'

Risk management is about achieving that balance. The ability to balance New Economy initiatives and Old Economy fundamentals is what will make the difference between successful organizations and the failures.

The organization needs to create a model and implement a system covering its whole universe of risk (Fig 11.1). The Universe of Risk Model™ comprises the following elements:

1 Corporate commitment.

2 Knowledge management.

3 Key issues and players.

4 The universe of risk: tools and methodologies.

5 Corporate survival and the dynamics of change.

These correspond to the sections in this book.

Checklists for risk assessment

The following are some typical checklists to aid risk assessment:

Cost factoring of risks (materiality)

To evaluate risks, some idea of the financial implication is needed, based on:

- direct-hit financial costs;
- reputation costs;
- operational costs;
- business loss cost potential;
- provisions for failure to identify and manage risks.

Risk ownership and assignment

Allocation of ownership of risk is followed by action on one of the following:

- Accept and manage risks.
- Assign risks.
- Risk derivatives.
- Residual risks identification.

Have we got it right?

What else do we need to assess? For example:

- Analysis of risk priorities for key external players (stakeholders).
- Gap analysis to define relative importance of un-managed risks to internal and external stakeholders.
- How do risks impact on the organization's legal and self-imposed duties for financial, environmental, ethical and social reporting?

- What risks did the organization fail to anticipate and manage in the previous 12 months?

Risk-related performance parameters

What risk parameter factors have impacted on:

- financial performance?
- reputational performance?
- board strategy?
- operational objectives?
- sales?
- cash flow?
- employee integrity at all levels?
- data integrity?

Risk management procedures

- Definitions: types of risks.
- The universe of risk.
- Planning.
- Legal, codes of practice, international and other requirements.
- Objectives and targets.
- Management programme(s).
- Implementation and operation.
- Structure and responsibility.
- Training, awareness and competence.
- Communication.
- Management system documentation.
- Document control.
- Operational control.
- Emergency preparedness and response.

- Checking and corrective action.

- Monitoring and measurement.

- Non-conformance and corrective and preventive action.

- Records.

- System integrity.

- System audit: verify systems, facts, events, near-misses.

- Board-level review.

Documentation review

1 Review available reports.

2 Obtain additional information.

3 Discussions with management and other employees.

4 Discussions with outsourcers and subcontractors.

5 Review liabilities, provisions and contingencies.

Risk identification

1 Evaluate risks.

2 Define nature of risks: financial, external stakeholder, etc.

3 Prioritize, accept, reject, assign, etc.

4 Identify opportunities in risk situations.

5 Identify risks in opportunity situations.

6 Risk identified as a potential for a capital gain.

7 Risk identified as a potential for a capital loss.

8 Residual risks: decision tree to identify vulnerable risk areas (less-than-smart management scenario, exposure, beyond business-as-usual).

9 Responsibility and authority; 'ownership' of risk; internal and external.

10 Change management.

11 Upcoming issues.

12 Materiality: what degree of risk exposure is tolerable?

12

Risk management in diversified financial companies

In recent years financial institutions and their supervisors have placed increased emphasis on the importance of measuring and managing risk on a firmwide basis – a co-ordinated process referred to as consolidated risk management.

Although the benefits of this type of risk management are widely acknowledged, few if any financial firms have fully developed systems in place today, according to a report in the New York Federal Reserve's March 2001 Economic Policy Review. The report, by NYFR Vice-President Beverly J. Hirtle and her colleague Christine M. Cumming, suggests that significant obstacles have led financial institutions to manage risk in a more random fashion. But they note that many large institutions are devoting significant resources to developing consolidated systems to cover diverse financial activities, customers and markets (Joint Forum 1999a). Many of the points they make are relevant to diversified companies outside the financial services industry. They define consolidated risk management as 'integrated or enterprise-wide risk management – a co-ordinated process for measuring and managing risk on a firmwide basis'.

While both parties agree on the importance of this type of risk management, support seems to be motivated by quite different concerns.

Supervisors of the financial services industry in the USA support it on the basis of 'safety-and-soundness'. In contrast, financial institutions appear willing to make significant efforts to develop consolidated risk management systems because they believe that those systems will help them assess the risk and return of different business lines, and allow more informed decisions about where to invest scarce resources to maximize profits.

The cost of implementing such systems, NYFR reports, results in a trade-off between information and regulation costs on one hand and the value derived from the consolidated risk management system on the other. In the past there have been technical hurdles to overcome for companies with a broad range of activities, even within the financial services sector.

Financial institutions in the USA and the EU are now involved in a wider range of activities than ever. These include banking, asset management, investment in companies which they help to manage. The Gramm-Leach-Bliley Act will enable affiliations including banking, securities and insurance underwriting in financial holding companies (FHCs).

Diversity of functions and mergers across geographical borders potentially extend the diversity of risk. The New York Fed believes that this complexity, by necessitating corporate intranets, aids consolidated risk management.

Diversity of functions and "mergers across geographical borders potentially extend the diversity of risk.

In 1999 the Fed issued guidelines for evaluating capital adequacy in light of the full range of risks facing a bank or holding company. Internationally the Basel Committee on Banking Supervision extended the framework to define the risk management process to include business strategy. It increased the scope to cover the activities of business unit chief executives.

An international forum of banking, securities and insurance regulators has published guidance for financially diversified companies to identify and manage risk on a group-wide basis (Joint Forum 1999a). The absence of an integrated risk management system would result in enhanced exposures and the transmission of material problems. The absence of an embedded system would also allow certain exposures to go unmanaged.

They rejected the 'silo' approach because risks are interdependent and cannot be segmented and managed solely by independent business units.

The Fed believes that consolidated risk management may allow a firm to recognize natural hedges – when one entity within the firm has positions or is engaged in activities that hedge the positions or activities of another part of the firm.

But this will only be apparent when there is an integrated, embedded system of risk management?

Firms that fail to recognize the diversification effects of such natural hedges may waste resources on redundant hedging by individual units.

A firm that has an embedded RM system will not have to waste time determining its aggregate position during times of crisis, market disruption, business continuity disruption or customer disaffection for whatever reason.

Reputational risk migrates across locations and international borders. Shell's Brent Spar experience started in the UK but the knock-on effects from consumer boycotts in Germany were what quickly led management to accede to Greenpeace's demands to review its oil rig disposal policy. Integrated and embedded RM creates interdependence between divisions within a diversified company. Financial risks taken by one business unit can impact on the availability of capital for another BU (the 'fungibility' of intra-firm capital). A company's internal capital market is a major area of corporate co-ordination.

The Fed sees two possible approaches:

1 Liquidity risk assessment involves knowledge of the company's risk exposures: the liquidity risk position should reflect the amount and type of risk that BU chief executives take on.

2 An integrated risk assessment approach would consider liquidity along with credit, market and other financial risks.

Leveraged risk was the subject of a report into the failure of a long-term management hedge fund in 1998. The conclusion was that there needs to be an integrated RM system which has under its umbrella all types of financial risk: market, capital, liquidity and leverage on capital. The Fed believes that debtholders and creditors will be drivers for integrated, enterprise-wide RM systems...

In agreeing to extend credit, these parties must take into account the moral hazard incentive that the firm has to increase its risk exposure – to the benefit of shareholders and the detriment of creditors – once credit has been extended. This situation is acute for financial firms which can change their risk profiles rapidly using derivatives and other liquid financial instruments. In the face of uncertainty, creditors may charge higher rates.

"" The Fed believes that debtholders and creditors will be drivers for integrated, enterprise-wide RM systems...

The way round this is for the firm to present an intregrated RM analysis that can be used to evaluate the exposures. Prisconsult's Risk Rating system evaluates a company's non-financial as well as financial risk rating according to five categories: R to RRRRR (see www.prisconsult.com).

A model embedded, enterprise-wide risk management

13

By Steve Barlow, Group Chief Internal Auditor, *Prudential*

When I was working for Andersens I shared an office with Steve Barlow, another 'experienced hire' as those of us who had not joined straight from university were called.

Steve was a great colleague. We often polished off lunch in half an hour downstairs in the staff canteen. The amount of professional knowledge sharing we managed in that half hour was pretty impressive. Steve, who had been head of internal audit at Pearson, was supportive when I joined.

He always had great client-friendly chat-up lines. He always initiated a client discussion with enquiries over personal matters. This generally meant he was discussing holiday plans – his and his clients'. I am sure it was partly because of his amiable manner that he brought in millions of pounds' worth of business.

Sadly for, he soon left for greener pastures at Prudential. He was recruited as Group Chief Internal Auditor to re-position the internal audit function to add more value. He makes the point for an embedded risk management culture, with internal audit being part of that: 'Internal audit is a key user of the output and makes an input into that.' He has worked closely with Group Finance Director Philip Broadley and Group Chief Executive Jonathan Bloomer to ensure that risk management was on course to be Turnbull compliant by the first quarter of 2001. His approach is very much one that I agree with – although different organizations may approach it in slightly different ways. And that is what this book is all about.

I asked Steve: How do you define 'risk management'?

I'd define it as the threat that internal and external events will adversely affect our ability to achieve our goals and hence impact value creation. It may be that something good WON'T happen, or that something BAD will happen. But taking well managed risks is essential for creating value.

Would you say that your company has an integrated risk management strategy which covers all significant risks (financial and non-financial) and all corporate global locations?

Yes, but not as 'integrated' as it could and should be. This is an ongoing issue which is being tackled as part of the 'full' embedding of risk management. The way that we manage risk is very much based on the fundamental principle that risk needs to be managed by all of the management and all of the people in the organization. So the best way to do that is to have a common, overall approach but to have the line managers actually responsible for risk management on a day-to-day basis.

> **Risk needs to be managed by all of the management and all of the people in the organization.**

The way that we manage that at the centre is we have checks and balances in our overall framework to make sure that there is regular review of how risk is being managed by each of our business units. The way that comes together is through what we call our dialogue process – and that takes place between the group chief executive and the group finance director and possibly any other executive directors who have responsibility for a particular business unit and the business unit's management team. They will meet regularly during the year to go through an update on how the business is performing against the business plan. In that meeting there is a consideration, an evaluation, an update of how the risks and opportunities are being managed by that local business unit management team.

So we have very much embedded the risk management process into the way that the group and the business units manage their individual business units; and the overall way in which the business is managed. We don't have a separate risk function *per se* at the centre. If you create a separate risk function you have not embedded risk management because you have created a silo of risk reporting. You need to channel it through the chief executive and existing relationships, and the way that he or she manages individual business units. We have an embedded system which is totally embedded. You don't actually see that it is risk because risk management is the same thing as the way the business is managed. It is very much driven back into the way that the chief executive is managing the business units. That is the culture and the philosophy at its most simple.

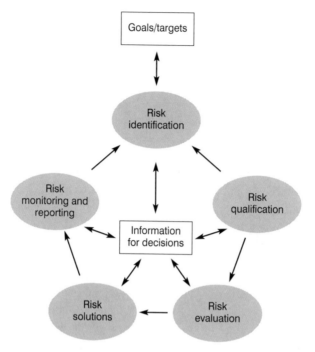

Fig 13.1   Prudential Group risk management cycle

Copyright: Prudential

Turnbull has led public companies to re-assess their risk management. Many organizations are groping their way forward. They are aware of the gaps in how they have managed risk in the past. Risk management is being re-written right now, isn't it?

I think that's right. I think a lot of companies are struggling with implementation, mainly 'over-engineering' and not recognizing that risk management is the same thing as good business management.

You need clarity with how you implement risk management, clarity with the way the business is managed, the strategic objectives of the organization. The chief executive and the board have always led the process of thinking through the risks, managing the company.

How do you risk manage your risk management? Say you were putting in a new IT or e-commerce system. How do you ensure that the risks are addressed up front, and not just left to the insurance guy to cover at the end of the implementation?

Implementation of these systems again – because of the size and complexity of the group – has to be managed on a decentralized basis. To give you a flavour of the scale and size of the group: in Asia we are already operating out of 11 different countries. So you have 11 different cultures and 11 different sets of regulatory risks. All you can have is an overall umbrella in terms of common approach to thinking about risk management.

The local IT director in Taiwan, for example, within the overall risk language that he is operating under, would consult with the local compliance function, for example, to understand what the compliance risks are; the local legal department to make sure he has fully understood the legal risks. But he would be the accountable person, responsible for making sure that a new system in that particular country was implemented in a way which managed the risks associated with that implementation. To try to do that somehow centrally is actually something which I do not think you can do.

The pieces that we are working on, and we need to improve significantly on, is something which you and I both believe is incredibly important – and that is knowledge management. This is an example of looking at risk from an upside perspective. What we ought to be doing is giving that person the benefit of the knowledge that the organization has and how we have tackled a similar implementation elsewhere in the group. Therefore what we are working on – and we are not perfect in this regard – is a corporate intranet which enables us to share knowledge and information about, for example, how new systems are being implemented in different parts of the organization. So this particular IT director is not implementing something on an 'island'. He can draw upon knowledge that's available elsewhere in the organization to help him improve and avoid potential pitfalls related to what he's tackling at this particular time.

> **Knowledge and information sharing are critical to risk management.**

So knowledge and information sharing are critical to risk management. Information for decision-making is at the heart of risk management.

Fig 13.2   Prudential's risk map

Copyright: Prudential

Don't you think that knowledge management, wonderful though it is, is dependent on people keeping it up-to-date? We both have experience of systems which are not kept up-to-date and so are useless when someone comes to use them.

Very much so. The whole area of how you deal with information overload, and how you make sure that the right people in the organization are given access to the right information, at the right time, to help them do their job more efficiently and effectively is one of the top five issues that we have identified as an organization that we need to do better.

The others are around:

- ways in which we manage our people: how we recruit, retain and develop the best people;

- how we leverage the IT capabilities across the group: leverage the expertise which we develop, for example, from the e-commerce perspective in terms of our internet bank egg;

- clarifying the role and responsibility of the group at the centre: and how it adds value to the whole organization;

- how we manage our capital across the organization: so that we exploit profitable and cash-generative initiatives and have a prioritization mechanism around that.

To be specific, the business potential of Asia is growing very rapidly, therefore it has capital requirements. UK margins are under pressure. A downside is our field salesforce in an internet-enabled era. So we are changing the way that we are selling to our customers. We are changing the ways in which we speak to our customers, moving to more remote, but hopefully interactive, methods through telephones, call centres and away from the 'man from the Pru'. That presents a different set of opportunities. The question is how do we profile our opportunities? Is it change in the UK or growth in Asia first? How much capital do we allocate to each? Those are obviously critical issues for the organization as a whole to address.

Strategically we as an organization need to be global. We have said that we are a multinational, multibrand, multichannel business having global scale. This was very much behind the strategy for the acquisition of American General. This, as you know, was the subject of AIG's competing bid for AG.

" " In terms of risk management, it is a stated objective that we are interested in acquisitions of e-businesses overseas and particularly in North America.

We operate in a global arena. Strategically I know that it is very much on our agenda to ensure that we are a global-scale player in the financial services sector. In terms of risk management, it is a stated objective that we are interested in acquisitions of e-businesses overseas and particularly in North America. That is driven from the core strategy of the business.

Prudential's senior management got together in Atlanta. You all prioritized all the important issues as you saw them. What can you tell me about that?

We discussed the five issues I talked about – plus a sixth which was how we dot com the organization. We linked in how to leverage benefits and how egg was a very big part of our future growth.

We had a discussion: 'destroy dot com'. The idea was to dot com all our legacy systems to make sure that we remained low-cost providers. The idea is that we can treat our customers as individual customer lines of one person. The benefit of the e-commerce proposition is that you can really get to know the individual requirements of each individual customer. And you treat each individual customer as a customer line of one. You can then tailor your service specifically to that person's requirements. That is one of the other objectives in terms of opportunities that we flagged up. As an organization we have a number of initiatives under way, not just in egg, to dot com the organization – from our back-office process through to our customer interface and front-end processes.

A lot of online banks and Old Economy companies have introduced dot com initiatives. The benefits are not always immediately obvious – and there are new risks. How are you addressing the challenges?

Security risk is critical to customer confidence. Therefore for any new e-commerce system implementation we have internal audit closely involved in ensuring that there is an appropriate security infrastructure in place. We have an overall group security policy and framework which is directed from the centre which individual business units have to comply with. Internal audit is tasked with making sure that there is compliance with that framework, in particular when new systems are being developed. Local management is made wholly aware that security is a business-critical activity. Jonathan Bloomer, when he has business unit dialogue meetings, if there is an e-commerce application that is in the pipeline, one of his dialogue questions of the business unit will be to get an update as to how the project is progressing.

Security will be one of the strategic issues he will make sure is on the chief executive's and IT director's agenda…The internal audit comes in to give assurance at a more detailed level that there has been appropriate coverage given.

Second, fraud control requires robust systems. What we are looking to do is maximize the system-generated controls to enable us to hopefully prevent fraud in the first place; and also to flag up examples of fraud. Our anti-fraud record is very strong. From the customer's perspective it is very important to make sure that we know who our customers are from a fraud and money-laundering perspective. When you join up to egg, you have to go through a process of being able to demonstrate that you are a bona fide person. Internal audit is responsible for ensuring that company policy has been applied. The time to do that is at the front end when the system requirement definitions are being put together. When the business case is being put together; and then being involved in the steering committee as the project develops. Ongoing, making sure that the procedures continue to be complied with.

Fraud control requires "robust systems.

Third, the customer experience is critical: getting them to understand what you are really trying to do. It is early days yet. We track people's requirements from an electronic perspective. If they have, for example, an egg card, we can immediately see what services they have and do not have. In an electronic environment, we know what the customer may be interested in.

There are legal implications to e-commerce. It is important that what you say online is accurate, that you are not making false claims, isn't it?

Yes. If we are saying that we have a product that is, say, market leading in terms of the interest rate being offered, whatever is stated in an electronic environment needs to be up-to-date and as accurate as if it were in an off-line environment. All the marketing literature going out electronically needs to be risk-managed. Egg has a compliance function which ensures that we know what the banking regulations are. Almost all their business is conducted online.

The risk map (Fig 13.2) is a common language and way of thinking about risk. We need to have a consistent language and way of thinking about risk across the whole of the organization to ensure that everyone talks in a similar sort of way. Take legal, regulatory and political risk: when you are having a brain-storming session with a board of directors, when people are talking about an opportunity or a risk, then the issue is captured in a consistent way so you can think about how you can manage that in a consistent way. You can compare and contrast across different business units how they are managing that risk. It gives you the benefit to leverage your knowledge as an organization so you manage more efficiently and effectively. The building block for doing that is having a common risk language.

Our business units are driven by their geographical location. Our business units are PC Asia (Prudential Corporate Asia) which operates out of 11 countries: there are sub-business units within that for Vietnam, China, Taiwan, Hong Kong, Singapore, Malaysia, Philippines, etc. The other business units are M&G, which is UK-based; egg; UK Insurance Operations – the old Pru life and pensions business and within it Scottish Amicable; in North America we have Jackson National Life and an asset management business, PPM America, operating out of Chicago which is affiliated to Jackson but separate from it.

Prudential Financial is a division of our UK insurance operations. Prudential Financial services is a business which incorporates things like our stakeholder proposition, pension schemes. Our strategy is to allow UK businesses to offer stakeholder pension plans to their employees through an e-enabled service. This enables us to bulk up. Selling a £3,600-a-year plan individually would not enable us to offer individual customers such a good deal. If you have 50 times £3,600 coming in that enables us to make money on a 1 per cent stakeholder fee. You have to think in an e-enabled way to offer that deal to customers. It also enables employers to set up a stakeholder pension scheme without setting up laborious, non-electronic processes.

The Prudential is one of the UK's largest financial services providers. Scottish Amicable is the lead brand in the independent financial adviser (IFA) marketplace, looking after the savings of 2 million people. It was looking for a secure and trusted environment when it launched an extranet to allow sharing with customers, suppliers and trading partners

" The bulk of transactions now take place over the net.

using web-based applications. So it uses digital certification technology, rather than names and passwords. Digital certification enables us to identify each individual IFA by interrogating their digital certificate. The bulk of transactions now take place over the net. The main security challenge was to manage access for thousands of IFAs. The aim eventually is to offer a completely personalized service for each IFA.

What about Prudential Securities?

That is not us. It's another company – Prudential of America. A lot of people get confused about that. It's a mutual with a similar background to us, about the same size. From a risk management perspective that's why we don't use the Prudential name in North America! I mentioned that our asset management business is called PPM America. We have an arrangement with Prudential of America that we will not use the Prudential name in North America and they will not use the Prudential name in the UK.

That is a legal risk?

In an electronic, global environment that is the type of risk you need to beware of. It's a most intractable situation because they have so much built up in their brand and we have so much built up in our brand.

Going back to the risk map and how you risk manage your risk management process, who knows about it?

All the business units, through the risk co-ordinator. We went through an education exercise when we rolled out this new risk framework. We primed business unit boards of directors in a series of workshops using this as the common language to make sure they were thinking about risk in a consistent way – and were capturing and classifying the risks which they were surfacing in a consistent way.

Notwithstanding what I said about embedded risk management, we do actually have risk reporting – but we do not make it a major thing. We major more on how the business is managed. We manage this on a quarterly basis with a stand-back, independent key risk report giving a full assessment under each risk heading.

Also, within the monthly management accounts, there is a heading where financial directors and business unit chief executives, when submitting their financial MI, have a heading to update whether there are any changes in the risk profile and whether there are any control issues which need to be surfaced.

Both of these come through to the finance department. They use it primarily to help the dialogue meetings as briefing material so appropriate questions can be asked by Jonathan and Philip, the CEO and CFO of the BU management.

Our new risk management framework dates back to when treasury were tasked by Jonathan to get us Turnbull-compliant. In 2000 we undertook two internal audits of our risk management process.

> **We found that we had a 'silo-based' approach to risk reporting.**

We found that we had a 'silo-based' approach to risk reporting. We were creating a risk function which was not properly embedded in the way the business was being managed. As a result of this review, I suggested leaving the risk reporting function at BU level, embedding it in the MI of the business. Otherwise it comes up to treasury and what do they do with it? You have to push it back to the BU level where most of the information is.

The core of a business is your financial and management reporting system. So you have to embed the risk management reporting within that. Otherwise it is going to be off-line to the way the business is actually managed. You need to have your risk information (RI) coming through on your corporate dashboard for the CEO when he is looking at the overall performance of the business. The way to do that is to push it back through one channel signed off locally by the business unit executive to the board and CEO.

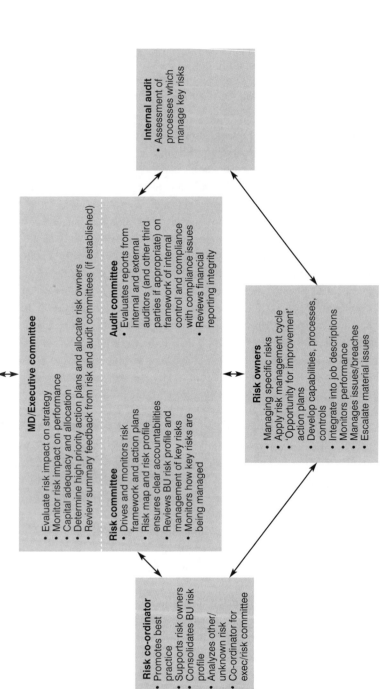

Fig 13.3 Prudential's risk management structure: how such a structure is applied is determined by each business unit

Copyright: Prudential

As a result of this internal audit, we made this change from treasury to group finance. We implemented Turnbull through:

■ having a common language;

■ a risk map;

■ rolling it out through the business units;

■ an ongoing reporting mechanism;

■ key risk reports;

■ embedding the risk reporting in the monthly management accounts.

Internal audit has played a role:

■ in reviewing the whole process and how it is implemented;

■ giving constructive advice which led to the changes we have implemented.

Internal audit is also involved in terms of any reports and issues we find which have a significant risk component. That triggers a loop back into the risk management process. That will lead management to update their risk profile. It will also lead internal audit to reflect upon the work that it is doing and make sure that its plans are updated so that it is continually looking at the key risks and the processes which should be in place to manage those risks. That is very much internal audit's role.

It needs to be independent of the risk management process. It is a key user of the risk information which risk process produces for it but it is also a contributor back into the risk process as a result of the work and the findings it has. It is independent but it sucks up information, contributes information back into the risk process. It also facilitates management in thinking laterally about their risk profiles and whether they are implementing appropriate risk management action plans related to their business strategy.

Risk owners are allocated risk. Who allocates risk?

Risk is allocated by the BU's CEO. In the group risk framework (Fig 13.3), we start with risk identification, quantification and evaluation. We then devise the solutions. So the next step on the risk cycle is to know who your risk owner is.

Pulling all this together is the information for decision-making. So throughout the whole process the BU CEO needs to monitor progress in relation to what the particular risks and opportunities are. The BU needs to clarify its business plan. It is very much a continuous process, driven locally within the overall management framework with central reporting.

The goals and targets are the strategic business objectives. We tend not to use the word 'strategy'.

The second outcome of the internal audit was the conclusion that risk planning needs to be integrated with business planning. We said, 'When you do your business planning, unless you have done a proper assessment of the risks and opportunities, then we cannot be fully Turnbull-compliant.'

> **When you do your business planning, unless you have done a proper assessment of the risks and opportunities, then we cannot be fully Turnbull-compliant.**

When the business planning cycle started we made sure that there was a proper consideration of risk, properly documented as part of the business planning process. Again it was pushing it back. Rather than saying, 'We are going to have a risk report,' it is saying, 'No. It is actually the business plan.'

Any organization that has a risk report, I would say is not really Turnbull-compliant in the spirit of Turnbull. It is not embedded. I am horrified that some organizations have a risk function at the centre. Any organization that has two or three people who call themselves 'risk', I think, has two too many. As an accountant who has specialized in business risk consulting and assurance for many years, I see it as a co-ordination role. The definition of risk management and the way business is managed should be one and the same thing.

There is a whole career structure, a profession, being generated off the back of Turnbull – which is patently what Turnbull did NOT want to happen. This is to an extent led by the 'Big Five' accounting firms. There are examples across a number of organizations which I am aware of where those organizations are not embedding risk management. They think the answer to Turnbull involves having lots of risk people. The CEOs of those companies need to ask whether those risk people are properly integrated.

This is a valid point. What historically is the corporate risk manager (CRM) has operated at the operational level – the people who used to deal just with insurance or chemical/disaster recovery. They have been in an insurance role. Now they are struggling because people are not talking to them early enough. The IT people buy the IT system and then just say 'Can you insure this?' whereas the CRM wants to be brought in at the design stage to design out the legal risk, the fraud risk, the hackers and so on. Then you have internal audit, which is part of the finance function so you have two separate functions, both charged with managing risks which have major financial implications. But they are at different levels in the hierarchy.

Yes. It comes back to the definition. If the definition of risk management is that your starting point is the strategic objectives of the organization, you have to look not only at the downside but the upside. Obviously someone confined to an insurance background is struggling because they are nowhere near involved in that. It has to be driven through the chief executive. The ultimate risk manager of the organization is your chief executive. All the systems and processes need to be aligned to provide him or her with the relevant information. He needs the assurance of knowing how risks are being managed across the organization.

> **If the definition of risk management is that your starting point is the strategic objectives of the organization, you have to look not only at the downside but the upside.**

Underneath that you replicate it with your business unit CEOs. All the systems and processes need to within an architecture which does not call it risk reporting. It needs to be the core way in which the business is managed.

What about upside risks?

Our definition of risk is 'the threat that internal and external events will adversely affect our ability to achieve our goals and hence impact value creation'. That is 'shareholder value creation'. What that means is that taking well-managed risks is essential for creating value. What that is saying is 'it is the risk that something good WON'T happen or something BAD will happen'.

What lots of organizations have got wrong is that if you value the definition of what business management is about, there is nothing different from the way in which the business is managed. Any manager will be looking at upsides and downsides. Any organization or function which is splitting off the loss side and only thinking about what can go wrong has totally got it wrong.

Wherever there is a chance for a capital loss there is also a chance for a capital gain.

Yes. It should be 50:50. Some organizations are driven from the regulatory perspective. Banks in particular are driven by the Basle Accord regulatory framework which requires loss information and capital adequacy to be captured centrally in the MI. This is a totally different concept and definition of what risk management is all about. It will be rolled out for insurance and other financial services.

From a commercial perspective, our modus operandi should be oriented towards what is appropriate commercially – upsides as well as downsides.

What does Prudential expect of the companies in which it invests?

M&G is responsible for all our corporate investments. We would monitor, as any financial institution would, the financial and general performance of the individual investment. Good corporate governance is something we would look to I am sure.

Tell me a bit more about how the workshops helped develop the system.

Workshops were, and are, used to help prioritize risks. We use them to 'pump prime' the whole process of facilitation and risk identification. We trained up a number of people to run facilitated workshops. We use interactive voting software to energize the sessions and make sure there is a focus on the key issues.

There's a first level of voting to prioritize the significant and likely risks. You see interactively on screen the consensus view of the group of the most significant and likely risks. Then you take these and use subsequent voting to answer the questions: What are you as a team going to do differently as a result of having identified those risks? What's the opportunity for improvement on those critical issues? What's the timescale for action?'

That helps the team as a whole to focus on the real things they are going to do differently. Because everything has been captured electronically, you can turn round and give them a report on what they have voted on.

With an embedded system, you have to get the business units to 'own' those risks. It is their risk management action plan. It's not ours. Some BUs do their own workshops now, which is great! That was the whole purpose of training up people. Notwithstanding the decentralization of risk, we have also done workshops for the board and for HR, at corporate level. This means we have expertise right across the group to run these workshops. It comes back to the beast that you're dealing with in a very large diverse group.

Do you monitor progress?

We certainly want to see the outputs because that helps us refine our overall approach and learn from one another. I do not see them all – I cannot with a group of this size. But I need to have an overall mechanism to have risks surface for me. If there are risks which we have identified which are not being managed locally, it is only on an exception basis. I have a reporting framework in place for escalation of any issues which are not dealt with locally through to me so I can brief top management at the centre and at the audit committee level. We also have a decentralized model in internal audit. I have got head of internal audit in each of my business units who would be involved in this risk process.

What feedback did you get from the workshops?

> **The most significant thing which arose was the consistent message that we needed to get our act together on e-business.**

It goes back to the fact that good risk management is good management. The most significant thing which arose was the consistent message that we needed to get our act together on e-business.

This led Jonathan to appoint an executive director for e-business and a central strategic team to co-ordinate e-business across the group. He has been facilitating knowledge-sharing across the Group. We have all been learning from egg and other e-business stuff going on elsewhere in the group. This has temporarily been contrary to our policy of decentralization. But what is the role of the centre? The role of the centre is to have mechanisms to put people in contact.

Why did people think they needed an e-business director? Was it because people didn't know where you were going or what?

That is a good question. Probably because it was so new, we had not yet embedded e-business in everything we do. E-business and strategy. It is not just an area of marketing. Every person should be doing e-business. In internal audit, in HR, wherever, we should all be setting up e-enabled systems. We have initiatives under way to improve the way we are using e-enabling tools. It is the same as picking up a telephone. E-business is becoming Business As Usual.

You mentioned Business As Usual. I always see that as a precursor to, what do we need tomorrow to move the company on? BAU is what worked yesterday – not what is necessarily going to work tomorrow?

BAU needs a mechanism to think out of the box to achieve competitive advantage. Strategy Away Days to brainstorm where the business is going, how you're going to steal a march on our competitors. This is the heart of good risk management. That is integral to the way Prudential is managed.

People risk is very much a stakeholder issue. We have an incentivization package, a remuneration structure, which is linked to performance. There are two levels. One level is related to the direct financial performance, the profitability

People risk is very much "a stakeholder issue.

of the company. The other element is related to what we call the leadership imperative. This is a set of values as to what constitutes a good manager.

Overall headings in our leadership imperatives are:

- Action-oriented.

- Strategic.

- People manager.

What about cultural challenges of operating in different countries? The challenges not just to profitability per se but the risk that local people have the wrong idea about the company? Sainsbury in Egypt, for example, lost sales because it was perceived as a Jewish company.

Our approach is to defuse risks by being multibranded, multichannel and multinational. So we do not just use the Prudential brand. We operate in the way which is appropriate for each individual market. You really understand your local customer, your local regulations, the local culture, the language. What drives our approach is understanding what are the products and services which are going to sell locally.

This is contrary to branding?

It is not contrary. It is important, if the Prudential name is used in a market that we have an appropriately consistent image that is presented. The overall framework for how the brand should be managed on a global basis is determined by the corporate communications people. In terms of letterhead, literature, etc. We decentralize brand management. In PC Asia, each country has a slightly different version of the brand. It is Prudential Singapore, Prudential Hong Kong…But it will be branded in the local language. In some, the Pru lady will not appear. They want to see a local company. It is getting close to the customer. The decisions on the *detail* of branding are delegated under the umbrella of the overall requirements of the centre.

PC Asia, which is based in Hong Kong, and is driven at the BU level by Mark Tucker who is the BU chief executive, with local BUs in Vietnam, Thailand, etc. will decide what is the appropriate way to market Prudential in each country.

❝❞ A well thought-out and structured acquisition is something which gives you global leverage.

A well thought-out and structured acquisition, if done with appropriate due diligence and research, is something which gives you global leverage – although to date, we have grown organically in PC Asia with the exception of joint ventures. Growth has been a mixture of organic, acquisition and collaborative joint ventures. That has been very successful. Each has their place in the strategy for growth in Asia.

■ Analysis

Prudential is very clear about how it wants to manage risk. It is rolling out the new risk management system in a way that gives individual business units a large amount of autonomy. This decentralized approach is appropriate to a large multinational company which is growing its international business. However, it keeps a tight rein on how risks are managed through group and business unit board meetings. There are quarterly updates for changes to the risk profile; monthly updates if there are significant changes; and bi-annual QA reviews by internal audit of the overall process.

The group does not appear to use quantitative risk management models which rank risks. The idea of quantum in risk is not an easy one to address. The scale of risk accepted by the chief executive, say, on a merger or acquisition issue, is a different order of magnitude from, say, an environmental issue managed by an operations manager. It is possible to assess gross and net risk in either case. But the potential for capital gain or capital loss, reputation gain or reputation loss, and so on, is not the same. So gross and net evaluations on a scale of one to five or one to ten, as used by some organizations, will not have the same significance for every risk.

Prudential was unsuccessful in its attempted takeover of American General. It agreed to terminate its merger agreement dated 11 March 2001 with American General Corporation of Houston, Texas, USA in consideration for which American General made an immediate payment to Prudential of the full termination fee of $600 million.

Prudential's risk management policy – summary

- Risk management is frontline BU responsibility:

  – proactively identify, understand and manage risks.

- Only retain/manage risks where they:

  – contribute to creating value;

  – withstand adverse outcomes;

  – involve processes and controls.

- Head office role is to:

  – set policy;

  – encourage risk-taking that adds value.

14 The risk maturity approach

By Susan Rucker, Partner, *KPMG*

S usan Rucker, a partner in KPMG's Assurance-Based Advisory Services practice, recently finished an assignment of helping to develop the firm's enterprise-wide risk management product suite. She is staying at the Waldorf-Astoria on Park Avenue, New York, while on client business. We meet in the lobby at midday and go down to the snack bar for a quick salad. We both have another appointment at one o'clock so we talk while we eat. Susan is focused and articulate. It is good fun to have a dialogue with another risk management consulting professional.

I start by asking Susan: How do you define 'business risk' at KPMG?

When we think about risk, we think about it in the context of business objectives and strategies. In that context, a business risk is something that will impede the achievement of a strategy or a business objective.

Do you have a distinctive approach to business risk?

We do. At KPMG, we approach it from two different levels – enterprise-wide and also at the process level, depending on the organization's needs as well as its maturity, if you will, in thinking about risks. We work with the client to help them understand where they are in the context of our proprietary risk maturity framework which helps them understand their risk approach as well as their risk aspirations. We compare them to other entities and talk with them about the way they handle risk.

There are different elements of the framework. An organization doesn't have to move to the same level of sophistication in each of the elements. We can plot where they want to go and then develop an action plan that will help them get there.

An important aspect of KPMG's approach is that we want to make sure that the organization understands their significant enterprise-wide risks. If senior management has not already done a risk inventory and assessment, we would facilitate that endeavour. But we would focus it at a highly strategic, enterprise-wide level so as to identify the 20 or 25 most critical risks, as opposed to the thousands of risks within an organization. For example, what are the risks that could put the organization out of business or seriously threaten its survival? Those are the ones we want to target for action.

Are you encouraging clients to establish embedded, integrated, enterprise-wide risk management?

Everyone's job has an element of risk management in it. How the organization chooses to communicate that fact, and to embed that, using your word, is

> **Everyone's job has an "element of risk management in it.**

up to them, based on the culture of their company. Some companies use very explicit frameworks and do things to communicate those frameworks such as develop unique vocabularies to discuss how they think about risk. They have board committees that oversee their risk management efforts, and you'll see aspects of the risk management framework become part of job descriptions and other aspects of how the organization communicates. Other companies choose to address risk in a more low-key fashion. For example, in the early days, the financial services industry imposed on its traders absolute limits on the risks they could and could not accept without providing an enterprise-wide context for risk management. What we are seeing now is that the consideration and establishment of enterprise-wide risk limits are moving up the chain to the top of the organization. This then sets a context for others in the entity to think about how this affects the way they do their jobs on a day-to-day basis.

As I said earlier, we also help organizations look at risk at the process level and to embed risk management there as well. Once you identify the risk from the strategic level you must move down to the process level to get it fixed and better enable the organization to achieve its business objectives.

What do you mean by the process level?

KPMG has a proprietary way of depicting businesses called business models. We have developed these models for almost forty industry segments. There are three kinds of processes in each of these models. There are what we call *core business processes*, which are those related to the major business functions. In a bank, a core process may be how they manage the deposit functions. There is a part of that process for setting up the account, another part to take deposits, and still another to handle withdrawals. There are also *strategic management processes*, which are those related to the development and implementation of the organization's strategy. Then there are *resource management processes* that are essentially common to all businesses but they are tailored to how an organization does business. The human resource process, for example, will help you answer the following: how do you hire people? Before you hire them, how do you identify the talent you want? Once you do that, how do you advertise? Get new hires on board? What is the process that you use to do evaluation?

We examine risk in processes within all three process categories. Every business has a set of processes that is unique to them, just as every business has a unique array of risks.

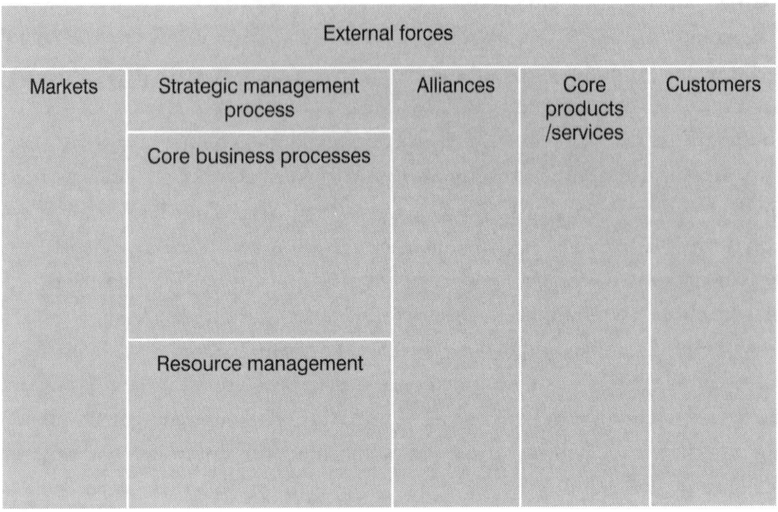

External forces				
Markets	Strategic management process	Alliances	Core products /services	Customers
	Core business processes			
	Resource management			

Fig 14.1 Business process in the context of the entity's industry and business model

Copyright: KPMG

Are we into forms? Or do you believe, as I believe, that the majority of these functions can be accomplished by the IT system? Keying critical phrases in the CV to requirements, matching the cost of purchasing gas here with the cost of purchasing energy somewhere else?

Are you asking about how to manage the risk? From a control standpoint or an embedded standpoint?

Yes.

> **In all probability, risk management will be embedded in systems in the future.**

In all probability, risk management will be embedded in systems in the future. If you think about the evolution of risk, most risk management today is historical. People have either forms to assist in the process or a way of looking back at performance results to determine whether they've been in compliance with risk management procedures and regulations.

In the future, risk management should become concurrent with business activities. For example, there may be embedded in the system information validation or checkpoints that function as controls related to identified risks. As someone is doing their job, they are actually getting feedback from the systems as to whether or not they are hitting the risk limits and/or optimizing risk appropriately.

If you think about it further, you can ultimately wrap predictive modelling around certain types of risk so that the predictive modelling can begin to impact strategic business decisions – not only at the company level but also at the process level. These models can help us answer the questions, What's this process going to do? Two hours from now? Twenty-four hours from now? Four years from now?

You have various levels of risk management within a company. Traditionally you have financial risk management. Then there are those managing operational or process risk. Third, there are internal and external audit – both of which are accustomed to remaining at arm's length from the strategic and process-risk management that you have described. There's often not a lot of dialogue between them. Because of corporate governance requirements and the way things are moving toward demands for a more comprehensive approach, there is a need for an ERM system.

Then you say, well, if the whole system is not going to drown in a sea of forms, audits, audits and yet more audits – for H&S, environment, finance risk, process, quality assurance and so on – there's a need to install technology to integrate all these checks and balances. In itself, that technology can save millions of dollars a year through simplification of the system and integration of resources and data. Not only is this more effective and efficient. It can add huge value. Do you agree?

In general, I would say that I agree with you. If the board establishes a risk management policy and begins implementing it throughout the organization, we believe that there will be a return. Quantifying this return may be difficult – the return related to establishing a risk committee is difficult, quantifying the return related to a derivatives or interest rate risk policy may not be. In the end, what you want, and what technology should enable, is to have your risk process enable the workforce to make the best decisions on a day-to-day basis by optimizing risk within the entity's risk appetite. The concept of optimization means that you take the right level of risk for your organization to balance risk and return, not the minimum level of risk which may sub-optimize business performance.

> **The concept of "optimization means that you take the right level of risk for your organization to balance risk and return.**

Some years ago there was a lot of talk about the 'paperless office'. One firm looked at replacing hard copies with electronic forms, e-mail and interactive systems. It had to design a form that was easy to use over the corporate network. It saved $25 million in processing costs. Many of these costs were people who were no longer required in the procurement function. Other companies who have established e-commerce functions now use two people to run the system where they formerly used 200 in a call centre. That kind of saving can be identified.

But going back to my question and your response, I am approaching it from the opposite direction. That if a company is trying to establish a good knowledge system, then risk is one of the areas that should be in there. My view is not that risk management needs to be technology-based but that an organization needs a master knowledge management system of which risk management is but a part. Otherwise you find you have all sorts of non-related IT systems which are not speaking to one another. Risk needs to be embedded in the rest of the organization's information system. There needs to be sharing – and instant access – to data.

In terms of quantification, do you assess gross risk and then see how this can be reduced to give a net risk figure?

At KPMG we do consider the concepts of gross risk and residual risk. Some level of risk is inherent in just about any situation. There are certain things you can do to optimize that risk, but some people say, 'I want to eliminate all risk.' That's probably not doable and not worth the effort. What you want to do is take a look at the gross risk and then say, okay, what is an acceptable level of risk. Driving to work, for example, poses a great number of risks, not all of which can be eliminated. I can't do anything about the risks posed by other drivers, but I can maintain my car, wear my seat-belt, drive carefully and so forth. In so doing I am creating an acceptable level of risk in exchange for the rewards of getting where I want to go.

Everyone understands that there is a risk-return equation. The higher the risk, the higher the reward. We talk about that a lot. But at some point, the risk gets so great that it outweighs the potential reward. The possibility of a negative return outweighs the possible positive return. Once you determine gross risk, you want to move to a level of risk (through management actions) that is compatible with your philosophy, your business objectives, and the way you choose to do business.

A lot of entrepreneurs that I talk with say that their approach is high-risk. If they don't take risks, there's no reward. It's the Star Trek approach. That's okay when you're a dominant entrepreneur but when you're looking at very big multinationals, that's probably not the way it is perceived. What's your experience?

Our clients have a broad range of personalities! Some people are very conservative in their business practices. Sometimes, that's driven by the leadership group, sometimes by the industry and the amount of regulation that they face, and other times by their customer base – and who they've chosen to target in various niches. There's no easily definable right or a wrong answer when it comes to how much risk you want to take. You have to look at your business circumstances. You will see different players in the same industry with very different risk profiles. Sometimes they can be very successful because they target the low-risk customers. Others will target those customers that are high-risk. For example, there are investment funds targeted at people that want high risk; others target people who want low risk. That translates to other industries as well.

We find that the best way to understand an organization's risk profile is to talk with someone within the company who is setting the tone. That may be the CEO. It may be the CRO or COO. Working within the division, it may be the division head. What we need to understand is the leadership philosophy of that person.

We will find people who say, 'I absolutely want my risk management systems to be non-invasive, to empower people as much as possible, to allow people to make their own decisions'. We'll find others who say, 'I need to minimize risk, to bring it down to a very low level'.

We know from long experience that if you try to get a company to do something that conflicts with their philosophy, it won't work. The amount of risk a company takes must be tailored to their own unique circumstances.

You need checks and balances. On the other hand, too much control and you stifle originality and the entrepreneurial spirit.

You do. And what we try to do is get leaders to understand that there is a balance. Actually sometimes the big issue is not an attitude that needs to be adjusted, but instead a lack of understanding of how the organization views risk. For example, many times we will see a wide diversity in the risk rating of a particular risk. You may see the person who's responsible for manufacturing say that a particular risk is absolutely the highest risk the company could take. The CFO may say it's the lowest risk.

> **Sometimes the big issue is not an attitude that needs to be adjusted, but instead a lack of understanding of how the organization views risk.**

So the question is, why would two people with two different jobs weight a risk differently? It is usually because of a difference in understanding of the risk. We have actually seen situations where we walk into a room and have six or seven people discussing a risk, and only one person rates that risk as high. But by the time that person has explained their rationale to the rest of the group, everyone else will rate the risk the same way. And vice versa.

This goes back to knowledge management. If you don't have all the available knowledge, you may not ever identify the risk, much less give it a consistent rating.

Better knowledge management systems can improve risk management. I think these systems are in their infancy in terms of their ability to capture and synthesize information to provide real-time input to decision-makers. These systems are also very limited in their ability to access information that is external to the company. Many times it is the marriage of internal and external information/knowledge that provides the biggest benefit to business people. If you think two or five years hence, these systems may be able to combine some sort of external knowledge scheme with some sort of internal knowledge scheme. Then you will begin to see a significant impact on decision-making.

I've been doing that for 15 years! It's all about something else: appreciation of public perceptions about the company and its products and services, its history, its capacity for change.

You have a strong IT risk competency. They feature elsewhere in this book. Tell me how ERM works with them.

KPMG has a group that concentrates on understanding the risks around information flows and the technology that enables those flows. Today more and more information is being handled digitally. As companies digitize, more and more of their information flows through systems – of their own and of their business partners. This can change the types and severity of the risks that an entity faces.

When we approach ERM engagements we bring to the table a multidisciplinary team that includes people with knowledge about risk, industry, technology and business process. This helps us to take a look at, and help the company understand, the risks they face and the way that they can optimize those risks.

A lot of people say the next step is to prioritize risk. But, to me, in an embedded, enterprise-wide, integrated risk management universe, all risks should be addressed and managed in some way. I agree with you that the company has to decide what level of risk it is comfortable with but prioritization misses the point for me.

> **" Most organizations can only deal with three to eight major initiatives at any given point in time.**

This is where we would disagree. Most organizations can only deal with three to eight major initiatives at any given point in time. Any good risk management system is going to have a series of management responses and controls.

You have to ask, what are the things that have to be built into the system to make a business work effectively and optimally? When you begin to identify risks that will impact the business and will require major change to optimize, you have to decide which are the biggest risks, and which can you put resources against to deal with in such a way that you change the way you manage them. That requires prioritization because most companies don't have unlimited resources to deal with identified risks.

Perhaps 95 per cent of the risk in financial terms may be in the hands of 5 per cent of executives, and they are going to be the CEO, CFO, chairman or COO. So you can't allocate the same risk weighting to all of your risks. Of course the major risks may require more detailed risk management. But all through the organization, there will be risks, small and large, to manage, and managing them should be part of every employee's day-to-day job.

Risks may also vary along the time continuum. If a location is suddenly subject to terrorism, riots or animal rights protesters, what may normally be a low-risk site becomes a priority for the company in terms of risk management resources.

In your example, 5 per cent of the people may make the strategic decisions on how much risk is acceptable and what direction the company is going to go in, but those 5 per cent cannot execute the risk strategy alone. They must determine how to delegate that execution, so that it does indeed become part of everyone's job.

In a conventional model, management sets the strategy. Managers are responsible for the execution. Are you saying the 5 per cent should be responsible for execution as well as strategy?

No. The 5 per cent may set limits around risks, or decide they want people taking more risk. But then they have to push the understanding of risk and responsibility for the day-to-day execution of risk management out to the individuals throughout the entity, and do this in such a way that the risk management system is sustainable and embedded in the operations of the company.

The conventional pyramid has strategy at the top, then, as you work down the pyramid, the tactical aspects, then operational and, at the base of the pyramid, execution.

To my mind, this is Old Economy. In the New Economy, more of a consensus approach exists, with various specialists at various levels contributing. However, that does not prevent a major part of the strategic and risk-taking decisions being in the hands of the top 5 per cent of executives.

At KPMG, we agree that risk cannot be only top down. We have developed our own proprietary risk maturity framework that helps think about risk throughout the organization (Figs 14.2 and 14.3).

> **At KPMG, we agree that "risk cannot be only top down.**

The first part of this framework is the risk strategy – we believe that you must understand the objectives and strategies of an organization, and link those to the strategy around risk.

Once the risk strategy is developed, it must be executed through the risk structure. This is the way an entity chooses to embed risk in its operations and culture.

The next step is measuring and monitoring – establishing criteria to measure risk and to help improve performance of the organization. Through the first three components, management will develop a portfolio of risks – those risks that have been identified, assessed and categorized across the entity.

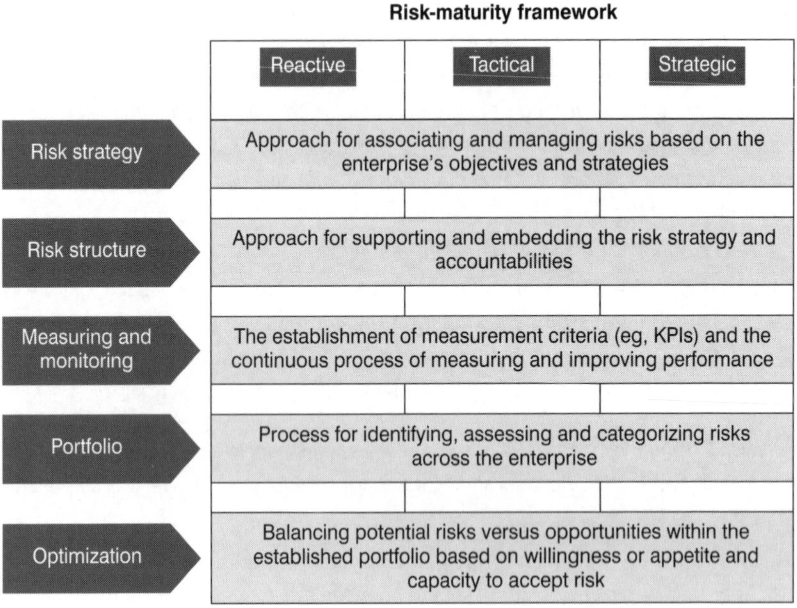

Risk-maturity framework

	Reactive	Tactical	Strategic
Risk strategy	Approach for associating and managing risks based on the enterprise's objectives and strategies		
Risk structure	Approach for supporting and embedding the risk strategy and accountabilities		
Measuring and monitoring	The establishment of measurement criteria (eg, KPIs) and the continuous process of measuring and improving performance		
Portfolio	Process for identifying, assessing and categorizing risks across the enterprise		
Optimization	Balancing potential risks versus opportunities within the established portfolio based on willingness or appetite and capacity to accept risk		

Fig 14.2 First, understand where you are...
Copyright: KPMG

KPMG

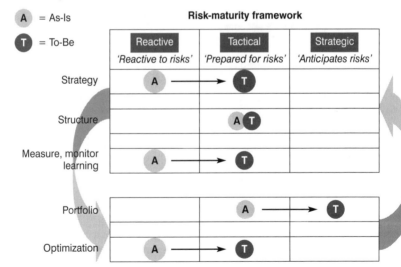

For example:

A = As-Is

T = To-Be

Risk-maturity framework

	Reactive *'Reactive to risks'*	Tactical *'Prepared for risks'*	Strategic *'Anticipates risks'*
Strategy	A ⟶	T	
Structure		A T	
Measure, monitor learning	A ⟶	T	
Portfolio		A ⟶	T
Optimization	A ⟶	T	

Fig 14.3 To allow you to determine your target action
Copyright: KPMG

Through optimization, this portfolio can then be put through a process of balancing risk and opportunities based on the willingness and capacity to accept risk. KPMG has developed an inventory of the characteristics of companies that are at different stages in each component of the framework – reactive, tactical or strategic. By comparing themselves to this inventory, they can understand where they stand in relationship to the components (their 'as is' state), and then decide where they want to move to within the framework (their 'to be' state).

Through this understanding of how they deal with risk today and how they want to deal with it tomorrow, companies can leverage the talents and efforts of all their personnel by embedding their own risk management framework within their organization.

In our work with clients and the risk maturity framework, we also leverage the industry-segment business models that were mentioned earlier. The business models help facilitate the risk identification process, support the analysis of identified risks and help provide a pre-populated framework that helps pinpoint where risks sit within the organization.

Finally, I would note that this work will present management with an array of choices. There will be choices to be made in how to embed the risk infrastructure, how to deal with identified risks, and what level of resources to devote to possible projects. Management should understand what criteria they will evaluate these choices against, and then rank them, assign responsibility, and monitor implementation. By doing this, management can begin to see the impact of their actions around enterprise risk management.

15

Information risk management

By Peter W. Morriss, Global Head of Information Risk Management, and Andrew Steet, Partner, Technology Assurance Services, *KPMG*

P eter W. Morriss has been involved in the risk assessment, audit, control and security of IT systems for more than 30 years. Andrew Steet has more than 20 years of experience in internal audit and IT audit. He is a council member of the Internal Audit Faculty of the International Chartered Accountants of England and Wales (ICAEW) and the Professional Issues Committee of the Institute of Internal Auditors (IIA) and is also the e-commerce spokesperson of the IIA.

I asked Peter to explain the consulting structure:

A client comes to us because they have a technology risk. Within KPMG there are three major areas:

1   Information Risk Management (IRM) – technology, which grew out of computer audit but now has a much wider remit.

2   Management Advisory Services (MAS) – basically internal audit from strategic review and design through to specific delivery contracts within different companies or parts of companies, depending where you are in the world.

3   Business Advisory Services (BAS).

How they split the bits between them may vary on the fringes. KPMG now have a Klegal firm which, although it is not part of Assurance, we do actually have some links between IRM and Klegal.

So that's the umbrella structure. I am responsible for information risk management globally, which is a chairman and oversight role, as opposed to an operational or functional management role. Major countries or groups of countries have operational partners in charge. I chair a group of those, plus one or two others who meet regularly to talk about various operational matters.

Within IRM we split up our services. Attest includes IRM specialists in statutory audit teams and the provision of MAS where opinions are given. Some of these opinions are beginning to be reported by way of web broadcasting methods using seals. We have issued word trust seals as a licensee through the English Institute. We are in the throes of issuing some reports using a KPMG seal. All the preparatory work has been done but you won't have seen an official one. That's really a line of reporting, it isn't a different service. It's merely a way of communicating: to the public at large or a closed community so that you have rights of access to certain material. The seal is not a new product. But the seal could involve all sorts of products. It's come about because of the web and the way people want to get access to information.

> **The IT aspects of "corporate governance are one of the things that chief executives think they don't have to understand until it bites them!**

Also we include in Attest, IT governance or IS governance which is probably getting closer to some of the thinking in your book which is corporate responsibility for IS within its wider framework of corporate governance. Our vision of it is designed to make sure that the IT aspects of corporate governance get to, or start with, whichever way you want to put it, the top table in a company. This hasn't always happened.

IT is one of the things that chief executives think they don't have to understand?

Yes, until it bites them! The approach is, increasingly, risk-based, not just doing things for the sake of it, because it's IT fashion or whatever, but because there is a corporate risk and therefore a corporate exposure and, following from that, a benefit to be had from mitigating that risk in some form of cost/reward ratio.

We are primarily focused on control and, how can I put this? Benefits realization? There is also the IS governance side and IT risk issues in due diligence.

In the large systems like SAP or Oracle or PeopleSoft, we would primarily get involved in controls design and security infrastructures – as opposed to functionality, having lots of programmers setting up profiles, actually installing the thing on people's boxes and so on. We come from the risk and control aspect.

So there's the big systems control and risk; the smaller systems selection and implementation and I would say we're looking at benefits realization as a separate issue. Lots and lots of people put in SAP and say, 'What have I got?' You know? That goes straight back to the fact that they didn't understand the change management up front! You've probably been there! So there you go. It seems familiar! So that's the systems side.

We have this four-stage model: Review – Architecture – Implement – Monitor which is a circular life cycle which is the basis on which most of our advisory services are conceived. IRM does not necessarily provide all aspects which the client needs. It may be us, it may be our consulting colleagues, it may be a third party. The idea is that the client gets the right answer from the right sources at the end of the day.

E-business control looks at the risks associated with going into e-business ventures – not necessarily the commercial risks like, 'Will I have enough customers?' but the IT-type risks in terms of security, access to websites, identification, authorization, very much focused to the IT issues and also, as well, from the corporate mis-management point of view, the business structure within which companies encourage or otherwise e-business initiatives to take place. We've done quite a bit of work helping vary large companies set up a better controlled environment where e-business initiatives are allowed to flourish but they are also thought to be under control.

Business continuity management starts with high availability and goes through to disaster recovery.

Project risk management is actually reporting on IT project management both in terms of setting up the systems in the first place for major projects and giving some assurance back to the management of the company that the reporting they are getting for the project is reliable and on time, that no surprises are building up and so on and so forth. Where people have been bitten by projects which are running perfectly until 95 per cent complete and then all of a sudden they hit a brick wall, you know? It never happens in real life of course! Sometimes, when coming into projects, within that service people begin to understand projects coming off the rails and we'll be asked to take a look and help them, perhaps reschedule it and get a grip, why it's gone wrong, when it has gone wrong. Again we don't necessarily provide all the technical solutions but we help to identify the risk and control issues which management must be aware of and take some actions on. It may be we can help them further with the solutions but that's where it starts.

> **People have been bitten by projects which are running perfectly until 95 per cent complete and then all of a sudden they hit a brick wall.**

Information systems security services cover a wide range of activities from security policies and guidelines at the top corporate or group level in an organization, how these are then cascaded and expanded through operational companies' divisions or what have you. Then, from the policy guidelines down to technical standards and from technical standards take that model – Review – Architecture – Implement – Monitor – now that's a huge and complex area of different types of product. Somebody may ask us to review, say, a Windows NT network and we would have specific tools, some specialized software, some using expert questionnaires. When I say 'expert', they are not expert systems, they are questionnaires produced by experts which are used by appropriately trained staff, including the experts, to identify risks and flaws in the systems and suggest suitable ways of sorting it out. That would apply to all major network operators and in the general network area, obviously, people are worried about internet access and those types of things. So we have products and/or processes. I quite like to call it a 'tool kit' because we talk about services but within those there are all sorts of tools and sub-tools and you can mix and match those to bring to the client. It is not a one-size-fits-all approach. I suppose this is where the professional meets the technical, picking the right bits and bringing them together for the client's needs. It's part and parcel of the process. But, although we break these service lines up, because it's helpful to have some structure, they are not rigidly exclusive.

As many different options as there are candies in a Woolworth's Pic 'n Mix?

That's quite a good way of putting it. Otherwise people think they can only buy bull's eyes!

IRM also covers things like reviewing certification authorities where these are being created and some of them volunteer for audit-type reports or security-type reports. Others have it thrust upon them by local legislation or what have you. It would include BS7799 review. We would help a client establish a BS7799 environment and advise them how to go about reaching that level of security and competence.

There are other elements of this which, in terms of the architecture and implementation where we work with major providers of solutions but not exclusively. People like RSA, Baltimore, the major players in PKI web-enabled business arena. Incidentally, I should have mentioned back-up of the high-availability. We work with ENC on data storage, data repository, design. We're also working with a number of clients on assignments to outsource security monitoring, it is going to be a big thing.

The philosophy and what has changed is that nearly all of our products have been re-focused since 1996 to a risk-based approach.

When you get to the review process, step one of our model, it has been very much *not* rush into the technology but step back and examine the risk of the context of what we do in the business. The context of what we do in the business is very important even if it's a network security review. Looking for the implications for the business is an important step at the beginning of the chain. I think that's different from how it used to be when people would rush in lower down, almost in isolation, partly, I suspect, because clients themselves had a piecemeal approach. It was like, somebody looks after this risk and somebody looks after that risk and they probably didn't know what each other was doing.

As more and more businesses are e-enabled, IT is the way we do business, not the way we keep the score. IT is the way we play the game. I think that is important because it puts IT at a different place on the business agenda, therefore a different place on the board agenda and therefore IT risk alongside other risks at the appropriate level.

> **" As more and more businesses are e-enabled, IT is the way we do business, not the way we keep the score.**

My colleagues and I have been talking much more to CEOs and CFOs and CIOs about IT risk in terms of business risk at board level or management committee level than we have been doing in the past. It is part and parcel of Turnbull and the German KonTraG. There are other countries as well, such as Australia, that have been more rigorous and vigorous than others in improving corporate governance.

Another area of interest, and this is a slight digression in a way, but it does pose interesting problems for corporate governance of IT, is where there is major outsourcing. You can outsource what suppliers do but you can't outsource the ultimate responsibility for this sort of thing. I think that's a challenge for some companies. They think 'outsource' means 'goodbye'! I don't think it does! It brings other risks. It is an extra dimension in the risk profile.

One of the things we've done with some of our clients is that we have run risk workshops particularly on the IT risk side – although we keep saying that you can't escape the business implications of the IT side in terms of identifying risk, the likelihood of risk, identifying the style of risk. Is it financial? Is it reputational? We are applying business measures to IT risks in terms of evaluation and therefore consideration of the priority in terms of other corporate risks and the investment that's needed to address them.

There are upsides and downsides. A lot of it is subjective but then it's all subjective. What is new to a lot of people is that we even dare to try to do it with IT risk. Okay, say we have a client that makes coffee and they have a frost in Brazil, they can recognize that they have a raw material supplier risk and I can work out that the price goes up 30 per cent. What happens if I lose my SAP system, it goes down for two weeks? My automated warehouse distribution system stops functioning for however many days, you know. That type of thinking is beginning to become more prevalent.

> **" Risk management isn't about preventing risk – because if you have no risk you have no endeavour – it's understanding the risk and making decisions with your eyes open.**

I think the other thing that's become accepted is that the risk management business isn't about preventing risk – because if you have no risk you have no endeavour basically – it's understanding the risk and making decisions with your eyes open. Management has a right to take risks in business but stakeholders have a right to expect that they do it with some degree of proper consideration.

We have started to get involved in due diligence because of mis-matches in IT systems when there is a merger or takeover. (Andrew Steet's area.) One of the main
things we look at in our due diligence work is the potential fit or otherwise of IT
between the two parties. Now sometimes if someone is going to buy a company
which will remain a stand-alone, it may not be a deal-breaker. If they are looking to
merge two businesses, which are more or less doing the same things very rapidly, we
would highlight the risk. Our view of the scale of the task, which could affect price,
could affect whether it went forward or not.

If you have big public deals, we would prepare documentation for deal rooms. A
lot of clients do not have documentation they can put in a deal room so that
prospective buyers and their consultants can actually see what their IT systems are
in a coherent way. It just doesn't exist. The biggest one we ever did was when the
(UK) railways were privatized. That was a huge task of documenting a deal room.
We had to describe the business functionality of the major systems, both financial,
managerial, safety and operational. We wrote descriptions of the major systems in
those four major areas in a standardized format. On those that were sufficiently
high-profile we actually went into quite a lot of detail on how they were managed,
how they were controlled, how they interfaced. If you buy a ticket for a train on an
ABCAT machine, what happens to the money? The point is that, in due diligence,
there is routine work which is documenting systems and sometimes being asked to
comment on quality, documentation, maintainability, backlog of subsistence
changes and so on. That's really a routine job. Then you have the strategic side: is
there a fit problem here?

*Do companies tend to dumb down and go for bought-in systems? Go for the system oper-
ated by the larger partner in the takeover or merger?*

There's no simple answer to that question. Very often people might buy a company
because it has an IT system which is pre-eminent in the marketplace.

One of our clients bought a huge pet foods business. It was quite clear from the
start that they were going to have very significant systems issues to bring, as was
their intention to bring, the acquired company into the corporate base. So much so
that they decided that they would wait two or three years before they even tried to
do it. Rather than do it tomorrow which was the original intention. That had an
effect on the deal. It didn't stop the deal but people suddenly realized that you
couldn't just press a button and have two amalgamated systems.

There are, within due diligence, sometimes contractual and licensing issues on
software which can have a lot of hidden costs if you don't pull them out in the deal.

You are not, for instance, just able to bring somebody on to your SAP box when you buy a new company without totally having to renegotiate your licence. It may not be possible. All of your Microsoft licences or what have you may not be transferable. If you sell a business, or if you detach part of a business and if you have a corporate licence and you sell off a quarter of your business, then that bit that goes is no longer covered by your corporate licence.

Is this generally found out or do companies get away with it?

Oh! If it's found out they get huge bills from the likes of Microsoft. There was an example a few years ago of Computer Associates who discovered a transfer and went big-time for the additional licence cost. I think they settled.

> **"" There was an example a few years ago of Computer Associates who discovered a transfer and went big-time for the additional licence cost.**

Are there penalties?

Directors can go to prison: it is a criminal offence. Normally, if you are working with clients and you know they have infringed, knowingly or unknowingly, we try to put the position and negotiate a settlement with the software supplier. The only people who win if you don't do it that way are the lawyers. Over the years you will see that software licences to large corporates have changed significantly.

It may be that, if you downsize your business because you sell a large chunk, you may be able to renegotiate your software contract anyway. Or at the time of an update. It is a complicated area and becoming more so.

There are two places in the UK that fight this battle for the software houses. The Federation Against Software Theft, known as FAST in the trade, represents a reasonable number of software suppliers. The other group, the Business Software Association (BSA), is American-based but active in Europe. They issue a regular warning, going for the big stick approach. It's like, 'if we catch you we'll send you to prison'. FAST tries to go for 'software is an asset and must be properly managed so get your whole house in order'.

Often you'll find, after the sale of a business, that you are paying money out for things you don't need or you're paying upgrade costs or maintenance charges on software you no longer use, all this sort of thing. So we try and come at it from a software asset management, or value proposition as opposed to a legal one. There are all sorts of aspects of due diligence which we can cover if they are necessary. If it is due diligence, in the same way that our financial boys will tear over the books, we can tear over the IT.

144

If a company that a client of yours is buying, presumably they recognize their responsibilities under corporate governance to report on the overall risk management function which does include IT, presumably your people, Andrew, review the whole IT infrastructure?

Yes. Increasingly boards of directors are recognizing that their corporate governance responsibilities under the Turnbull guidance extend, not just to all risk management and control, but could also be interpreted as specific risks such as information technology.

I sit on the Technical Developments Committee of the Institute of Internal Auditors and the Internal Audit Committee of the Institute of Chartered Accountants. I am also the e-commerce spokesman of the Institute of Internal Auditors. Both bodies that I sit on did a lot of preliminary work to support Turnbull's guidance. We came up with a view that, for the majority of FTSE companies, the three key risks that they face are:

■ Reputation risk: for example, the issue with Nike when children were found to be used as slave labour. So the issue is what does that do to your share price and your market loyalty?

■ Technology, because technology risk covers all aspects of business.

■ Environment.

So technology risk is seen as possibly the major risk facing FTSE companies.

How are things moving?

If we go back in time to the mid-1980s, when I was working in industry, firms like KPMG would categorize businesses into three groups:

■ Computer-dominant, the top stream – basically banks and airlines, which were totally dependent on their IT infrastructure.

■ Computer-significant, a middle stream – companies which used computers, needed computers but which would not go out of business if computers went down for a whole week or so.

■ Computer-insignificant, a third level which were companies that did not use much IT, maybe they outsourced payroll to a bureau; that's probably as far as they went.

Today the vast majority of the FTSE 200 would be categorized as computer-dominant in that so much of what they do is dependent on their IT infrastructure to the extent that they would not be able to continue in business for a day without it. Their e-business risks include:

- strategy;

- project management;

- operations, policies and procedures;

- technology (applications and infrastructure).

Although the categories of e-business risk are not different, speed of realization, circumstances in which they arise, and impact on the business may be very different.

The role of the internal auditor

16

By Richard Gossage, Head of Group Risk, *The Royal Bank of Scotland Group*

Richard Gossage is Head of Group Risk at the Royal Bank of Scotland Group. Until July 2001 he was Head of Group Internal Audit, with a staff of 343 professionals and a budget of £23.4 million. In 2001 he explained the role of internal audit to corporate risk managers at AIRMIC's annual conference in Birmingham.

He strongly believes that internal audit should remain an arm's length function, detached from the CRM function in any organization. Auditors guard their independence – and ability to audit and criticize other functions – jealously.

RBOS won the battle to take over major British clearing bank NatWest. Its management is 'unbelievably focused!' he told me. It must have been to pull off that coup! He brings the same discipline and focus to the art of internal audit and risk management. RBOS has some excellent risk management models. He suggested to AIRMIC that they should examine how businesses stay healthy in risk management terms.

Who does the corporate health check? Who advises on treatment and cures? It's the profession of internal auditing. The role of the internal audit function at RBOS is to continuously assess how risks are being managed and controlled throughout the group; report regularly to the group executive and group audit committee on the results of these assessments; and to influence the continuous development of the risk management and control process through sharing best practices.

What does this actually mean?

You have to ask: are all internal audit functions the same? Do they differ around the world? Do you need different solutions for different industries? And what is the interface with corporate risk management functions?

> **You have to ask: are all "internal audit functions the same? Do they differ around the world?**

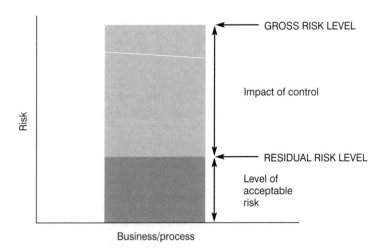

Fig 16.1 RBOS risk map
Copyright: RBOS

What's your strategy?

The strategy is two-fold: first, to provide independent and robust assurance. Second, we have to champion change for the continuous improvement of risk management and control. We do this in a number of ways:

■ Being a centre of knowledge, innovation and creativity to the benefit of the group.

■ Being partners with our stakeholders, to meet the needs of the group and its customers.

■ Aligning our processes to business objectives and processes.

■ Investing in quality people, processes and technology.

■ Delivering a high-quality and cost-effective service.

How are the key deliverables changing for publicly quoted companies?

Our basic structure comprises a divisional and group monthly control report. Then every six months there are divisional and group opinions. We have to ensure that we are Turnbull compliant and report on this annually. We supplement this with assurance to external stakeholders, individual audit reports and advice and best practice notes.

There are three performance parameters we apply. First, adequacy: this is an assessment of whether or not a risk management and control process is properly designed and fit for the purpose. Second, effectiveness: this is an assessment of whether or not a risk management and control process operates correctly in prac-tice. And finally, sustainability: a period between audit opinions where processes operate in a steady environment without there being a critical control failure.

There are five levels of internal audit assurance:

- The highest level (Assurance Level 1) is where risk management and control process exceeds capable levels in terms of adequacy effectiveness and sustainability.

- Assurance Level 2 is where risk management and control process meets acceptable levels in all material aspects in terms of adequacy, effectiveness and sustainability.

- Assurance Level 3 is where risk management and control process meets acceptable levels in terms of adequacy, effectiveness and sustainability for the majority of material aspects in terms of internal control – but a limited number of specific improvements are required.

- Assurance Level 4 is where risk management and control process falls significantly below acceptable levels and considerable improvement is required.

- At Assurance Level 5, the risk management and control process is failing to such a degree that loss of our banking licence and our business licence would be at risk.

The current factors (past and future) impacting on the internal auditor are Turnbull et al.; the Financial Services and Markets Act; Basel II; and the rise of operational risk.

Classification level	Financial	Customer	Reputational
	Potential or actual loss which affects either the profit and loss account or balance sheet within any 12-month period (ie loss of profit of loss of assets).	Actual or potential impact arising from either operational failure or management failure which leads to an inability to: • Provide a quality service to our customers, or • Execute our business, or • Comply with laws, regulations or policies and procedures	Actual or potential impact to the reputation of the Royal Bank of Scotland Group in the external environments, UK and overseas. This includes the views held by all the regulatory bodies that regulate any element of our group's business or activities.
Major Is this an issue the Group Chief Executive and, ultimately the group audit committee need to know of?	In excess of £10 million in a 12-month period.	• Affecting more than 25 percent of a business's customers or staff. • Total failure of major supplier. • Loss of key system for a trading day or failure to meet a business critical process deadline • Management failure at executive level.	• Likelihood of a actual adverse comment in any national media • Likelihood of a actual censure by any of our regulators.
Significant Is this an issue the Chief Executive of the business needs to know of?	Between of £1 million and £10 million in a 12-month period.	• Affecting between 5 percent and 25 percent of a business's customers or staff. • Partial failure of a third party supplier. • Loss of key system which causes major operational or customer impact • Management failure at operational level.	• Likelihood of an actual adverse comment in the local press, or equivalent • Any event which may affect our standing with any of our regulators.
Important Is this an issue the senior operational/unit manager needs to know of?	Between of £250,000 and £1 million in a 12-month period.	• Affecting up to 5 percent of a business's customers or staff. • Deteriorating performance of supplier. • Loss of key systems which causes a minor operational or customer impact • Management failure at unit or supervisory level.	• Any event which may tarnish our reputation with a specific customer, group or third party.

Fig 16.2 Business impact of a potential or actual control failure classification criteria

Copyright: RBOS

Types of risk 17

Risk management identifies two types of risk – macro risk and micro risk.

1 Macro risk

Macro risks are external factors which have the potential to affect the overall viability of the organization. They include:

- *external financial risks* – including business portfolio valuation; claims and litigation costs; financial markets; interest rates; cost of borrowing; cash flow; liquidity; credit; market pricing; currency trading; financial instruments; currency; equity; commodities; natural resources; taxation; pensions strategy; back-up systems; other treasury; the euro;

- *legislative and regulatory risks* – including legal and regulatory compliance;

- *political risk* – stability of regimes and economies; EU expansion; international terrorism;

- energy risk.

Legislative and regulatory risks, branding and reputation risks and energy risk are among the top quadrant of risks about which companies are most worried. I will deal with these briefly in turn.

2 Micro risk

Micro risks are internal factors which have the potential to affect the overall viability of the organization. They include:

- operational or process risks – liabilities with regard to processes such as manufacturing, service provision, transport, distribution, business continuity, health and safety; environment; chemical toxicity; radiation; resources sourcing, utilization, optimization and waste management, accidents, incidents and near misses.

- financial risks;

- environmental, social and ethical risks;

- branding and reputation risks;

- people risks.

Environmental, social and ethical risk

Environmental, social and ethical risk has been rising up the agenda since the mid-1980s in Europe and a lot longer in the USA.

I have been connected with environmental consulting since 1987 when I designed the first comprehensive corporate environmental policy in the UK for client Shanks & McEwan as they were then called. But I still encounter people who ask me, 'What exactly is environmental consulting?'

"" I started out by asking the client to consider the effect of their activities on the environment every day of their working lives.

I started out by asking the client to consider the effect of their activities on the environment every day of their working lives.

Under Section 4.3.1 Environmental aspects of ISO 14001, Environmental Management Systems, any organization is asked to 'identify the environmental aspects of its activities, products or services that have or can have significant impacts on the environment. The organization shall ensure that the aspects related to these significant impacts are considered in setting its environmental objectives'.

These aspects include 'emissions to air, ground and water; defacement of the landscape and effects on human health'.

For organizations who are bottom-line focused, perhaps a better way of putting it is triple bottom line.

The triple bottom line approach is probably more easily understood – if only because it is shorter. The danger here is that people slip back into ignorance. Triple bottom line is generally taken to mean: (1) environmental, (2) social and (3) financial issues, risks or effects.

But triple bottom line can also be read as: (1) the environment benefits, (2) operational efficiency benefits and (3) the bottom line benefits. From things like:

- reducing waste, which just happens to have operational cost benefits (related to process waste, 'shrinkage', ie theft and waste disposal) and therefore bottom-line benefits;

- reducing energy consumption, which just happens to have operational cost benefits and therefore bottom-line benefits;

- reducing consumption of natural resources, which just happens to have operational cost benefits and therefore bottom-line benefits;

- replacing hazardous materials with less-hazardous (and often less costly) materials;

- creating a caring corporate culture which may attract more caring staff;

- creating an attractive office and landscaped environment which may attract more caring staff.

Legislative and regulatory risks

Organizations may have historical liabilities from previous site owners (M&A managers please note) such as asbestos, contaminated land or contaminated water.

Asbestos is a risk on which I have been constantly advising clients. Any building in the UK pre-1980 is bound to contain it. And it will cost millions of pounds per site to encapsulate or remove – which can harm even the most ambitious property development projects.

It is estimated that asbestos liabilities in Europe will peak between 2017 and 2021 depending on the country. That means the peak. Which means that the incidence that you see today is going to go up and up and up and up. It's enough to keep most people up at night if they think about it.

> **It's enough to keep most people up at night if they think about it.**

You only have to consider the millions of metric tonnes that were imported into the UK, to understand the scale of a problem which will not go away. Epidemiologist Dr Julian Peto calculated the possible incidence in the *British Journal of Cancer* 1999, in his country-by-country survey.

Contaminated Land Liabilities

Contaminated Land (England) Regulations 2000 and Statutory Guidance and similar legislation in the rest of the EU mean that clean-up costs will be incurred by many companies. Remediation costs will vary according to the scope and nature of the remediation specification. They:

- are usually non-recurring;

- may enhance asset value;

- need to be minimized through sound knowledge of cost-effective techniques;

- require evaluation of 'source-pathway-receptor' risks;

- are based at the very least on the 'suitable for use' approach;

- legally require evaluation of what is reasonable.

Input to legal issues management

Tony Cherry is Head of Risk Management at UK solicitors Beachcroft Wansbroughs. As well as co-ordinating the firm's risk management services he works day to day in his own area of technical expertise, relating to product, workplace and environmental risk. His quantified risk plans, based on actual corporate experience, are reproduced in Figs 17.1 and 17.2.

Legal risk management, he suggests, should be based on the pre-emptive approach as follows.

- Not crisis management – that's the point.

- Early assessment of legal risk.

- Prediction of legally related behaviours.

- Legal risk assessment of issue management strategies.

- Management of hostile legal relations.

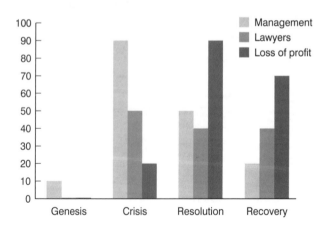

Fig 17.1 Risk out of control

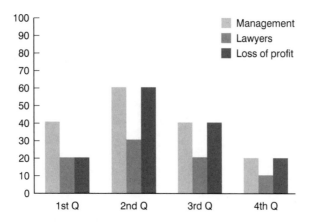

Fig 17.2 Improving the outcome
Copyright Beachcroft Wansbroughs, solicitors

Mergers and acquisitions, global securities offerings and international licensing and distribution strategies may pose potential antitrust or competition, securities and intellectual property issues. This is a scenario in which enforcement and litigation risk management should be practised on a global basis.

18

Branding and reputation risks

There are a large number of branding and reputation risks which are interwoven. Here I pinpoint a selection.

Nike

There is no doubt that campaigners pushed Nike, the US sports shoe group, into action to require its suppliers to treat their workers better after allegations of sexual harassment and physical abuse of workers at Indonesian contract factories used by the company. This is the kind of campaign, with damage to corporate reputation, which many companies now fear.

" This is the kind of campaign, with damage to corporate reputation, which many companies now fear.

Nike commissioned and released a full report into conditions at the factories in response to allegations contained in a report by the Global Alliance for Workers and Communities. Nike promised to address worker concerns on verbal and physical abuse; sexual harassment; overtime issues; health and safety; and annual, sick and menstrual leave.

Nike confirmed it would implement harassment training and introduce a grievance system. It would strengthen existing workplace policies and penalties, including the reporting of serious injuries and deaths.

Sandoz

Shortly after midnight on 1 November 1986, Swiss police detected a fire at the warehouse of Sandoz. The fire at Schweizerhalle near Basel was the first such incident in 100 years of company operations.

The warehouse contained 987 tonnes of pesticides, and the fire took 160 firemen six hours and 30,000 litres of water per minute to get under control. The water flushed chemicals into the Rhine including, it was estimated, 200 kg of toxic and highly persistent mercury. The bottom line, apart from the physical damage and insurance liability, was that Sandoz's shares fell 16 per cent, Ciba-Geigy by 5 per cent, and Roche by 3.4 per cent.

The social bottom line was panic. As often occurs after such incidents, people opened windows instead of closing them – probably to get a better view. In Basel 10,000 residents held a protest rally against the company. They threw dead eels and bottles at company and local government officials. Across Europe, demands were made for stricter environmental liability laws.

The bottom line for the environment was the death of half a million fish and a 60 km pollution slick which moved downstream.

The company's own fire brigade managed to prevent the spread of the fire to other warehouses storing sodium, which would have exploded in contact with water. This meant that there were no fatalities from the incident.

But the timing – the German and French authorities were alerted at 3 am – led many, including the company, to believe it was an act of sabotage. Only four days previously the site had been inspected by the Swiss fire protection service and declared safe.

It was not until November 2000 that the German state TV network broadcast a programme in which Vincent Cannistraro, 59, formerly head of counter-terrorist operations for the CIA, told viewers that a special Stasi unit, the AGMS (the Working Group for Ministerial Special Problems), was responsible.

'The Stasi worked on commission for the KGB,' Cannistraro claimed. 'They used the catastrophe contingency plan prepared by a Zurich insurance company, which had inspected Sandoz's site. Thomas Auerbach, a Stasi archives researcher on AGMS activities, confirmed this. The Stasi were renowned for their expertise in explosives sabotage.'

> **'The Stasi worked on "commission for the KGB,' Cannistraro claimed.**

Around the same time, all Germany's leading chemical companies suffered incidents. The reason? The Soviet authorities, deeply embarrassed by the Chernobyl nuclear power plant explosion in 1985, wished to deflect attention away from their own environmental shortcomings and ordered the sabotage of chemical companies in the west according to Cannistraro.

The political bottom line was the escalation of support for the Green party in Germany.

For Sandoz, the incident was traumatic.

I was fortunate to persuade Dr Jean-Jacques Salzmann, Sandoz's Head of Corporate Safety and Environmental Protection, to address a conference I ran on 17 November 1987 on *The Environmental Impact of Industrial Activities*. He told in his own words of the effect on the local population: 'The year in which Sandoz celebrated its centenary had been progressing successfully,' he told us. 'And then came 1 November.

'A fire in one of our warehouses quickly developed into a disaster never before experienced in the 100 years of our existence. It was an accident that severely damaged the reputation of our company among the general public. It released emotions which surprised and dismayed us.

> **" The conflict is all the greater since all political groups agree that the chemical industry generally, and in Basel in particular, is indispensable.**

'The confidence of many residents of the Basel area in their chemical industry had been shaken. The conflict is all the greater since all political groups agree that the chemical industry generally, and in Basel in particular, is indispensable.

'In the long term, beneficial co-existence of the chemical industry and the population is impossible without the confidence and goodwill of the local population. Regaining this confidence is, therefore, one of our main concerns.'

Tell it all...

John Harvey-Jones has also written about trust. In his book, *Making It Happen – Reflections on Leadership*, he writes, 'Trust, once it begins to deteriorate, quite suddenly flips over and becomes a sort of galloping corrosion of suspicion which is very difficult to halt. Trust is tremendously difficult to build up and all too easy to destroy, so it is worth taking all sorts of actions, even if they appear to be finicky, to avoid losing it.'

When advising clients on how to manage threats to corporate reputation, I always advise them to be honest, 'up front' and apologetic. But also to react quickly with a statement. As in life, the person who apologizes – even if it is not his or her fault – is forgiven more readily than the person who hides or tries to blame someone else.

> **" The chief executive who faces the TV cameras and admits certain deficiencies is building up that elusive reputation for trust. A safe pair of hands. Respect.**

The communications executive of my client Waste Management put it succinctly: 'Tell it all, tell it straight and tell it fast!'

Managing public relations crises is all about minimizing the damage to corporate reputation or brand. The chief executive who faces the TV cameras and admits certain deficiencies is building up that elusive reputation for trust. A safe pair of hands. Respect.

When Perrier had an incident which involved contamination of their bottles with bleach used in sterilizing them, the chief executive handled the situation well on two counts. She immediately took responsibility for the incident without making any excuses. And she reassured the public by withdrawing bottles.

19

Protecting the brand

By Heiko Haasler, Marketing Director,
Brand Protection,
De La Rue International Limited

Brand management is a growing professional discipline. At De La Rue, Heiko Haasler is responsible for product development and communications. He has worked with a number of consumer goods and technology companies as a strategic consultant.

De La Rue is better known as the cash-to-secure-transactions group, the world's largest commercial security printer and paper-maker, involved in the production of more than 150 national currencies and a wide range of security documents such as stamps and vouchers, as well as brand protection. The company is also a leading provider of cash-handling equipment and solutions to banks and retailers, as well as a range of identity systems to commerce and governments world-wide. But it also acts as a strategic partner and adviser on other aspects of security, integrity and trust.

Haasler explains how brand owners can protect and differentiate their brands in a number of ways:

First, enabling customers – the consumer – to authenticate the product ('this feels authentic') and to assure them that they are paying a brand premium for a quality product. Most common examples are holograms, security threads, colour-changing foils and heat-sensitive inks which can be included in the packaging, the label, swing tag or directly onto the product – parallels with bank notes are obvious. Customers include Calvin Klein, Bayer, Visa, Johnny Walker to name but a few.

Second, allowing customs inspectors and investigators to check consumer products in the field (and intercept rogue shipments) by covertly marking and tagging products. These taggants (invisible chemical or bio-chemical markers) can be detected using special hand-held devices. Further examination can be provided in our lab, for forensic analysis in court proceedings, for example. Again, some of this technology is adapted from the bank note business. Here we work with leading sports-wear and spirit brands.

Third, providing track and trace information on the movement of goods, so that the brand owner knows exactly at any point in time where their products are. We call this 'supply chain visibility'. In other words, we make our customers aware when things go missing, are diverted or overproduced. This involves a fairly complex set of security technology and information systems. We are operating this sort of system for Microsoft, for example (the sticker under PC helps us track the distribution of Windows software).

Fourth, giving brand visibility at point of sale – where the appearance or messages of the product change to engage the consumer (a stereogram, for example) which provides authentication at the same time. We are working with major video and games publishers such as Disney and Columbia TriStar.

What is the financial value of brand image and why is protecting the brand an important risk management issue?

Brand dilutions by copycat products are a risk that managers have to face when putting together a strategy to maximize the potential of the brand. It's a delicate balance, extending the brand's range and increasing revenue streams without losing sight of its integrity. Now imagine how the scenario can spiral out of control if the image of the brand is placed in the hands of retailers and grey market traders, whose focus is on short-term profit rather than the long-term integrity of the brand. The brand is only a financial asset to the brand owner and not to those whose hands it passes through en route to the consumer. Even worse, the image may be distorted by anonymous counterfeiters and copy-cats, whose profit motives could not be further from that of the brand owner. How much greater the task then of seizing back control of the brand's personality.

> **The brand is only a financial asset to the brand owner and not to those whose hands it passes through en route to the consumer.**

With all this in mind, it's no surprise that in the UK, the government's support for the principle of world-wide parallel trade sent a shiver down the spines of many luxury and fashion brand owners. In these sectors, a company's market capitalization is inextricably tied to the name and that 'certain something' that says a product – and by implication its purchaser – is sexy or aloof or avant-garde or just down right rich – it's hard for a product to be any of those things when it's on the shelf next to a tin of beans.

Brands at the top of the luxury, fashion and lifestyle ladders are selling a dream but it is one based on very solid, commercial foundations of design, product quality, packaging, pricing and the right communication channels. It's a heady marketing mix made even more interesting by the absolute need to ensure that these star products are seen in the right milieu.

Typically companies will spend about 15 per cent of turnover on building a brand through marketing and advertising but less than 1 per cent on brand protection – a woefully inadequate amount. For a company to set about developing a brand without considering at the outset how the brand is to be protected is like pouring petrol on a fire – the more they promote the brand, the more consumer demand is created and that simply fuels sales of infringing items be they counterfeit, lookalikes or grey imports.

Global brands are built on complex supply chains, passing through many hands – some friendly, some threatening – until they reach the consumers. As the chain is stretched, the links get weaker and products can simply slip through holes and disappear.

Outsourcing of production and distribution means that crucial brand information has to be entrusted to suppliers, which can leave brand owners vulnerable to abuse: from counterfeiters, who steal new designs and have fake versions on the market before legitimate items have even been launched; from manufacturers, who produce a batch for the brand owner and one for themselves; from distributors, whose lower-priced parallel imports undermine legitimate stockists and leave the global pricing strategy in tatters.

However, the case for outsourcing manufacturing, logistics and distribution is a strong one: companies can save millions in costs as well as improving turnround times and achieving higher levels of quality and predictability. Fortunately operational efficiency, cost savings and brand control do not have to be mutually exclusive.

The key is to take control of the supply chain without losing the benefits of flexibility – making the production and movement of all goods visible to scrutiny, without complicating or slowing down the process. An effective 'track and trace' solution can deliver visibility, security and authentication from start to finish, anywhere in the world. It identifies each item in the supply chain and quickly answers a range of questions such as: whether it's genuine, where it is, where it should be and how it came to be there. Any discrepancies in the movement of goods in the chain can then be identified and offending partners can be removed. Global 'track and trace' solutions can be used in a variety of industry-specific ways, for example: for the protection of high-value goods and components in the IT and luxury goods sectors; to record audit trails and service information in engineering and automotive industries for safety and warranty purposes; as a safety and quality control mechanism in the medical field; and to minimize exposure in case of product quality or tamper issues where items can be recalled on a selective basis. The implications for risk management are clearly evident.

Track and trace solutions rely on product tagging and here the range of options, covert and overt, are numerous and varied: from standard or secure bar codes to

> **" The key is to take control of the supply chain without losing the benefits of flexibility.**

covert data-carrying tags on packaging and products. In addition to track and trace-ability, electronic devices such as printed circuits and notch-filters confer tamper evidence, enhancing packaging security. Bespoke detectors allow remote authentication from outside the packaging.

Optical devices such as high-security holograms add publicly recognizable authenticity to an item and can be incorporated into other security features such as tamper-evident tear tapes and shrink sleeves.

Security print features such as intaglio or micro printing add an extra degree of brand recognition as well as protection, while taggants can be incorporated into packaging to provide covert security. The covert nature of such technologies means that they can provide forensic evidence of authenticity in cases of dispute.

And finally, in the range of security solution, traditional bank note technologies, such as watermarking and woven threads, are increasingly incorporated into product packaging, confirming that today's most powerful brands exist as global currencies in their own right requiring the very highest level of protection.

20 Energy risk

E nergy has become a commodity like any other. The energy needs of large organizations represent a significant part of their operational expenditure. Utilities and market traders deal in a wider variety of energy products than in the past. They are multinational companies with incredible procurement and distribution powers. Deregulation of energy markets globally has created great opportunities for them. But the markets present risks to energy consumers.

World energy consumption is projected to increase by 59 per cent between 1999 and 2020. Worldwide energy use will grow from 382 quadrillion British thermal units (Btu) in 1999 to 607 quadrillion Btu in 2020. In Part V Corporate survival and the dynamics of change, I talk to Mary Harris of PA Consulting about energy risk.

Much of the growth in world-wide energy use is expected in the developing world. Energy demand in developing Asia and Central and South America is projected to more than double between 1999 and 2020. The areas are expected to sustain energy demand growth of 4 per cent annually throughout the forecast, accounting for more than one half of the total projected increment in world energy consumption and 81 per cent of the increment for the developing world. World oil prices have been extremely volatile for the past three years. In 1998 consumers benefited as oil prices fell to $10 per barrel, a result of oversupply caused by lower demand in southeast Asia, North America and Western Europe.

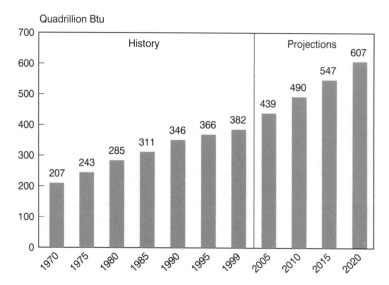

Fig 20.1 World energy consumption, 1970–2020

Sources: **History**: Energy Information Administration (EIA), Office of Energy Markets and End Use, International Statistics Database and *International Energy Annual 1999*, DOE/EIA-0219(99) (Washington, DC, January 2001). **Projections**: EIA, World Energy Projection System (2001).

Table 20.1: Energy consumption and carbon emissions by region, 1990–2020

Region	Energy consumption (quadrillion Btu)				Carbon dioxide emissions (million metric tons carbon equivalent)			
	1990	1999	2010	2020	1990	1999	2010	2020
Industrialized	182.4	209.6	243.4	270.4	2,842	3,122	3,619	4,043
EE/FSU	76.3	50.5	60.3	72.3	1,337	810	940	1,094
Developing								
Asia	51.0	70.9	113.4	162.2	1,053	1,361	2,137	3,013
Middle East	13.1	19.3	26.9	37.2	231	330	451	627
Africa	9.3	11.8	16.1	20.8	179	218	294	373
Central and South								
America	13.7	19.8	29.6	44.1	178	249	394	611
Total	87.2	121.8	186.1	264.4	1,641	2,158	3,276	4,624
Total world	346.0	381.8	489.7	607.1	5,821	6,091	7,835	9,762

Sources: History: Energy Information Administration (EIA), *International Energy Annual 1999*, DOE/EIA-0219(99) (Washington, DC, January 2001). **Projections:** EIA, World Energy Projection System (2001).

In 2000, world oil prices rebounded strongly, reaching a daily peak of $37 per barrel, rates not seen since the Gulf War of 1990–1991. The high prices can be traced to a tightening of production by the Organization of Petroleum Exporting Countries (OPEC) and several key non-OPEC countries (Russia, Mexico, Oman and Norway) and a reluctance by oil companies to commit capital to major development efforts for fear of a return to low prices, in concert with unexpectedly strong demand recovery in the economies of Asia. Unrest in the Middle East has also exacerbated the price volatility. Oil companies were also reluctant to refill abnormally low stock levels, because they feared a return to the low price environment of 1998.

The industrialized world also was affected by the high world oil price environment of 2000. Concerns in the United States about a recurrence of the previous winter's shortage of home heating fuel oil for the northeast – given the very low stock levels of August 2000 – led the Clinton administration to allow industry access to as much as 30 million barrels of crude oil from the nation's strategic petroleum reserve.

In the EU, Spain and France expressed the desire to follow the US lead, but the International Energy Agency, the United Kingdom and Germany opposed the move, and the stocks ultimately were not released. Multiple strikes to protest at high fuel prices were launched or threatened throughout Western Europe in the third quarter of 2000 by truckers, farmers and taxi drivers (whose livelihood is immediately affected by the cost of fuel).

In the **USA**, electricity prices increased sharply in California, New York and several other states in 2000/2001.

The energy crisis in California and the USA's western states was acknowledged in the Government's 2001 *National Energy Policy* (NEP) – published five months into the George W. Bush Government. In defining 'The Energy Challenge' it acknowledges that, 'The point has been reached where demand is occasionally exceeding supply'.

California's energy consumption has been growing by 7 per cent a year according to the NEP records. The situation was exacerbated by droughts which reduced supplies of water to hydro-electric power stations in the Pacific north-west and caused rolling blackouts. Power shortages were predicted to continue, 'until more supply is added'.

Consumers, Press and media, the anti-capitalist lobby and politicians think differently. Their spin on the situation is that the large energy supply companies, particularly the market traders who deal in, rather than actually generating, energy have 'manufactured' an energy shortage to allow them to raise prices. Companies like Duke Energy, Dynergy, Enron, the Mirant Corporation, Reliant Energy and the Williams Companies whose profits have escalated in the first years of the 21st century, including the months of the Californian energy crisis, were singled out for attention. Pipeline and energy market trader Enron's revenues – $101 billion in 2000 – are rising exponentially. This was cited in stark contrast to the financial difficulties of the retail energy sector, public and private sector consumers.

Wholesale power costs in California rose from US$7 billion in 1999 to US$27 billion in 2000. The latter figure was set to double in 2001 when Californians demanded that the power companies refund US$9 billion in 'over-charges'. But power suppliers claimed that Californian utilities owed them billions of dollars.

Utility companies had made their purchases almost exclusively from the volatile spot market (the California Power Exchange). Later, when the exchange began offering some access to forward markets, utilities failed to fully exploit the opportunities to buy forward. At the same time, consumers of Southern California Edison and Pacific Gas and Electric were not exposed to the true cost of power because retail prices remained frozen as part of the original deregulation laws. Meanwhile, in San Diego, where price caps were lifted, consumers were effectively placed on a variable rate mortgage which led to a tripling of bills. Prices rose because of all the demand pressures, including a rise in gas prices, a major fuel for electricity generation. Some customers did protect themselves from the risks of the spot market by switching to companies which offered fixed prices – but at the expense of locking themselves into long-term contracts.

Enter the US Federal Energy Regulatory Commission. FERC controls prices through the spot market for electricity, declaring any price above a benchmark of 85 per cent of the highest clearing price subject to a refund. It is a market-based system rather than a rigid price cap.

Local politicians and the government urged FERC to extend price restraints on electricity supplies to western states. FERC agreed that the market had become 'dysfunctional' and that the high prices could not be justified. Emboldened by new government appointees, FERC did the government's job for it and set price caps. The energy supply industry reduced wholesale prices in California from $300 to less than $100 a megawatt hour. But the pressure on government to demand further cuts was irresistible.

Some pundits, and the environmental lobby, say that price rises are no more than a market response to profligate consumption of cheap energy and that a re-adjustment was always going to be inevitable. Maybe so, but the market loves a shortage. It is said that some traders have played on market volatility to lock some intensive energy users, desperate to manage their risk, into long-term, guaranteed-price energy outsourcing contracts. Consumers 'hedging' against future energy price spikes against need also to consider the risk of getting locked into high-priced energy contracts when there could be a downward correction in energy prices. This might happen because of government action or through future over-investment in new capacity and a competitive marketplace (see interview with Mary Harris, page 178).

NEP recognizes that the stifling regulatory environment has delayed new power plant development. Despite sustained economic growth in California and the associated increase in demand for power, authorities did not approve any significant new power projects in a decade. Long-term solutions must address the need for more power stations.

The complicated and lengthy approval process needs to be tackled, say power generators and traders, to quicken power plant siting and construction timelines. Price caps, which prevent consumers from understanding the real cost of power, they say, discourage consumers from conserving energy. There needs to be price stability.

Energy market traders would like American utilities to rely less on the volatile spot market and purchase more power through long-term contracts with them. The rationale, they say, is to protect them from spikes in prices. But this may be at the expense of agreeing artificially high prices in contracts up front.

Power bottlenecks also exist, say the North American Electric Reliability Council, in Minnesota, Wisconsin, Ontario, Michigan, New York City, the Midwest, the South, the Southeast and the Southwest.

Energy risk through market deregulation, outsourcing contracts, and market domination by traders, increasingly from outside the EU, without a history of power generation or supply is also becoming a feature of the **European** energy scene.

The increasing tendency to import fuel and power supplies is a medium-term risk of great concern to the European Commission which is keen to promote renewable energy generation.

There are lessons to be learned from the American experience. California's crisis is blamed by many on the Clinton administration's poorly-drafted deregulation legislation. In many countries, deregulation was intended to increase competition and reduce prices to the consumer. Instead, it has often created the conditions for generators, the retail sector and market traders to make excess profit and to develop the very monopolies which deregulation was intended to prevent.

In the **UK**, the InterContinentalExchange, the over-the-counter (OTC) market for energy and metals products has acquired London's International Petroleum Exchange. It is linking up with the London Clearing House to offer a centralized service. The facility will introduce competition into a market increasingly dominated by multinational players. It claims that it will remove the credit risk element from commodity trading, allow members to use capital more efficiently and boost its trading activity.

OTC trades are customized, one-to-one transactions between large-scale investors, such as investment banks. In recent years, some contracts have become increasingly standardized, leading to centralised clearing. This can reduce risk exposure and operational costs – at a price. Like any outsourcing activity, the customer needs to weight the risks of performing the activity in-house with those of paying a premium to allow others to manage the risk.

Under the deal with the LCH, which already clears for the IPE, ICE will initially offer the clearing option on two of its busiest contracts – West Texas Intermediate crude oil swaps and Henry Hub natural gas swaps. LCH has applied to The Commodity Futures Trading Commission (CFTC) to become a 'derivatives clearing organization' – a new designation under the 2000 re-structuring of US derivatives regulation.

Companies outsourcing their energy, or any other commodity trading, need assurances that the outsourcing company is itself settling its bills on time – something that some of the largest multi-national traders have been accused of not always doing.

In **India**, energy pricing has been the issue at the $2.9 billion Dabhol Power Project near Mumbai which came on stream in May 1999. Enron threatened to withdraw from this US$2.9 billion project to provide electricity to the Maharashtra State Electricity Board (MSEB). At issue, says the Indian government, is the fact that the tariff for MSEB is three times higher at its most costly point than that levied by Indian producers. MSEB had refused to pay bills totalling some US$45 million when Enron launched arbitration proceedings in 2001. MSEB responded by rescinding its contract to draw down power. Enron is selling its shareholding.

In **Japan**, Tokyo Electric Power (Tepco) is attempting to defend its operating environment. A host of new companies are threatening to enter its patch after a partial deregulation of the electricity supply market in 2000. Tepco's large industrial and commercial customers now have the option of alternative supplies.

The main threat comes from industrial giants such as Nippon Steel that have long generated much of their own energy and have growing surpluses. The next stage of deregulation will come after a review of progress, scheduled for 2003. But there is a growing possibility of competition from overseas companies.

Tepco has delayed development of 22 power stations because of Japan's economic recession. It is promising to develop nuclear plants, but, with the threat of competitors entering the market, Tepco cannot afford to invest in what could be under-utilized generating capacity. Deregulation might allow it to purchase additional gas generators, such as Tokyo Gas, although this might be prevented by monopoly watchdogs.

With world energy markets in such a flux, intensive energy consumers need to carefully examine their energy-related risks.

CORPORATE SURVIVAL AND THE DYNAMICS OF CHANGE

In this section I talk to a selection of Old and New Economy companies about their approach to risk management. The discussions took place during the first half of 2001. Ernst & Young's first-quarter profit warnings analysis for the year showed the highest rate of warnings (136) recorded since their analysis started in 1998, and a rise of 77 per cent on the previous quarter. Slowing world growth, continuing troubles for the software and computer services sector, and the economic impact of foot and mouth disease in the UK were contributory factors. Other key sectors hit during the quarter included general retailers, and engineering and machinery.

The TMT sector saw a continuing downward trend. Software and computer services generated the largest number of warnings, 14 per cent of the total. 'Earlier over-investment in Y2K issues, the risk of recession and a drop in demand from the internet sector influenced the slide in profits in the IT sector,' said Ernst & Young. 'In the coming months trouble is expected for more of the larger and well-regarded players operating within the technology sector as their investments through corporate venturing and vendor financing are further exposed to the downturn. More warnings are also expected from telecommunications network companies.'

In the retail sector, nine of the 11 profit warnings were from companies involved with clothing, and six of these nine were from discounters or other value-based operators. Some of the discounters' problems have resulted from an overcrowded market and competition from middle-market operators.

Alan Greenspan, chairman of the US Federal Reserve, offered hope that the American economy had stopped deteriorating. But he added: 'The period of sub-par economic performance is not over. And we are not yet free of the risk that economic weakness will be greater than currently anticipated and require further policy response'.

> **We are not yet free of the risk that economic weakness will be greater than currently anticipated and require further policy response.**

British economist Peter Spencer, adviser to Ernst & Young's Item Club, in 2001 said the British economy was at risk of recession. No matter that he had in mind that old-fashioned contradiction a 'growth recession', a cyclical downturn in which output grows at a snail's pace. The Treasury and the Bank of England should therefore get together with their counterparts in euroland, and even America, to drive the euro higher and remove currency risk for British firms, he said.

What George W. Bush's National Energy Policy means for the utility industry

21

By Mary Harris, *PA Consulting*

P*A Consulting in 2001 was very quick off the mark to analyze the Bush administration's National Energy Policy. Mary, can you summarize the main points in the NEP – and assess whether more certainty will be introduced into the energy supply and trading arrangements in the USA?*

First up, Bush's NEP is a balanced supply-demand analysis that focuses on infrastructure and technology. It has a stronger focus on conservation and efficiency than we expected. There is also reference to energy security, especially with regard to oil imports into the USA.

The California crisis and the NEP put energy issues centre stage. Energy users need to assess their risks. The crisis has focused minds wonderfully. What we should look at in the report is the new aspects of energy policy introduced just five months into a new administration which clearly favours the energy industry.

If you ask me what we can learn from the NEP, it underlines a number of policy directions:

■ Bush believes in market solutions: he wants to remove impediments to market forces. The NEP represents a significant shift in this respect towards markets in the energy sector. Their refusal to impose electricity price controls is indicative of a non-interventionist approach.

■ The NEP refocuses on long-term strategy. If risks are to be avoided, long-term issues must be addressed. Supply-demand imbalance has been building for decades. Low prices for too long have made people complacent.

■ Nuclear power will play a valuable role in the future: but he doesn't suggest any statistics on new plant.

■ There's no analysis of global emissions and climate change: a great worry to the Europeans and others. You wonder if he's depending on more nuclear to reduce our emissions.

- Clean coal is seen as another important fuel of the future to meet increased electricity demands over the next 20 years. This is a change from coal's recent 'dirty' image, the great polluter, the generation of carbon emissions.

- The US government wants to see comprehensive electricity restructuring – achieved by legislation, encouraging competition and repealing the Public Utility Holding Company Act (PUHCA) and parts of the Public Utility Regulatory Policies Act (PURPA). This is all broadly consistent with the Clinton administration.

- The strongest, and most controversial, proposal is to provide federal authority for acquisition of rights-of-way for new electricity transmission. This is what's held back new transmission investment for years. It risks pitting state and local interests against national, federal and commercial interests.

- We are likely to see New Source Review (NSR) regulations introduced. These would establish rules for upgrading existing generation units and refineries. Suggestions that the Environmental Protection Agency may ease off on the enforcement of New Source Review requirements may provide the power section with more certainty so that sensible investment decisions can be made.

- Multi-pollutant legislation is likely to be introduced to establish a flexible market-based programme to cap emissions of sulphur dioxide, nitrogen oxides and mercury from electric power generators. Carbon dioxide is, significantly, omitted from this list.

I would expect a lively debate on all the recommendations for legislation in the NEP.

What the NEP ignores

The report was written largely by the incoming members of the Bush team. So, from a commercial perspective, there are some noticeable omissions:

- Demand side is not seriously addressed, although more energy efficiency is advocated.

- The fundamental changes taking place in the electricity industry are not appreciated. It is unlikely that there will be drilling in the Arctic during Bush's term of office, despite the hints given during the election.

- What will happen is that measures which were initiated during the Clinton era, such as reform and repeal of PUHCA, will make a big impact on energy supply.

- Bush has also made it clear that he wants the Federal Energy Regulatory Commission (FERC) to have more teeth: and its actions have shown that it hears what he is saying. He can achieve what he wants by leaning on them: he does not need to antagonize his energy sector supporters or consumers by acting himself.

- Risks are not addressed despite the fact that the shift to electricity markets will lead to some very volatile spot markets. This risk should not be underestimated.

Environmental groups were not happy with the NEP, were they? The government is hostile to Kyoto. It wants to see more exploration in areas of outstanding natural beauty such as Alaska. They see Big Capital in the ascendancy.

The electricity generation and supply industry has made it clear that it wants action to blunt the teeth of campaigners. The commercial sector wants to blunt their power. Although you have to remember that the Clinton administration never ratified Kyoto. But they were quieter about not doing so than Bush! Nevertheless it is true to say that the major energy companies, Bush supporters, are looking for the upside after years of downside risks. They want:

> **The electricity generation "and supply industry has made it clear that it wants action to blunt the teeth of campaigners.**

- rights of way for new transmission lines;

- market-based tariffs to facilitate investments;

- the role and powers of FERC and other federal agencies in a deregulated energy and utility marketplace to be clarified;

- to know the final position on Kyoto, emissions reductions and emissions trading, so they can plan accordingly;

- how government will 'skew' the marketplace; by regulation, legislation, R&D grants, fiscal policy and international commitments.

But it is hard to see how the legal and environmental campaign risks will go away. They seem to be growing stronger all the time. Considering adverse reactions to proposals to drill in the Arctic, it is hard to see how this could be implemented during the first term.

In California, natural gas pipeline capacity is controversial. The failure of projects during the 1990s was a result of opposition from the intra-state carriers and sometimes the California Public Utilities Commission. The intra-state opposition to inter-state capacity continues. They could be resolved by controversial changes in the Natural Gas Act. The NEP does not address this. Nothing in the NEP oil and gas proposals will make the risk management task of utility executives any easier in relation to oil and gas markets and gas price and cost volatility.

> **They need to develop business models and risk models to deal with the new situation.**

Electricity generators should not expect any help from the Bush regime in dealing with the risks connected with purchasing natural gas. They need to examine their risk exposure in relation to fuel purchases. They need to develop business models and risk models to deal with the new situation.

What happens next? There are huge risks and prizes to play for on all sides. Profits for energy merchants, power-generation companies and integrated electricity utilities across the United States rose in the wake of the California energy crisis. Energy-merchant and power-generation company earnings rose more than 30 per cent, while integrated electricity utilities were up 12 per cent, according to Merrill Lynch's global power and gas research group on Wall Street. The low-cost producers have locked in margins through long-term contracts, and have the merchant capability to take advantage of the inherent volatility in the energy sector. At the same time, the California crisis has created a political and legal overhang on the industry as everyone passes the buck for an energy crisis that many say they saw coming. Public outrage at all this forced some companies to pull back prices.

It will be interesting to see the detail of how lobbying from various sides, including senators and congressmen, changes the NEP. As I indicated, the situation is complicated by the federal structure in the United States. There is a patchwork of state regulation and ad hoc reliability council areas served by a multiplicity of investor-owned, municipal and federal utilities. The US electricity sector has progressed more slowly than its equivalents in the UK and Australia. There is a need for informed reform of the electricity sector. This would introduce more certainty into the marketplace and reduce some of the risks – for generators, retailers and consumers.

What is clear is that power and heat companies will be building an unprecedented number of energy plants. PA's database indicates that in excess of 245 GW of new capacity is under development: 51 GW come on line in 2001; 67 GW in 2002; and 60 GW in 2003. This is amazing: 215 GWs of extra capacity in five years, leading to a 30 per cent increase in supply in the period 1998–2003! Or, to put it another way, as much as the rest of the world built in three years!

A more realistic risk assessment indicates that, say, only 75 per cent of this projected capacity will be built. Excess capacity will have been requested to hedge the bets on siting approvals. There will be contractual and gas pipeline problems. Gas pipeline access is another risk. That could affect up to 30 GW by 2006. It is conceivable that there may be a glut of energy in five years' time – perhaps 50 GWs of excess capacity. Energy prices could fall.

The complexities and risks of energy purchasing are leading many energy-intensive consumers to outsource their energy trading. With price caps and volatile spot markets, energy risk is becoming an ever-more-complex matter, don't you think? In the EU we are also seeing facilities management in general being outsourced to multinational supply companies who can play the market on their behalf. Who are the major players?

This new capacity is being built by increasingly large power generating and trading companies who wish to assemble unregulated power generation asset portfolios often in the 20 to 40 GW range. Two companies are targeting generation portfolios of 60 to 70 GW. By 2005, eight or ten large power producers will own more than 25 GW.

With the exception of California, supply will be able to meet the growing energy demand. More than 90 per cent of the planned new capacity will be gas-fired. NEP forecasts that, over the next 20 years, 38,000 miles of new gas pipeline will be required.

> **NEP forecasts that, over "" the next 20 years, 38,000 miles of new gas pipeline will be required.**

This means that many new plants and pipelines will be built by cash-rich players, such as Enron, who are power generators and traders but who already have large and growing pipeline networks?

Yes, perhaps not build but own the output. Six of the leading power wholesalers are in the top ten gas wholesalers. But we are now seeing the emergence of very powerful, multi-energy traders with smart, diversified asset networks – pipelines, power plants, gas, coal, oil, wind farms – with a wide spread across the whole USA.

Is Bush's identification of a valuable role for nuclear power in the future feasible?

There has not been a nuclear power plant commissioned or conceptualized in the United States for the past 20 years. The financial risks, the burden of building, operating and decommissioning the plants are so large that few firms are interested in taking them forward. The big issue in the USA right now is not whether new plants are built but whether those plants reaching the end of their useful life, or reaching the end of their licensing period which is the first 30 years, will be able to be relicensed and stay in operation. The Bush administration is looking at whether we will decommission at the end of their licence period the 100 nuclear power units that are operating or whether or not they will continue to operate for a period of 10 or 20 more years.

> **The big issue in the USA "" right now is not whether new plants are built but whether those plants will be able to be relicensed and stay in operation.**

Also the environmental problems and the potential environmental health problems? The world saw what could happen with a nuclear incident at Chernobyl. You did some work following that in the environs of Chernobyl, didn't you?

Yes. I was part of a team from the USA and the EU that was tasked with coming up with an action plan to address the social problems related to closing the Chernobyl plant. It was agreed that the plant would be closed in 2000 and it has now closed all of the units. Three of the units continued to operate after the fourth exploded and it had been operating continuously from 1986. But it is an old plant design. It was built without containment. It is a rather unstable and particularly risky nuclear plant design. That could never possibly by built under American, Japanese or European standards.

Dealing with the social ramifications of that – everything from managing the public health of the people in the region to decommissioning the plant safely, to maintaining the integrity of the sarcophagus over the exploding unit, which still emits radiation and has some highly active radiation in its rubble – all this was part of the work we did.

What can the West learn from that incident?

I think the lesson of Chernobyl is really not one of technology. Obviously it would be great to have technology and enough redundancy in systems to be able to overcome human error and stupidity. In the case of Chernobyl, we know that it was caused by a planned failure that was designed as a systems test. It involved shutting down all the energy to the plant, all the water to the plant and then letting it go into a turn-off situation when they could then bring it up. Well, of course, most of the nuclear plant operators who had reviewed this procedure had rejected it and said, no, they would never do this with their plant. It was a fairly ridiculous idea. At Chernobyl it went wrong in the first ten minutes. There's no substitute at all for people with proper training and integrity. Systems always have to be monitored and managed. There's hardly a way to design around people who override the technology.

Except good management and a good culture in the company?

Well, that goes without saying. You do want to have good management. And you want to have management that has the appropriate training, understanding and skills for the industry that they are operating. You don't take a highly trained professional from one field and think that they could be inter-changeable with one from another. I'd be unlikely to think that an excellent brain surgeon could run an IT company.

The USA had its own early problems with nuclear power – Three Mile Island.

Yes, that was 1979 when a hydrogen bubble formed in the reactor.

It's not so easy just to restart nuclear programmes. What's been happening in Europe is that all the guys who used to go into nuclear because it was considered high-tech and the smart place to be for the most brilliant mathematicians, theoretical chemists and physicists, all these people with first class degrees are finding they can get extremely well-paid jobs in the City and that's where they are going. They are not going into nuclear power. It's a declining industry. So the workers in the nuclear industry are ageing and there isn't a new stream of people coming up to replace them. Three Mile Island was so long ago that most readers of this book probably won't ever have heard about it.

Right. The nuclear industry is thought of, as people in the business say, as 'the mortuary business'. They are in the business of decommissioning plant. For those that are operating, it's certainly not the high times of building and producing. I think there's an excellent culture in many of the plants that exist but it just isn't attracting people the way it did.

So I wonder how realistic the Bush plan for more nuclear energy is?

I think the Bush plan is not necessarily to build new plants but to not close down the ones that exist too quickly.

22

The competitive universe – product risk and process risk

**By Brian Fullerton, Global Director
of Risk Management,
*Merrill Lynch Investment Managers***

I am sitting in an Italian restaurant, eating my monkfish with black truffle shavings, and talking at twice the speed of thought with Brian Fullerton. Merrill Lynch Investment Managers' Global Director of Risk Management looks and speaks a lot like Bill Gates. There's the same youthfulness. The same open-neck shirt, smart casual jacket, thinning hair – and the voice brimming with enthusiasm for his subject. And yes, again, it's IT. But this time, IT in the service of making big bucks for Merrill Lynch clients. Brian's plate of risotto goes untouched as he enthuses about what MLIM does. He talks about the asset manager that has more than $500 billion in active management:

We are a stand-alone division of Merrill Lynch. We manage all sorts of mandates globally – growth, institutional and retail mandates, both pooled vehicles, like major funds, and separate accounts for individuals and for institutions. We're one of the key business units in Merrill Lynch. We are a separate arm of Merrill Lynch. One arm does asset management and one does capital markets and investment banking. Then we have two brokerage units that provide advice to individuals: one an international arm and one a US-based arm.

Like many companies in the financial services sector, you are changing fast, aren't you? It must be a hell of a job to risk-manage a company changing at this kind of pace?

It is. We have a lot of different aspects of risk management at Merrill Lynch. We have a whole side that deals with capital markets where ML is risking its own capital. It is putting its capital at risk. That's a traditional risk management function in protecting ML's capital so we can be in business every day. Whether it is doing underwriting for clients or whether it is making a market for different instruments. So that's what risk management does in our capital markets and investment banking.

We also have risk management involved in our client advisory groups, making sure that our strategies are sound, the advice we are giving is appropriate, how it fits into what's right for the client. The flow of information from different parts of Merrill – our flow where we are actually working on investments solutions and investments that the client will be involved in. The capital markets side, underwriting securities, figuring out how those advisory clients will be able to tap into those two other parts of Merrill. So it's a complex organization with 68,000 people to support all over the world.

Where do you sit in the company structure?

I have a direct line to the Head of Asset Management and a line to the Head of Corporate Risk Management. I work with both of those gentlemen; Jeffrey Peek, Executive Vice-President, is Head of MLIM, and Arshad R. Zakaria, Senior Vice-President, is the Head of Corporate Risk Management. Mr Zakaria oversees all risk management and corporate credit functions world-wide. He joined Merrill Lynch in 1987, and has served in investment banking with a particular focus on equity-linked products and on derivatives. He was named a managing director in 1991, and served most recently as head of the Global Corporate Finance Group in investment banking.

We have risk engrained in many different things that we're doing. One, it's a quality control aspect. Second, risk management is one of the services we deliver. Clients want performance of their assets but they want that within some risk tolerance. So it's actually part of the product that we deliver. If you think about what an investment management firm offers, it delivers a specified set of returns at a certain level of risk. That's what we're trying to focus on. It's engrained in what we do.

On one side we have particular measures as we define products. We ask, what are these products meant to do? Then we check that that's what that product does. Sometimes it's quantitative measures. Sometimes it's more to do with the characteristics of the services we deliver. We are extremely data-dependent. One important risk management tool is our ability to slice and examine our portfolio in many different ways.

It's also how do we conduct our operations? Do we make mistakes? The process risk involves making sure that we optimize the client order flows. And minimize operational mishaps.

How has your huge investment in IT made this easier?

For example, matching clients who are looking for high-risk-high-return investments with suitable punts – and then tracking the performance in real time.

You are in the business of second-guessing risk. It's endemic to what you do?

That's right. It is really part of the service we provide. We know the markets are going to be volatile. We say, this is what we think you can expect.

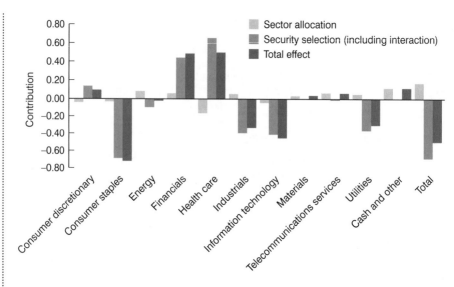

Fig 22.1 Total effect breakdown, month ending 29/06/2001 portfolio vs. S&P 500

Copyright: Merrill Lynch

" **Ninety per cent of the work is in the data: knowing how to pull it together, understanding what data is important.**

The hard stuff, the mathematics, is about 10 per cent of our problem because there are a lot of smart people out there. We have made progress in defining how we are going to look at risk quantitatively, for example risk reports tracking error, performance attribution and truth in advertising. Ninety per cent of the work is in the data: knowing how to pull it together, understanding what data is important, always reacting to the last crisis, what the history has been, never knowing how to face the new crisis that may come up and how that will play out. Data is a huge part of what we do. The risk is that the data's not there.

IT is the only way to attack that sort of problem and to manage that. Our quantitative models are a small part of our spend on risk management, and data management is a huge part of our spend. We use that for every part of our product. Risk management is a separate discipline but it is also integrated into our investment processes.

Let's home in on those quantitative models. Can you describe them?

We use a lot of measures where we examine a portfolio, an investment risk, for example. We'll identify what are the sources of volatility. How is this portfolio going to behave? We'll then use our fiscal models to say, look, these are the potential outcomes you have. We'll measure how this product behaves relative to peer groups and relative indices. We'll have a sense of where we're positioned relative to our competitors. Then we ask how: how do we enhance the investment process? We take these tools back to our portfolio managers.

There are a lot of models available but there are some key questions. What are the assumptions of the different models? Are you going to use more than one model? This gets back to quality control and the competitive nature analysis. What is in your portfolio? How does it compare to a benchmark? Or to a competitive universe of other products? That's where we spend a lot of time, analyzing this stuff.

A good fund manager will achieve dexterity in using these tools to analyze whether the portfolio is performing to target. He can play with a lot of variables such as a greater financial investment by the client, an increase or decrease in portfolio risk, adjusting the targets, a bull market or a bear market, and then see how this might affect returns? Is that it?

Yes. Our quantitative tools allow us to do very powerful analysis.

What else do the quantitative tools do? Can they input personal data – like the client likes croissants and strawberry jam for breakfast?

I am not sure we track what our clients' have for breakfast! But we track what they expect from our investments.

Do the quantitative tools also tell you something about your most successful analysts and their analytical methodologies? Or what kinds of products clients like? Or whether it is the high-risk or low-risk products which make more money over the three-, five- and ten-year period?

Yes, we use tools to estimate the contribution of our analysts and to construct portfolios with various risk profiles. In a nutshell, the tools allow us to leverage the intellectual capital of our portfolio managers and analysts.

What are the sources of return and the sources of risk? What do we think is causing that investment not to do so well? We spend a lot of time working out how we can enhance our best products.

Can you be more specific?

Let's start with what we call a truth in advertising review of our products. We ask, what is this product supposed to do? And then, how can we measure that?

Portfolio vs. S&P 500
29/12/2000 to 29/6/2001
US dollar

MSCI_SECTOR_PA2	Portfolio			Benchmark			Variation			Attribution analysis			
	Average weight	Total contribution		Average weight	Total contribution		Average weight	Total contribution		Allocation effect	Selection effect	Interaction effect	Total effect
		Return	To return		Return	To return		Return	To return				
Consumer discretionary	9.37	16.05	1.48	12.60	11.72	1.21	-3.23	4.33	0.28	-0.28	0.57	-0.23	0.06
Consumer staples	11.00	-17.23	-1.63	7.73	-11.55	-1.06	3.27	-5.68	-0.57	-0.52	-0.43	0.03	-0.92
Energy	5.60	6.79	0.31	6.67	-3.24	-0.22	-1.07	10.03	0.53	-0.11	0.59	-0.28	0.20
Financials	18.70	-1.37	0.40	17.15	-2.52	-0.45	1.55	1.15	0.85	0.31	0.18	0.45	0.94
Health care	16.45	-8.09	-1.66	13.24	-15.52	-2.18	3.21	7.42	0.53	-0.47	1.14	0.46	1.14
Industrials	9.85	-8.71	-1.15	10.82	-0.51	-0.01	-0.97	-8.20	-1.14	-0.20	-0.84	0.15	-0.89
Information technology	15.35	-17.54	-1.08	19.57	-17.49	-3.54	-4.22	-0.05	2.46	0.17	0.27	0.81	1.25
Materials	1.34	4.96	0.12	2.49	4.28	0.11	-1.15	0.68	0.01	-0.03	0.04	0.07	0.07
Telecommunications services	2.11	-11.77	-0.10	5.89	-2.56	-0.09	-3.79	-9.21	-0.01	-0.03	-0.52	0.31	-0.24
Utilities	2.41	-19.63	-0.57	3.84	-12.42	-0.49	-1.44	-7.22	-0.08	0.16	-0.49	0.06	-0.26
Cash and other	7.83	-0.65	-0.19	0.00	0.00	0.00	7.83	-0.65	-0.19	1.32	0.00	0.00	1.32
Total	**100.00**	**-4.05**	**-4.05**	**100.00**	**-6.72**	**-6.72**	**0.00**	**2.67**	**2.67**	**0.31**	**0.52**	**1.83**	**2.67**

Holdings Data As Of
Portfolio 29/12/2000 to 29/6/2001
S&P 500 02/1/2001 to 29/6/2001

Fig 22.2 Performance attribution

Copyright: Merrill Lynch

The US market is very well specified. Let's take a large cap growth fund. Well, we manage that to ensure that that overall portfolio is large cap and that it is actually invested in growth securities. Because you have to understand that the individual managers – if you don't have this stuff in place – might very well be tempted to take that large cap growth bracket and move it into a small cap value product if that market's where the returns are.

But that won't work for our clients. When clients put together a portfolio, they are allocating to a specific asset class or return profile. If they allocate to a US large cap growth fund they don't want to find that's not what it now is just because it doesn't work. It doesn't go the way we think.

We're lucky. We have quite a product line. We have a credible presence in Europe, having acquired Mercury (Asset Management/MAM). We have a lot of products to offer clients. If someone wants to invest in our global products, they don't want to find that it's actually invested in the UK markets. It's common sense. But it's a discipline done outside the portfolio team. It says, what is this product supposed to do? How are we checking to make sure it's doing that? And giving feedback. Hey! Why so much in a given country? This is supposed to be a global fund!

The days are long gone when people just said, get the best returns you can. They hired just one asset manager, gave them money and that manager did what he thought was right. That's not what we offer. We offer a very disciplined approach to building client portfolios. For that to happen, everybody has to play their position.

> **The days are long gone " when people just said, get the best returns you can.**

We'll look at different categories and we say, you know, global small cap. Well, we'll say, what do the clients expect in this category? What are the terms of our competitors?

What do the clients expect? How much risk do you need to take to give those kinds of returns? Are we taking enough risk?

Risk is part of our overall strategy. We have to incorporate it into a lot of aspects of our operations – from the first part. We in MLIM do not take capital positions for ourselves. We are building investment portfolios for our clients. So we have quality control measures.

That's a very important part of what we do. Looking at our products from the sense of what kind of quality controls can we put in place for our 'manufacturing' processes? How do we build those products in a way that we deliver what the client expects?

The quantitative models analyze those portfolios. We're an active manager. We want to give clients out-performance relative to the benchmark or the competitive universe. We're very focused on that.

We need to take enough risk but we don't want to take too much. The level of risk that is appropriate depends on client expectations. They don't want you to take more. So we're trying to walk a balance. It's a grey line. It's very much an art judging how much risk we should take. We spend a lot of time assessing and managing risk throughout the firm. We work with the people producing the products and the portfolio managers.

It's very important for you to manage your online legal risk, isn't it? Because if you claim you're doing anything, it's a commitment, a claim?

Absolutely. For the longest time we've had to manage legal risks because, in the institutional business, you sign compliance documents. In some cases today, we do so online. We put all our information online. Online has become a huge way for us to distribute information to the client. Let them know what we're doing with their money.

It's also a way for us to get information out, to give them information on how they should build their portfolio. We think that's important because, if they build their portfolios correctly, and they have a good sense of the risk inherent in that portfolio, then both of us will be happy because we can deliver successfully on that mandate.

Our worst nightmare is someone who wants to have returns that are inconsistent with the amount of risk they are willing to take.

I'm getting the impression that you're working very closely with the fund managers? You're the risk manager but you're working very closely with your fund managers? Is that right?

That's exactly right. That's where we come from. It's not only quality control. It's also improving the process. Integrating into the investment process to try to make better decisions. Although we also work with the groups you mentioned: legal as well as marketing, to make sure that the products and the messages are appropriate. Marketing departments view all these quantitative and advertising measures and use the information for product and channel management. Investments can be complex and we want to convey them correctly to our clients.

Each manager is actually running a whole portfolio of securities. An average portfolio may have 100 securities in it. These quantitative and process tools are a great way to look at a portfolio. That's why they are a great way to manage your overall business too because you have a portfolio of businesses.

What we're talking about is managing complexity, isn't it?

Absolutely. I think it starts at a product level. But we've spent a couple of days talking about our different businesses. We've talked about the community of risk. How to pick out which new areas we are going to invest in. Where we are going to put our resources. We are in a lucky position to have more opportunity than we can actually meet in the short term. We have to choose which investments we are going to make. For each one we are looking at what's the potential upside of this? What's the potential downside? It's a risk analysis of the opportunities that we have.

It is predicted that the majority of online punters will be located in China by 2007. Are you active there?

We've an active sales office in China. There are a lot of good opportunities. We're meeting with a lot of strong institutions there. So we're very excited about the opportunity there. We're one of the few players that have a global reach. We have a very strong commitment to Asia. We've been there for a very long time. We think we can deliver a very good product there. We manufacture product in Tokyo as well as Singapore and Australia. We have representatives and analysts in other places like China.

What are you doing right now?

My team is global. Everywhere we manage money, we need to do the things we talked about. Watching the quality of the products. Using our tools to improve the investment process. We're currently looking at some new offering which we are going to put out. When we have a new product, we look at what are the things this product is supposed to do? What are the natural competitors of this product? What do the clients expect from us? How should we manage this product? How can we give more information back to the portfolio managers about what's going on with their product? What can go wrong? What quantitative and process tools should we put in place?

> **The interesting thing is "" that all this stuff doesn't replace the good, old-fashioned investment sense that people have always had. You have to have that.**

The interesting thing is that all this stuff doesn't replace the good, old-fashioned investment sense that people have always had. You have to have that. It's like saying that good engineering and technology companies or a car manufacturer don't need inspiration. The way the world has moved is that we can make things better, faster and cheaper. The creativity still needs to be there.

It is a huge risk. We tend to a strategy of buying off-the-shelf software and integrating it. So we have a lot of integration risk as we pull together the commercial pieces. We go to the person who has the best credit risk model. We don't want to use the third or fourth best because it's the same vendor. We won't buy the total solution. We'll buy pieces and put them into our own final framework. It's important for us that the managers who need the information have the best analytical software. We need to present the world the way we want to build our portfolios, not the way someone wants to sell us software. So that's a big IT challenge for us.

We have some interesting tools. I'd just like to go over two. One is a risk tool. We take a portfolio and say, where are the big risks in this portfolio? We also look at it relative to a benchmark. Then we say, which securities are the cause of that risk? That's on the forecast side.

On the other side, after it happens, we use a tool to understand our returns. We can pick up on how accurate our forecasts are. So we can say, what are we doing right when we do things right? What else has to do with it? The sector allocation? Or is it in specific stocks that we do best? Security selection is what we call that.

Is it certain industries or countries we do better in? We call that sector allocation. Is it certain types of companies we do better in? The size of companies? We look at our data in a lot of different ways and ask, what's driven these returns? We want to know what we're good at and we also want to know where we are falling down so we can go back and try to improve that process over and over.

2000–2001 saw the re-emergence of a bear market, particularly in TMT stock and emerging economies. How was your year?

Our performance over the all-important three- and five-year periods remains excellent. We are building a global business. We have asset management in London and New York and a good size in Asia. That's an unusual book of business and it makes risk management technology more important because we are trying to put together global teams. We'll all offer a global product which will have a US component, a European component, an Asian component. Getting those pieces right so we can share that information is difficult. We have made great progress towards that in 2000/2001.

Jeff Peek is in New York. Chief Investment Office Bob Doll is in New York. The Chief Operating Officer, Peter Gibbs, is in London. In China there has been a lot of interest from different institutional investors and reinsurers who are looking overseas to make investments. We can really solve some problems that they have and build a partnership with them.

Is the IT language English or Chinese?

Well, we are not manufacturing there. When our sales effort to them begins it will be in Chinese. The interesting thing actually is I had a client come visit me. My world is quantitative people, people with PhDs from MIT, Berkeley. A member

> **In China there has been a "lot of interest. We can really solve some problems that they have and build a partnership with them."**

of my team did this presentation on What Risk Is – it's knowledge, it's management – in Chinese because we have that sort of workforce, we can do that. The clients were a little surprised to come to Princeton, New Jersey (outside New York) and have the presentation given to them in Chinese. The funny thing was that one of the delegation was the college roommate of the guy in my team. They were undergraduates together in China. My guy came to the USA and became further educated. It's a small world. That's the kind of opportunity we have. It's an amazingly connected world.

I saw a speech by your CEO that said an awful lot of ML people went to Wharton. Where did you go?

I went to Wharton. You know, there are some MBA programmes that are very quantitative – such as University of Chicago and Wharton we have a lot of people from there. The MLIM CEO went to Harvard. That's not at all unusual.

Competitor risk has surfaced for you as people surf the net and buy financial services online from people like Charles Schwab. How are you managing that risk?

One, we use the internet quite heavily ourselves to deliver information to our clients. Some like to access their information online. We are happy to be driven by clients' choice of what they want. The investment management business has been impacted a little differently than the brokerage and the financial advice part which compete directly with Schwab. We don't really do that. We compete with other people that manage portfolios. There's one called Metamarkets that put their portfolio up on the internet. That's the concept that investing is part entertainment and part returns. We don't really go that way...

Roulette, you mean?

I don't know. Most people want to be involved with their decisions – that's our clients. Others want to make the investment decision. That's not really where we want to go because we are looking for a different kind of client that was very serious about their portfolio and how they want it put together. So we're using the internet as a way to service that client. That's our strategy today. It's been extremely effective for us and it will continue to be.

What is your customer profile – in terms of how much is invested per month?

From £50 a month in an ISA or any of our products, right up to discretionary asset management where people wouldn't get into it until they had £1 million plus to invest. There's this huge band in between, the 'mass affluent' as they are described now. These we can now access via our tie-up with HSBC, which is basically internet-based.

It's a way to leverage ourselves. The distribution is not our business. Our part is manufacturing great portfolios that give good returns and manage the risk effectively. Through HSBC we access more clients. One of the things we do is retirement plans, and servicing those plans.

Now we've put all that information out there it is very confusing for people. I guess we're going to have to get better at helping people navigate through the complexities of our organization. We put it out there. We try and be very open. But it's very confusing. We just separated our asset management business from our client brokerage business because our asset management group is one of the biggest in the world. We have more than $500 billion in assets. That's bigger than most stand-alone asset managers.

Merrill Lynch is one of the world's leading financial management and advisory companies with offices in 44 countries and total client assets of about $1.6 trillion. As an investment bank, it is the top global underwriter and market maker of debt and equity securities and a leading strategic adviser to corporations, governments, institutions and individuals world-wide. Through Merrill Lynch Investment Managers, the company is one of the world's largest managers of financial assets. Our financial advisory business is one of the biggest stand-alones. Our investment banking and capital markets are one of the biggest!

In asset management we have tremendous sharing opportunities. We have one research tool we call Bull's Eye where we post our research so we can share it. So someone in London will go visit a company and they'll write up whether it's good or bad, what's going on. Someone in Princeton who's managing a portfolio can access that. Similarly, someone in the USA can visit a company in Silicon Valley and write that up for all our international colleagues. There's tremendous leverage, the stuff the intranet enables us to do.

Is this made available to clients?

No. This is our opinions of companies. We have to be very careful about that because we can be wrong as well as right. But we have to have opinions. We put out something different for our clients. Typically, we focus our message to our clients on their portfolios. We put out so much – an amazing challenge for corporations is how you manage the information you put out there so people can figure it all out.

> **I think the more companies develop their websites, the more they want out of them in terms of what they can do.**

I think the more companies develop their websites, the more they want out of them in terms of what they can do. We're going towards video and audio interaction with customers. The big thing is content management.

This has now become an essential discipline in everything we do. We always talk about the content. What are we doing to create content. What are we doing to distribute that. That's the power of the web. It's made every group think about that. We do most of our work for our portfolio managers and our management. Some for clients but mostly to look at our facts and make sure they're right for ourselves. That's where we spend a lot of time.

The thing's shifting. It used to be getting out all the stuff you're working out. Now it's, what are the different people who are going to use the web, internally and externally and from us? How can we use the web? If we're not making that particularly easy for you, what do internal and external clients want with it?

We've been amazingly open about the stuff we've put out there. But is it what people want? There are so many different groups. People from college who want to decide whether they want to come and join us. An individual retail plan. A powerful institution, pension fund.

Motley Fool (fool.com site) has discussions posted with various investors.

One of the scary things we've seen with some of those online discussion boards is you don't necessarily have to be qualified to comment. That's why we're cautious about putting out our opinions. Sometimes you go and look at a company. There are the hard numbers. But something seems wrong. Employees don't seem motivated. It doesn't seem like they're behind the strategy. We don't think that's a great place to invest. Now if we're hesitant, we share that internally. We have to be very careful about sharing that externally.

It's interesting when you read some of the information out there from non-investment professionals.

> **They sometimes have great insight. Sometimes they don't. There are terrible cases where people are manipulated.**

They sometimes have great insight. Sometimes they don't. There are terrible cases where, you know, people are manipulated.

If you were giving advice to a company that is just thinking about their knowledge management system, advice on mistakes you'd made in the past, what would you say?

I'd say this is one of the most difficult things to do. I think the only way to do it is start at two ends. One end is, you know, ask, what are you trying to get out? And then, what are you trying to put together? Because if you start either way and just start working on it, there's a massive problem of data, how to get all that right, it's a never-ending thing. It'll be years before you get anything out.

If you don't get the information flow correctly, the processes and the data clean, it'll never be any good. You need to work from both ends. It's so complex. We find we have to make these partnerships with people at one end: the business users of that information. At the other end are the professionals who know how to manage data, how to 'clean' data, how to access data and put all that together.

How do you keep data up-to-date? That's the biggest problem?

Our data changes instantaneously. We plug into all sorts of data sources. You have to ask, at what frequency do you need this data? You don't need everything instantaneously. But there are some things you do and you have to identify that because, one, the costs for real-time data are huge; and second, it can cause more confusion than insights.

The third point is that all this data is great but you still need analysis. So we have to build in time for that. You look at what different risk tools mean, what different analyses mean.

The risk is of too much data – the So What? paradigm.

Yes. It becomes mind-numbing. It's not effective. People can't deal with that.

What has been the cost of investment in technology at Merrill Lynch?

It's been one of our biggest investments – infrastructure, technology and data management. It's the people who do that as well as the tools.

The hidden costs.

The hidden costs. If you add all the aspects together I think that would be our biggest single bet – technology and the human capital involved in that.

A TECHOLOGY FUND
vs ML Tech 100 Index
Thursday, July 26 2001

Risk summary

Benchmark	Total risk	Benchmark risk	Beta	Active risk
ML Tech 100 index	27.1	29.2	0.9	5.9

10 most overweight assets

Stock	Portfolio	Benchmark	Active	% Active risk
Cash_USD	7.7	0.0	7.7	0.0
CELESTICA INC CAD NP	2.4	0.0	2.4	-2.9
TMP WORLDWIDE INC	1.8	0.0	1.8	0.0
GEMSTAR TV GUIDE INT	1.8	0.0	1.8	-0.4
LAM RESEARCH	1.7	0.0	1.7	-1.5
First Data	1.6	0.0	1.6	-0.3
Veritas Software	2.1	0.6	1.5	-1.5
Tyco International	1.4	0.0	1.4	-0.3
TAIWAN SEMICONDUCTOR	1.3	0.0	1.3	-0.4
ALTERA CORP COM	3.0	1.7	1.3	-1.7

10 most underweight assets

Stock	Portfolio	Benchmark	Active	% Active risk
Computer Associates	0.0	2.3	-2.3	8.5
Citrix Systems	0.0	2.1	-2.1	9.1
BMC Software	0.0	2.0	-2.0	9.4
Electronic Data Syst	0.0	2.0	-2.0	2.3
SUNGARD DATA SYS	0.0	2.0	-2.0	3.1
E-BAY INC	1.0	2.9	-1.9	8.4
ELECTRONIC ARTS	0.6	2.4	-1.8	5.3
TAIWAN SEMIC-ADR	0.0	1.8	-1.8	4.3
Apple Computer	0.6	2.2	-1.7	4.7
KLA-TENCOR CORP COM	0.9	2.5	-1.6	4.4

Sector exposure

Sector	Portfolio	Benchmark	Active	% Tracking error
CONSUMER DISCRETIONARY	7.0	6.8	0.2	8.2
CONSUMER STAPLES	0.0	0.0	0.0	0.0
ENERGY	0.0	0.0	0.0	0.0
FINANCIALS	0.0	0.0	0.0	0.0
HEALTH CARE	0.0	0.0	0.0	0.0
INDUSTRIALS	6.4	1.3	5.1	10.8
INFORMATION TECHNOLOGY	77.2	91.8	-14.6	60.9
MATERIALS	0.0	0.0	0.0	0.0
TELECOMMUNICATIONS SERVICES	1.6	0.0	1.6	2.8
UTILITIES	0.0	0.0	0.0	0.0
UNCLASSIFIED	0.0	0.0	0.0	0.0
Cash	7.7	0.0	7.7	17.3

Fig 22.3 MLIM risk exposures report

Copyright: Merrill Lynch

Industry exposure				
Industry	**Portfolio**	**Benchmark**	**Active**	**% Tracking error**
COMMERCIAL SERVICES AND SUPPLIES	4.7	0.0	4.7	7.9
COMMUNICATIONS EQUIPMENT	10.9	11.4	–0.5	8.7
COMPUTERS AND PERIPHERALS	10.4	14.2	–3.8	7.2
DIVERSIFIED TELECOMS SERVICES	1.6	0.0	1.6	2.8
ELECTRICAL EQUIPMENT	0.3	1.3	–1.0	0.2
ELECTRONIC EQUIPMENT AND INSTRUMENTS	9.4	6.0	3.4	11.3
HOTELS RESTAURANTS AND LEISURE	0.5	0.0	0.5	0.9
HOUSEHOLD DURABLES	0.0	1.3	–1.3	0.0
INDUSTRIAL CONGLOMERATES	1.4	0.0	1.4	2.8
INTERNET AND CATALOGUE RETAIL	1.0	3.8	–2.8	–2.1
INTERNET SOFTWARE AND SERVICES	3.0	4.2	–1.2	2.1
IT CONSULTING AND SERVICES	0.8	7.3	–6.4	0.9
MEDIA	5.5	1.7	3.9	9.5
SEMICONDUCTOR EQUIPMENT AND PRODUCTS	26.9	25.9	1.0	19.7
SOFTWARE	15.7	22.9	–7.2	11.1
Cash	7.7	0.0	7.7	17.3

Fig 22.3 cont'd

■ Analysis

This conversation was really interesting because Brian talked about product risk, process risk, competitors and working closely with the people in, what in a manufacturing or a service industry, would be called 'operations' and 'marketing'. He talked about MLIM's excellent knowledge management. He also commented on the high-level skills Merrill employs. In a world dominated by the cliché, 'our people are our most valuable asset', and where good people are becoming increasingly hard to recruit, he indicates the multi-degree and multi-disciplinary skills which the world's five-star employers are seeking.

Biotech start-ups 23

By Peter Keen, *Merlin Biosciences*

Peter Keen, Managing Director of UK operations at Merlin Biosciences, is sitting in his sunny penthouse office above London's St James's Square. The building is full of glass, light and sculpture inside a magnificent Regency shell. I pause at the top of the atrium on the way out and realize it reflects Merlin's business philosophy – high-tech in a traditional business framework.

But it's by no means sunshine all the way! Merlin is a venture capital firm specializing in the life sciences sector. The companies in which Merlin invests discover, develop and commercialize bio-technologies. They are a high-risk but potentially high-reward investment. If they, and Merlin, get it right, the outcome is big bucks and ultimately a takeover by a mega-pharmaceutical company.

But many other companies have got it wrong, or made claims for their products that they have later been unable to substantiate. Business confidence in the whole sector can be undermined by problems, of a scientific or financial nature, at just one biotech company. So Merlin has a vested interest in their getting it right. And in avoiding investments in companies that do not have scrupulous science and integrity. The outcome also needs water-tight patents and a commercially-positioned product line.

Peter explains the investment strategy and how he hopes Merlin's hands-on VC style will steer biotech start-ups away from the icebergs:

Our start-up fund, the Merlin Fund LP, raised £39 million primarily from UK-based investors and from the Finsbury Life Sciences Investment Trust (FLIT). It is a venture capital fund investing in *start-up biotech companies*.

Our second fund, the Merlin Biosciences Fund, raised €247 million. West LB committed €37.5 million. This is for *later stage, pre-IPO biotech companies*. Another commitment of €50 million was made in 2000 by the European Investment Bank's (EIB) European Investment Fund (EIF). The initial €37.5 million was followed by a top-up of €12.5 million based on our raising more than €200 million. This came from European-based financial institutions, pension funds and private investors.

So €247 million has come in...

The way a venture capital fund works is that you draw the money down as you require it. So an investor like EIF will say, 'I am contractually obligated to give you within ten days of your asking for whatever money you want between €0 and €50 million. We are obligated to generate returns on people's money. If we draw it all and put it in the bank earning 5 per cent interest, rest assured the investors don't wish to receive 5 per cent. They can do that themselves. What they expect is for the money to be put to work and put into higher risk-higher-reward ventures.

The Merlin Biosciences Fund invests in European lifescience companies. Roughly 50 per cent has been allocated to UK biotechs. Technically, we can invest a small proportion outside the EU. We have a 'Eurovision Song Contest' definition of Europe! We've invested in an Israeli biotech company. The fund invests €5 million to €12 million per company, taking a significant minority equity stake.

Finsbury Life Sciences Investment Trust, previously the Reabourne Merlin Life Sciences Investment Trust PLC, is a publicly quoted investment trust, launched in 1997. Its objective is to achieve long-term capital growth by investing in life science companies based in the UK, Western Europe (including Scandinavia) and Israel. FLIT invests in both quoted and unquoted biotechnology and healthcare companies. It is managed by investment bank Close Finsbury Asset Management Ltd. Merlin Biosciences advises FLIT's unquoted life science portfolio. Reabourne Technology Investment Management Ltd advises the quoted portfolio. FLIT's top ten portfolio investments include Merlin Fund, Shire Pharmaceuticals, Celltech Group, Teva Pharmaceutical, Biacore International, Alizyme, Gyrus, Cambridge Antibody Technology, Smith and Nephew and Zeltia.

The fundraising environment for biotechnology companies has been tough. Dozens of European biotechnology companies have put flotations on hold because of hostile conditions in the public capital markets.

If the fundamentals are sound it will happen – when market conditions are right! Neurotech is France's largest private biotechnology company. With Apax Partners we raised €35 million in a pre-IPO financing round in 2001. This was our first French investment and the largest cash call for some years in the sector. Neurotech is developing genetically engineered eye and nerve cells to replace damaged tissue. They could also act as implantable drug factories. Diseases such as adult-onset blindness and dementia are difficult to treat with the pill-based medicines, and especially the complex molecules developed by biotechnology companies, because of problems getting them across the blood-brain barrier, or into the eye. Neurotech will use the cash – which is to be paid in two tranches linked to its progress – to put its first treatments into clinical trials and to buy new technology. Payment of the second block of cash would value the company at about €70 million.

In 2002–2003 we hope to take three companies public – Cyclacel, which develops anti-cancer drugs; Microscience, which specializes in vaccines; and Ark Therapeutics, which develops cardiovascular drugs.

Over the next three years Merlin hopes to expand its presence outside Europe, targeting the USA, Canada, Singapore, Australia and Japan.

When you invest in companies, do you always take a seat on the board?

We would expect to because we don't see ourselves as just providing capital. Investors do not commit money and pay us a fee without expecting us to do more. Equally important is our added-value contribution. I've been in the biotech industry since the 1980s, 12 of these years in operational management. I've seen mistakes made and learned from those.

Inevitably companies go through a 'sweaty palms' period. What it actually means is that you have to keep cool. You use the experience of the stakeholders in the business to make the company succeed.

> **I've been in the biotech industry since the 1980s, 12 of these years in operational management. I've seen mistakes made and learned from those.**

That's where Merlin contributes added value. One of the ways that you do that is by having a non-executive seat on the board. Although much of the board-level interaction is strategic. You meet as a board every month or two for three hours. There's a limit to what you can achieve in that timeframe. You have appropriate governance control but in reality it's the work you do with the executives; and with the chairman whom we expect to be strong and independent. It's the concept of no surprises. We're aware of what the pitfalls are. How to help grow the company by identifying additional technologies to purchase and identifying key recruits.

People run their portfolios in different ways. We have our target model of €5 million to €12 million. We would never sit on the board post the company going public except in circumstances where we are locked in to shareholders. We would generally resign at the IPO because we would wish to have the flexibility to sell. We could not do so if we were party to inside information.

Would investors expect to see a good return on their investment by the time of the IPO?

Every situation is different. Where we see there being significant growth in the period post-IPO, we would be tempted to stay in. However, we are paid as managers of a private equity portfolio. There are lots of other people out there who are paid to run public portfolios. You have to understand what the interests of your investors are. They don't want to be paying us a management fee to run a portfolio of companies anybody can buy.

There are companies where we do not see the IPO as being the exit. We see the IPO as a stepping stone to achieve the ultimate exit which we believe for these companies will be acquisition by one of the major companies in the field. It is as an appropriate middle step to achieving that end game that the company goes public.

Tell me a little more about how your expertise translates into growing the companies in which you invest.

For the pool of investments in the Merlin Fund companies, we actually wrote the business plans for them. We identified leading edge technology. If you were an academic and you realized that you had something with commercial potential, what we did was provide the full range of support of which the business plan is the end result of six to nine months' intensive work. We provided the seed capital to get the intellectual property into a corporate entity. It is a long iterative process to put the business plan together. We see significant chunks of intellectual property coming out of academic institutions.

The risk with academic ideas is that they may not pass the clinical or financial tests?

It's getting better. People are getting much smarter. But we have to protect the intellectual property. Someone might say, 'I'm going to speak at this conference in a month's time' or 'I'm going to publish this paper. I'd better patent the work first before I make the public disclosure.' Then what happens is that the patent is done in a rush. To construct a proper patent, you need to ask, what is the commercial end-point of my intellectual property? How do we get there? What are the other hurdles that need to be jumped?

It requires a full analysis of what other people are doing. It requires an innovative approach to ensure that everything that is going to happen to that IP from a commercial standpoint is covered by that patent application. Now, if you're an academic interacting with colleagues and you have a short deadline to construct the patent, how can you possibly put the correct IP strategy in place? The answer is 'you can't'.

Academics are becoming more commercially focused?

There is a greater degree of support for them in terms of the breadth, depth and quality of the technology transfer. But there is still a lot of IP that has not been properly protected.

The whole basis of science to date has been that 'science is for everyone'. Academia is a sharing culture.

The risk management starts there. We ask them, 'what is the vision? What can we create with your technology?' Just having the science is not enough. It has to be converted into a business opportunity. We have to convert them from thinking they can put the science into the company, draw £25,000 a year in consultancy fees, and that's it. Building a business is a lot harder than that!

So we say to them, 'First up, understand the vision of the business that you are trying to create. Test whether that business opportunity stacks up in the market-place.' There are many here-today-gone-tomorrow business ideas. Technologies are quickly overtaken by improvements.

One of the risks for early-stage investors is to understand what the business is going to be in year five. It's going to be in year five or year six that we are potentially going to be looking to realize our investment. Unless we understand what the business is going to be like in five years' time, unless you, as one of the founders, believe in and know where you want to be in year five, then we don't have a basis to make that initial investment.

Statistically, what you bring to the party on day one will fail.

Only one in 12 pharmaceutical 'discoveries' makes it through to commercial development.

Something that's in Phase I clinical trials has a 10 per cent chance of success. Another way of looking at it is that, if you've got a clinical discovery in Phase 1, the risk of failure as you progress through clinical trials and regulatory approval to commercial development is 90 per cent.

> **Statistically, what you bring to the party on day one will fail. The risk of failure as you progress through clinical trials and regulatory approval to commercial development is 90 per cent.**

One of the key factors to ensure in the early stage company is that it has critical mass. You want to ensure that, when the lead product fails, you still have a business. That means you have to wrap up in your business a number of complementary technologies. Sometimes they become a bit of a rag-bag. But we try to add technology that adds some sort of therapeutic focus so they can get some interaction through various research projects. As a consequence, when something fails, you still have a business there.

That comes back down to, 'We're founding a company round a particular technology. You're a major stakeholder in that business. You have to understand that, for us to succeed as partners in your business, we will have to bring other technologies in.' You will potentially be diluted as a shareholder. You may have to pool resources, perhaps with a professional competitor in another field, to ensure that what you land up with is a sustainable business. It's no good backing just a small number of programmes: that's a recipe for failure.

To summarize, what are the key issues which minimize the risk?

Number one is critical mass. Number two is buy-in for the long-term strategy of the business. Number three is flexibility. Absolutely key! The founders have to be flexible in terms of recognizing that 'the skill sets that you bring to the company today may not necessarily be the skill sets that are required later on'. So you can be the chief scientific officer in the early days of the company. But once something moves from research into development, and we're being very theoretical here but, you know, you're an academic researcher. What do you know about clinical development? That is what's going to translate your discovery and get it into the market. That requires specialists. Again, you're not going to be the top dog. Your importance in the company diminishes.

We try to communicate to the founders the evolution of the business from day one. This comes back to, where does the business want to be in year five? We talk to the founders and say, 'This is how it is going to evolve. This is how your role will evolve. This is how, as the company raises the chunks of money it needs to grow, your shareholding will dilute. Are you comfortable with that? Do you understand that that is what's going to happen?'

For those that say, 'Well, we want to be running the show, I don't want my shareholding to dilute,' then you have to say, 'Sorry, we don't have the basis of a partnership. The deal is your IP and know-how, and our money, financial skills and commercial strategy. We need to have the basis of something that can work. If you don't confront those up front, all you're doing is storing up problems for later on.'

When companies heap up problems, they become the subject of takeover, sometimes by a company they would regard as a lesser player, perhaps offering shares rather than cash, which is what they really want. They cast around for a cash-rich company to take them over. Then we get down to director risk – huge egos and a preference for putting bids together rather than getting stuck in and solving problems down at the ranch.

It's interesting that you immediately associate takeovers with problems. Statistically, if you look at UK biotech, those companies that have engaged in merger activity or have been taken over are the problem companies.

There are one or two notable exceptions. Take the Celltech and Chiroscience merger. Two very successful companies. You have:

$$\text{success} + \text{success} = \text{even greater success}$$

In many of the merger situations that have taken place you get:

$$-1 + -1 = -3$$

What you need is mergers between successful companies to make even more successful companies. That generally hasn't happened. When you try to analyze the reasons, it normally comes down to one thing – management egos. No-one wants to relinquish the job of CEO having developed a successful company. Sometimes you also get investor egos. They say, 'We've backed a successful company. Why should we take a smaller shareholding?' Or you get arguments between the investor groups and other shareholders. You need to think of the end game. Don't look too short term. Look at the bigger picture.

The markets want to back the larger companies – the £150 million minimum market capital businesses. Why? Because they are large enough to cope with failure. When you're small, it's much more

> **What you need is mergers between successful companies to make even more successful companies. That generally hasn't happened.**

difficult. Everything's more visible. The share price gets hammered. It's not obvious what you're going to replace failure with. It takes a long time to recover. In a large market cap company, failure is not fatal. Investors in the public arena see safety in size.

How does the VC get companies to critical mass quickly?

In the past five years private equity has had to finance companies for longer. In 1997 you could get a company away with a market cap of £80 million. You can't any more. So investors are having to stay in longer and put in more money and that is going to have an impact on your returns. You want to get to £150 million market cap as soon as possible. That means you must be driving consolidations of two £75 million companies and start the process of making the company public.

How soon? Within two years? Five years? You haven't consolidated up front, have you?

No. We consolidate maturing situations. To comply with Chapter 20 requirements, you need a couple of products in clinical trial. But that is not enough now. Investors want to see at least one product in place, preferably more.

Which companies in your portfolio have been consolidated?

A relatively small number. A lot are early-stage. Morphochem, founded in 1996 and based in Munich, has acquired technologies and has operations in Princeton, USA, and in Basel, Switzerland. A biopharmaceutical company focusing on protein-protein interactions to develop novel therapeutics for major diseases of unmet medical need, it is a pioneer in 'chemical genomics' – a novel drug discovery paradigm based on the association of intracellular responses to potential therapeutics in whole cells – which promises to radically improve the productivity of the drug discovery process, generating highly specific clinical candidates with fewer side effects.

In 1999 Vectura acquired the company Co-ordinated Drug Development (CDD) and the 35 employees at the Centre of Drug Formulation Studies, a department of the University of Bath. The centre is still located at the university but at arm's length – although the university is a significant shareholder and an excellent partner in the business. Merlin had brought together leading research institutions in drug delivery technologies in 1997 to form Vectura. In 1998, the Merlin Fund invested £1.75 million. In 2001 the Merlin Biosciences Fund invested £2.8 million and the Merlin Fund invested a further £1 million. The fact that the university committed £1 million (although gave only £800,000 because it was over-subscribed) to this latest round gave incoming investors a lot of confidence.

This speciality pharmaceutical business focuses on application of novel drug delivery technologies in the development of proprietary therapeutics. Its goal is to enable better life-cycle management for pharmaceutical companies and better treatment outcomes for patients. Its core competency is application of particle science to the creation and design of innovative technology platforms and enhanced-performance pharmaceuticals.

Cancer therapy company Cyclacel, based in Dundee, Scotland, acquired Fluoroscience for its assay technology. Vascular therapy company Ark Therapeutics acquired Quattrogene, based in Finland, which has complementary technology. The two professors had been collaborating at the University of Kuopio in Finland. It was a natural move to bring them together.

It sounds very incestuous?

" I think it's fair to say that, if you're doing what you were doing two years ago, then you're probably doing it wrong.

If you've been around as long as I have you tend to know everybody. My first company was on the Cambridge Science Park in 1983 when CSP was not as it is today! I have watched it grow. But you have to work hard to keep on top of it. The business models change. I think it's fair to say that, if you're doing what you were doing two years ago, then you're probably doing it wrong.

What's changed?

Certainly the pace of technological innovation has changed. Many things that were done in the lab, chips, experiments, things like robotics. Science has soared on an exponential curve.

The use of computers for digital analysis?

Yes. Combinatorial chemistry, the human genome. All that sort of thing has opened up huge potential opportunities. The other thing that has changed is that the pool of available ideas coming out of academia has increased exponentially. The ideas were there before. Five years ago there was a feeling that commercial exploitation of your work and advancement as an academic were mutually exclusive objectives. Now we still have research assessment exercises. There's still this desire to publish rather than to patent. But university tech transfer groups have got hold of that patent side. Now you publish and patent in a much better way. There are groups of people pushing that pool of IP out to the likes of ourselves and other groups with the resource to help the founders create opportunities.

I guess it's like football, golf and tennis – once people see the mega-bucks to be made they all want a piece of the action and the whole profession becomes intensely competitive.

Yes. In the UK and EU you now see the emergence of a group of academic-based millionaires. Once there are a few that have made millions from exploiting their science, a lot of people will say, if he can do it, with my technology (because it's always better than his) I can make a million. It's kick-starting the commercialization of science.

What we did at Merlin in 1997 onwards was we enabled those scientific entrepreneurs to have their cake and eat it. What we said was, you carry on doing what you're best at, which is science. Leave the formation of the company, the writing of the business plan, blah, blah, blah down to us. Of course we need your time. We need to understand the science, the vision of where you're going.

What we'd often say is, we'd like to hire your number two into the company because, if you were head of department, while you may have had intellectual input, making the breakthrough, making the difference, there was somebody working at the bench who was implementing it. That was the guy that we wanted to get into the company to be taking the research forward.

How long does a commercial patent take to develop?

If you take the average life of a patent which is 17 years, it probably takes seven years of that to get it to commercial development. If you have ten years left when you get to the marketplace, you're doing very well. If you're sharper about it you can develop subsequent improvements, process patents round that.

Biotech companies tend to specialize – some in vaccines, some in therapies, some in diagnostic tests. They focus on areas where they think they will get a quick result.

From a portfolio approach, we have companies involved in those activities as well as the higher-risk-higher-reward end.

What's the higher-risk-higher-reward end?

Normally reward is associated with risk. If you're developing a vaccine, you may be able to get the product to market faster. But the market potential for a vaccine is a lot lower than the potential for a new drug. There aren't many vaccines that sell more than $250 million a year. You have your polio vaccine once and a booster every ten years. If you have an ulcer, you're taking Zantac every day. The blockbuster drugs are the ones you take every day for chronic conditions.

I'm fascinated by the use of the term 'technologies'. Why are they called technologies?

In developing a new drug, somebody has to make a breakthrough in understanding the biology and understanding how to make a chemical or, dare I say it, a biological product. At some stage somebody has to make an innovative step to solve the problem. Sometimes it may be by taking the biological model and screening hundreds of thousands of chemical compounds against that biological target. It was actually the technology of high throughput screening that helped make that process that much more efficient. Fifteen years ago it would have been a lucky hit. Now it's something you can leave running on a chip overnight.

You can devise chemical structures on a computer screen which should be interacting with a particular biological target. Then you pass it to the chemist who has to make it.

We have a company where we believe we have developed software, that will predict the biological interaction of a compound, not at the receptor site, but in terms of side-effects. Why do most drugs fail? Because of toxicology side-effects. If you can predict those for any given molecule you can rapidly improve the development failures. Products will not drop out at the same rate.

It may reduce the time for clinical trials.

It may. DNA profiling is also shortening the time horizon. Drugs will be able to be matched to genetic profile of the patient more accurately – 'personalized' – so they will be more effective. Not so hit-and-miss. No more taking five years to find the particular drug for a particular person, if you're lucky.

There are all these technical aspects which all have risks inherent in them. How do you limit risk?

There are some things that you just can't do anything about. Investing in science is inherently risky. Why is it that all the major companies take products all the way through the clinical development process and, at the end of the day, it doesn't work? With all their might and muscle and money, risk is inherent.

> **There are some things that you just can't do anything about. Investing in science is inherently risky.**

We focus on those areas of risk that we can control. What makes the difference? Venture capitalists say there are three components of a successful company: management, management and management.

What I stressed earlier about ensuring that the key players are in tune with each other on where they want to take the business is absolutely fundamental. It's the first part of that process.

Why do businesses not reach their true potential? Because you as an individual want to take the company down one road; we as a sophisticated investor who always think that we know best want to take it down another way. Net result – chaos.

Another way risk is managed is in the evolution of the management team.

The constantly rotating universe of skill sets required by a business at different stages in its maturity.

The necessity for people to be flexible. On average, the successful US biotech companies have had three CEOs. Get good non-executive help in as well. Use guys who can steer you down the right paths, open doors, use their contacts.

You limit risk by recruiting the best people that you can possibly afford. Don't employ a £30,000 a year person and expect them to produce the output of a £130,000 a year person. You have a window of opportunity. You are science's leading edge at a moment in time. But the world isn't standing still out there waiting for you to develop your product. So you have got to get there as fast as you can. You do that by recruiting the best people.

Cutting corners always gets found out. We are in the most heavily regulated industry that exists. If you cut a corner five years ago, when your file gets before the regulators you are going to get found out. Doing things properly takes longer than cutting corners. You can be entrepreneurial. The smaller biotech companies can be more fleet of foot than the bureaucratic large pharmas – but don't equate being entrepreneurial with cutting corners. The latter always comes back to haunt you.

We are in a situation at the moment where we have a CEO who won't take advice. He thinks he knows what's best. He may well. But we feel disappointed that he doesn't listen to other people's counsel and consider that, actually, they may have a point. So we keep coming back to management issues. Many business problems come back to management. Science you cannot so easily control. People risk? You can.

If you were to take a representative sample of successful US biotech companies – and I use the USA as an example because the population is much greater and they will have had three consecutive CEOs as I said in a time scale of seven years – I can only think of one company where the founder is still the CEO. That's Frank Baldino of Cephalon in Philadelphia.

I've been involved in recruitment for many companies in the Merlin Fund. I can't say we get it right all the time. It's not a case of learning from experience and never making the same mistake again. Recruitment is one of the areas where I never cease to be amazed at things that occur as a result of people. As far as issues in respect of people, I am still surprised, still haven't got it 100 per cent right. Things you would never expect. If you bet a thousand quid that person A would never do that – and there you are, following day, they've done it! When you are dealing with the breadth of companies, and all sorts of individuals, from the introverts to the extroverts, to the egotists to the publicity-shy, all sorts of things occur. Over time you can narrow it down but you can never get it 100 per cent right. There's always something about the human being that others will regard as daft decisions, irrational...

It's all very well talking about how to minimize risk. Business since the year dot has been based on taking risks. If you're not taking risks, you're not growing the company.

> **We're investing at the highest risk end and in the highest risk technology that it's possible for people to throw their money at.**

I understand the point you're making. We believe we're investing at the highest risk end and in the highest risk technology that it's possible for people to throw their money at. What we're talking about is minimizing an element of risk in an overall venture that is incredibly risky.

Success with the science is the real, real risk. What you do is create the framework to ensure that the science has the greatest potential. I've seen people spend tens of millions of pounds successfully developing a piece of science for it to have no intellectual property value at the end of it. Your money's down the drain! The patent position you thought you had didn't exist or was capable of being got round by others. You have to ensure the IP is right. Success means finding the optimum way of exploiting the idea.

One of the risks that the TMT sector – which is similar to the biotech sector in some ways – ignored during the 'easy money' days of 2000–2001 was excessive cash burn. Even hardened Old Economy executives have been blown out of the water because they ignored this risk. They thought the money would never stop flowing in.

One of the ways that you minimize financial risk is on a drip feed basis. Venture capitalists love doing this! I was only discussing this with one of our guys on the software side this morning.

In the USA people have a 'go for it' attitude. Which means that for every stage of development of a US biotech, they are given on average one-and-a-half to two times the amount of money that we give the equivalent EU company. Their approach is, well, why don't you just get to there and we'll see if you've met that milestone and if you have then we'll give you some more money. What's that doing? That's minimizing the risk of putting all the money in in one go when it all disappears.

What committing larger amounts of money does is to give the company momentum. Management can concentrate on what they're paid to do which is get on, run the business, get the science there. In the EU, every 18 months, we're expecting management to forget about the business for six months while they go off and raise some more money. Raising money is a huge distraction for management.

The US model is to put more money in at each stage. What does that also do? It means you can attract the best people. If you're a very experienced executive in a large pharma company, the last thing you've ever done in your life is worry about where the money is going to come from next month to pay your salary. You've got your final salary, pension scheme and all sorts of options. I'm going to try and attract you and give you bucketfuls of equity, share options and so on. Then I'll say, come and join us and by the way we've got 15 months' money left. You are not someone who is used to the dynamics of an emerging bio-pharmaceutical company. This is just not going to happen.

Throwing lots of money at something doesn't always produce results. Ernst & Young's eighth annual European life sciences report shows that the extra sums of money invested in the USA do not generate a proportionate increase in the number of commercial products. Every €1 of additional capital raised by European biotechs was converted into a €30 increase in value, whereas their US counterparts managed only a €5 increase.

I'm not familiar with that piece of research. I'm looking at it from the perspective of the early-stage investor. The greater availability of capital in the USA gives you the greater chance of success.

Ernst & Young certainly agree that Europe cannot afford to remain in the shadow of the USA.

There's a lot more merger activity in the USA.

All these factors combine to make investors very edgy about investing in biotech in the UK.

It comes down to time horizons and the degree of risk that is acceptable. If you are a pension fund you may regard biotech as too high-risk. But if you're running a £1 billion portfolio and on average your pensioners are 20 years away from retirement, should you not be allocating a small proportion of your fund to high risk? Because with high risk potentially comes high reward. With low risk comes low reward. You put your money into Treasury bills and you're guaranteed just 5 per cent for the next 25 years.

Your average venture capital fund over the last umpteen years has delivered a 20 per cent return. Who are the major providers of money to the UK venture capitalists? Primarily US and European institutions. The vast majority of the money for our large fund came from continental European institutions. What are we doing? We're taking UK technology. We're backing that technology using the skills of a group of people based in London and Cambridge with investment funds. We're running a UK and European fund and we've only been going five years. When those companies are successful, the profits go back to Europe. Most of the other life-science investors in the UK invest a lot in the USA.

A final word on risk management?

Sometimes you just see a situation and say, I'm going to back that! Then you do all your due diligence around a mind set which is that you're looking for the due diligence to give you the excuse to do the deal. It feels right. No amount of analytical

" Sometimes you just see a situation and say, I'm going to back that! It feels right. No amount of analytical work is going to change that.

work is going to change that. Conversely there are times when everything stacks up and logic says you should be doing this deal but something just says, no! It doesn't feel right. The old gut feel!

The European Investment Fund (EIF)

Merlin received €50 million in 2000 from the European Investment Bank's (EIB) European Investment Fund (EIF). EU leaders at their Lisbon summit had told the bank to make Europe the world's most competitive, knowledge-based economy by 2010. The EIF became able to invest in venture capital organizations specializing in biotechnology.

'The market didn't want to touch biotechnology in 1999,' says Jacques Lilli, a senior EIF venture capital officer. Not only did the EIF become by far the largest investor in Merlin, it provided advice on the structuring and strategy of the venture capital vehicle and suggested having a managing director on the European continent to promote its Europe-wide ambitions.

Neither the EIB nor the EIF, with just over 50 staff, can invest directly in companies. Instead the EIB seeks specialist fund managers as partners to ensure investments are subject to commercial discipline. 'We create specialized intermediaries so that we become a fund of funds,' says Philippe Maystadt, the former Belgian finance minister, who took over as president in 2000. 'We favour a tripartite structure with public sector and private investors and the EIF.'

Biotech futures 24

There is no doubt that the biotech industry is a key growth industry of the future. It displays the characteristics of an emerging sector – a large number of new entrants and massive competition to become dominant quickly.

Ernst & Young's eighth annual European life sciences report, *Integration*, published in 2001, confirms the year 2000 as, 'the best ever for European biotech. Fundraisings, valuations, revenues, employment and the number of companies all reached record levels'. Alliances, mergers and acquisitions were up 54 per cent on 1999, indicating, 'a global trend towards greater interaction between biotech companies, and the need to attain critical mass.'

It highlights the competitive nature of the industry _ the high risks involved and the urgency to 'prove' that New Economy ways of treating disease work without side effects. This is the sine qua non of continuing investment, whether from venture capitalists, the bond market or the stock market.

Ernst & Young believes that size matters: 'Europe's biotech industry is still very much secondary to that of the US, which has been flooded with new capital. The US biotech industry is pulling further away from Europe. Its vastly superior resources mean that US companies stand a greater chance of dominating their chosen niche within the sector.

'Technology is moving fast and data is growing exponentially,' says Dr Glenn Crocker, Ernst & Young's life sciences senior consultant. 'Companies must collaborate to put all the pieces of the jigsaw in place, and diversify risk. Alliances are the lifeblood of the biotech sector.'

Companies must "collaborate to diversify risk.

Integration is going to be a key issue, he believes that a single pan-European high-tech exchange is needed to encourage investment through a more liquid capital market that will generate higher exit valuations and tradable volumes (eight out of the top ten European biotech companies now have dual stock market listings, evidencing the need to develop a broad investor base); a Europe-wide science strategy is required to avoid dilution or duplication of effort; the integration of taxation policy across Europe remains problematic; regulatory processes need to be integrated across Europe; and consistency must be brought to patenting and pharmaceutical pricing policies. The report notes that:

- strategic alliances have dominated the league table of European biotech deals since 1996 as pharmaceutical giants looked to biotech to fill product and technology gaps;

- 403 alliances were announced across Europe in 2000, up 54 per cent on 1999.

- biotech-to-biotech alliances are booming, as big pharmaceutical companies are no longer necessarily preferred partners;

- European biotech indices in 2000 outperformed the London Stock Exchange, NASDAQ and the pharmaceutical sector, as investors differentiated biotech from high-tech stocks. Despite a 39 per cent fall in NASDAQ in 2000, European biotech share indices were up 50–75 per cent;

- investments in the industry topped €6.5 billion in 2000 (€1.1 billion in 1999);

- 39 European companies were floated in 2000, increasing the number of public biotech companies in Europe by 52 per cent.

- €3 billion was raised in biotech IPOs (€0.3 billion in 1999) with an average amount raised by these companies at IPO of nearly €80 million, almost double the previous best;

- European biotechs are more financially secure than ever before; 60 per cent of European public companies have at least four years' cash (at current burn rates), up from 46 per cent in 1999;

- the market capitalization of many companies increased by at least 100 per cent. In some cases valuation grew by 500 per cent;

- the increase in public valuations had a knock-on effect on private equity fundraisings, with more than 40 companies raising more than €10 million in 2000 (compared with 18 in 1999);

- Europe's public biotechs have 278 products at various stages of the drug development pipeline;

- all the financial performance indices increased significantly in 2000, with industry revenues up 38 per cent to €8.7 billion, R&D expenditure up 48 per cent to €5 billion, and the industry net loss up 42 per cent to €1.6 billion.

- the total estimated number of European entrepreneurial bioscience companies increased to 1,570 (up 16 per cent). This is around 300 more than reported in the USA.

The question is – are biotech companies heading for the kind of fall we saw with the dot coms in 2000/2001?

The UK still dominates the European sector – 48 of Europe's 105 public companies are British. They generate 25 per cent of Europe's biotech revenues (€2 billion). About 128 of the 278 products in the pipelines of Europe's public companies derive from UK biotechs. More importantly, the UK also accounts for 13 of the 27 products listed in 'Phase III' (the final pre-commercial stage).

The UK's leading players, such as Cambridge Antibody Technology and Oxford Glycosciences, remain strong. But Ernst & Young predict that many of the next generation of Europe's leading biotechs may come from outside the UK, particularly Switzerland and Germany, where 'massive state-funded expansion of the biotech industry continues to reap rewards'. Their report records 330 biotech companies in Germany, compared with 281 in the UK.

More significant, according to Ernst & Young, is the fact that German companies formed only relatively recently, such as LION Bioscience and Evotec, are moving into the top tier of European biotech and starting to acquire US and UK companies.

The USA is even more powerful. The market capitalization of US life sciences company Amgen is €70 billion – equivalent to almost the whole of Europe's biotech industry. Average revenues per biotech company in Europe are €6 million. Those of the USA are €19 million. Average R&D spend in Europe is €3 million. In the USA it is €9 million. The average number of employees per company in Europe is 40. In the USA it is 127.

'The average European public biotech market capitalization is €0.7 billion compared to that of the USA at €1.3 billion. Total equity financing raised in Europe was €6.6 billion compared to the USA at €33 billion. The top ten US biotech companies out-capitalized the top ten European companies by about four to one,' says Crocker. 'It is likely that a majority of winners will come from the USA.' US companies raised €4.1 billion since IPO and have a combined valuation of €20 billion. Compare this to their European counterparts which raised €0.3 billion since IPO and are now valued at €12 billion. But every €1 of additional capital raised by European biotechs increased value by €30. US biotechs added only €5 in value.

> **The average European public biotech market capitalization is €0.7 billion compared to that of the USA at €1.3 billion.**

25

The global biotech industry – high risks and high rewards

By Jonathan Pockson, Chief Financial Officer, *Microscience*

*J*onathan Pockson gave up a safe job in an established pharmaceutical company to become Chief Financial Officer of a biotechnology start-up. The risks were great. Why did he do it?

Certainly not for the salary, in fact many who join start-up biotech ventures are happy to take a reduction in salary. I have been in biotech for nearly ten years now. and I feel the excitement of bioscience. You must have self-belief and something of an entrepreneurial drive to go into the industry. My colleagues and I gave up secure career paths with a large organization. Glaxo's research budget, for example, is in the billions a year. Our R&D budget is of the order of £5 million.

Then there is the challenge of running a business – literally everything related to the business, all the decisions, working out exactly where we are going to go. Obviously we have governance and strong controls in the company but we can to some extent determine our own destiny.

> **The wealth creation in biotech companies can be incredible.**

And, although biotech is risky, it is very rewarding, the achievements within the company and the scientific advances and also financial reward is measured directly by these achievements. The benefits will come through the share options. The wealth creation in biotech companies can be incredible.

What levels of financial reward are we talking about?

In 1997, when we were founded, we took the decision to be in the vaccines business. In 2001 the world market for vaccines was of the order of $5 billion, relatively small compared with a single drug like Insulin which itself has a value of more than $64 billion a year. Compare this with the combined market value of about $2 billion for the drugs that we have under development. By 2010 it is recognized that the vaccines market will have grown to greater than $20 billion. We should reap the benefits of this dramatic growth.

The growth in this market is creating a great deal of interest among the major pharmaceutical companies.

Vaccines are really creating interest as evidenced by the large payments made by pharma companies to enter the vaccines marketplace. A selection of recent human vaccine deals shows the extent of these deals done by major pharma concerns with biotech companies.

Table 25.1 Recent human vaccine deals

2000	SB/Medimmune S. pneumoniae vaccine (pre-clinical)	$30 million + royalty
1999	AHP/Aviron flu vaccine (Phase III)	$400 million + 40 per cent royalty
1998	GW/Powderject hepatitis B DNA vaccine and others (Phase I)	$300 million + royalty
1998	SB/Corixa theraputic vaccines cancer/infectious diseases	$204 million + royalty
1997	GW/Cantab DISC HSV vaccine (Phase I)	$50 million + royalty

Recent deals that have been done with biotech companies are big deals. Take one – a flu vaccine. Aviron, a large biotech company, could receive up to $400 million in licence fees, milestone payments and financial support from American Home Products. Powderject has the potential to earn in excess of $300 million in licence, option and milestone payments from Glaxo to obtain rights to their vaccine developments. We also know what royalties involved are because Rod Richards, our Chief Executive, negotiated these deals when he worked in Glaxo. So we can sit at the same table with these powerful pharma companies and know the royalty rates we can achieve.

You work through all the years of development, you try to achieve a successful Phase II result and the value creation achieved can potentially be phenomenal.

It's a competitive area. How have you sought to manage your risks?

We review various aspects of risk management at board level. Our first risk-based decision was to concentrate on vaccines – an area of operation where we believe we can show rapid results. Our aim is to get a product into clinical trials as quickly as possible. Second, we have acquired and developed valuable intellectual property Third, from early on we recruited an experienced management team. People who know how to run biotech companies and know what is involved in getting product through clinical trials and the regulatory authorities. Also it goes without saying that the science and the scientists are without doubt second to none.

The development of pharmaceutical products including vaccines involve risk, you have to mitigate the risk. You need to be able to choose product areas where you will have a lead. You are going to have to develop a better product – a smarter mousetrap. Products also take a long time to develop; you need to be able to predict what the market and your competition will be like in five to ten years' time – that is difficult and highly risky.

> **You need to predict what the market will be like in five to ten years' time – that is highly risky.**

We were attracted to vaccines because, on the one hand, the vaccines market will grow very fast. On the other, genomics and other new scientific methods developed today will create a range of 'new' vaccines for tomorrow.

The race has started in genomics to find genes that will make great targets for vaccines. Young, small, fast-moving companies like Microscience are establishing today the intellectual property position in vaccines. These companies will be of substantial value within five years.

We are currently developing five vaccines based upon our genomics and proteomics research platforms. We focus on the discovery and development of innovative, rationally designed vaccines for prophylaxis and treatment of disease in areas of significant unmet clinical need. Our business strategy is to proactively manage scientific and commercial risks by leveraging the company's discovery platforms across a range of vaccines.

You have to be always conscious of the various risks. If at present the product is an injectable product, are you going to produce another injectable product or an oral product? If presently the dosage is four times a day, can you produce a single-dose version?

For one of our products, for typhoid, we have decided that we are going to go for a single dose oral vaccine – and this is critical. At present there is an injectable product or a four-dose oral regime; obviously a single-dose vaccine will be preferable. We are developing a single-dose oral vaccine; this will give us substantial advantage.

Did you develop your own platform technologies?

Our proprietary functional genomics and vaccine technology was developed at Imperial College of Science, Technology and Medicine – the premier European medical research institute. This technology formed the basis upon which we developed our expanding product portfolio. We can return to this platform at any time and generate further vaccines for our pipeline.

We have three granted patents and have filed more than 50 additional patents – which underpin the product developments, providing long-term intellectual property protection beyond the projected product launch dates. As many as 300 individual gene targets have been included within these patent filings.

Microscience, through its Signature Tagged Mutagenisis (STM) technology, has identified a number of bacterial genes that following mutation will lead to the death of the organisms in the host but not in the environment. The human body's immune system will react against such bacterial mutations and thus defeat the potential onslaught of the disease. This new approach to vaccine development has the further advantage of reducing the current reliance upon antibiotics; many organisms are becoming immune.

With STM we can reduce the risk of failure because this platform technology actually finds the genes that cause disease. Microscience owns STM and we are the only company that can exploit its potential. The technology is being used in many academic centres around the world; it is ideal for novel research. Many PhD students are looking for projects in microbiology and the screens they can undertake in various pathogens make perfect academic projects. However, should they wish to commercialize their discoveries they will have to come to us for licence. We therefore have a handle on all the STM genomics developments outside our company.

We at Microscience have used STM to develop vaccines for typhoid and meningitis B as well as using it to develop the company's oral vaccine delivery system.

Our research budget is not large and so we have to be very careful to focus our scientific development – we focus on commercial goals.

We make sure that each scientist – and we have 43, the majority of whom are PhDs – concentrates on a specific set of tasks in their everyday life in the laboratory. They are rewarded on success in developing those projects. This is a relatively new concept – to pay a scientist for commercial performance. Not many companies give their staff a bonus on successful project achievement.

Rod (Richards, Chief Executive Officer) and I debated this concept of a company-wide bonus scheme at length and decided to give it a go. It has proved incredibly successful. Our scientists are now in focused teams. Each scientist knows his budget so if there is a variance from budget they have to get authorization for a budget variance. That is very unusual and it creates a very exciting environment in which to work.

We have strict guidelines in establishing the bonus for each scientist. The project leader will evaluate each project and decide which aspects are bonus-able. This kind of scheme raises an ethical question because science has to be rigorous. You cannot cut corners in drug development. So we have to balance. We want to make sure that the scientist strives to achieve

You cannot cut corners in "" drug development. So we have to balance.

his or her goal in a particular year. We want it done properly with all bases covered. The objectives set for each scientist are vetted at associate director level, above project leader, and by the R&D committee to make sure they are valid, ethical and achievable. Finally the board approves the overall bonus-able objectives for the whole company.

We have achieved this because we are small. But we regard it as vital. What it has enabled us to do is get five products into development extremely quickly, cheaply and efficiently. It is products in development leading to clinical trial that creates the substantial value in our business.

Yet your development costs can be smaller than they would be at, say, Glaxo for the same R&D?

Only up to a certain point in time. I haven't seen their costings but all of our experience tells us is that our development costs are lower in the discovery and early development phases of a vaccine. Biotechs are arguably more efficient at the earlier stages of development. After Phase II, programmes are driven by regulatory authorities in the USA and Europe. Thereafter, cost will be comparable as products enter clinical trials.

Let's go back to the products you are developing. There are huge clinical risks involved – the product may not work? A competitor may win the race to market? With the mega-bucks involved there may be a temptation to 'fudge' the results?

Our clinical development risk is very tightly controlled through the requirements of the regulatory authorities. The pharmaceutical industry is one of the most regulated in the world. The process of developing any pharmaceutical, including vaccines, is incredibly complicated and is fraught with substantial regulatory risks right from the outset. We know exactly where we are going before we commence any Phase I study.

The development of a vaccine takes five to seven years from initial discovery phase through to getting it out on the market. What is critical to the risk management of a bioscience business is not to rush the initial safety trials.

The Phase I clinical study is to demonstrate that the product is safe for humans. Phase I trials are generally done on healthy volunteers. Phase II proves the efficacy of the product. It is safe and it achieves the standards. At that stage and depending on the market size for the product, its value will grow substantially. What we at Microscience do, because of our financial constraints, is go to the stage of proving efficacy (Phase II) and then we will license out the product, generally to a large pharmaceutical company.

What is critically important in our clinical risk management is to recognize that before we enter Phase I we have a phenomenal amount of regulated development work which must be done. Each of those boxes on the chart has to be ticked. The tests are rigorous in terms of developing a master cell bank. At this stage, the regulatory authorities need to know the characterization of that cell, that gene, down to the n'th degree. If you don't have it by that stage, regulatory authorities may potentially ask you to start again. Many biotech companies have lost three or four years of process development because they did not properly follow the protocols and tried to cut corners. It never pays to cut corners because if the regulatory authorities don't ask you to repeat studies certainly a potential licensing partner will!

Many biotech companies have fallen down by talking up their research as if they were in Phase II when in reality they were not. Our strategy is to go rigorously through each of these processes and not move on even to Phase I until we have achieved them. This delays the start of Phase I but we have the confidence of knowing that after Phase I we have a commercially viable product. We will not have to go back to square one. If we license out the product, the pharma company will not have to start again. They won't say, 'Sorry! We won't give you the up-front payments you are asking for because we have to start again!' That's how we handle the development risk.

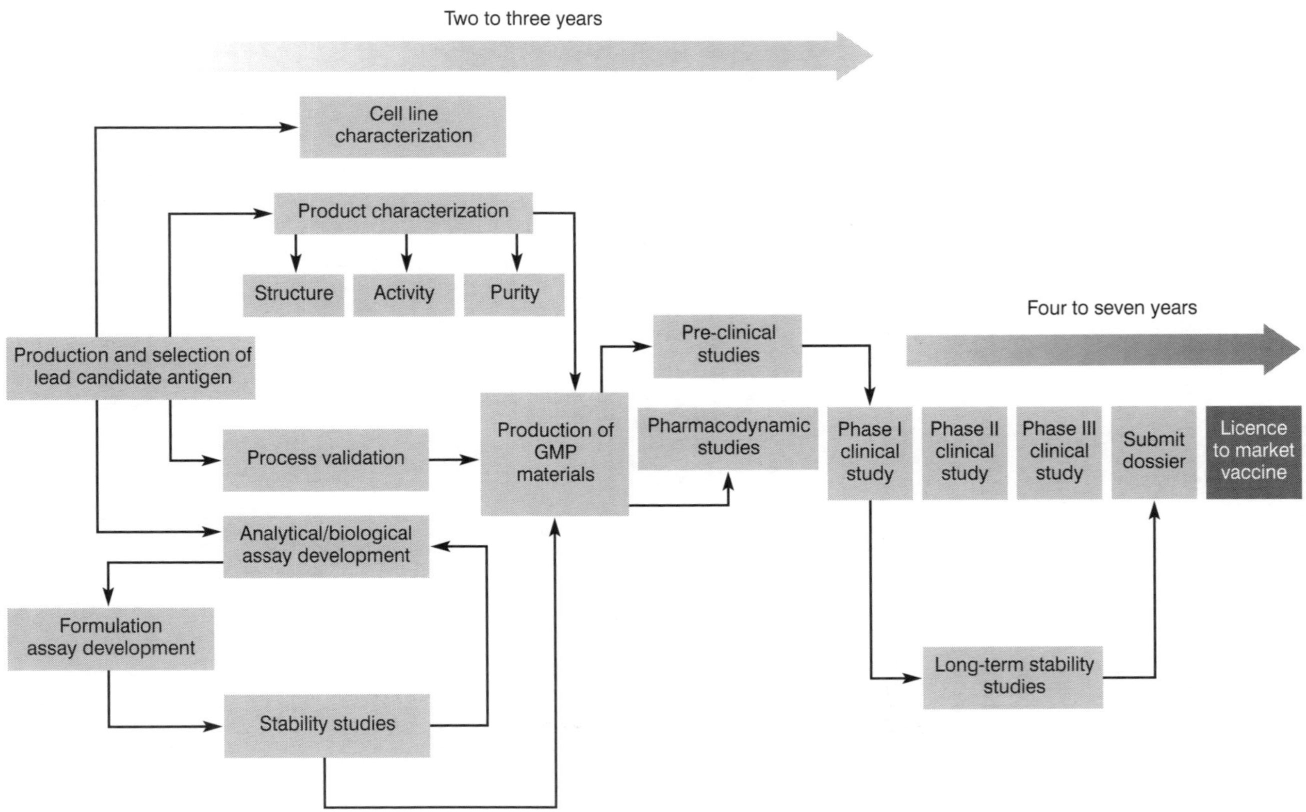

Fig 25.1 Vaccine development process

Presumably you have the staff with experience of going through these trials and knowing what is expected – and you have the management checks and balances to ensure the process is ethical?

Yes. The company hasn't been going many years but each of our scientists had standard operating procedures and good laboratory practice drilled into them when they came to us. Many of our scientists have experience of clinical trials. Our research and development committee will vet all the procedures within our development programmes.

But thalidomide went through all this presumably and we know what happened with that?

That went through Phase II studies successfully. It proved to be efficacious. But the birth deformities had not been predicted in advance. What that did was make the regulatory authorities post-thalidomide even more cautious. The hoops we have to go through today to even get into a Phase I study are enormous. To give you an example, we are about to enter into a Phase I study in the USA for our typhoid vaccine. In order to set up just the first meeting with the FDA (Food and Drug Administration) has meant the production of detailed dossiers covering all aspects of the product protocols, manufacturing processes and the studies carried out to date. That's just to get in the door for a first meeting. The safety profile of drugs is now perhaps the most important factor that the regulatory authorities consider. There is a vast amount of research reading done by scientists to try to anticipate the performance and the side effects of the drugs being developed. This knowledge base combined with the physical side of laboratory work and testing in animal models gives us an indication of how safe and successful the products we are developing are likely to be.

> **" " But thalidomide went through all this presumably and we know what happened with that?**

Our technology platforms are very exciting. I have already referred to our STM technology which we acquired from Imperial. We combine the findings from this technology with our Protein Vaccinology Technology developed by the company. These 'gene finder' technologies enable us to search a gene sequence of a bacterium, for example, and quickly establish those genes that causes virulence (disease) and reside on the surface of the cell of the bacterium. This gives us prime targets for the development of novel vaccines and anti-bacterial therapeutics. These technologies are yielding significant opportunities.

Our clinical risk strategy is to develop opportunities for collaborative programmes utilizing STM in both the animal and human health field. The broad applicability of STM across a wide range of pathogens present the company with the potential to enter into joint development programmes with other biotechnology/pharmaceutical companies. The company is actively pursuing these opportunities in both the animal and human health field. The opportunity for Microscience to develop novel types of small molecule compounds based upon the STM methodology is particularly exciting.

The upside risk is that they are doing your R&D for free? The parallel is Linux in the IT sector. You have an unlimited, unpaid research base?

Absolutely. We have tabs on what leading academic centres round the world are doing. Generally, in academia, scientists are allowed to utilize under free licence technologies for research purposes, generally royalty-free. The moment they want to commercialize their findings – and there is a movement round the world today for academics to link with commercial organizations – that's when we step in to negotiate a licence agreement.

The risk is that others will use STM to develop and commercialize a vaccine without telling you?

Remember the research and development process is not a swift process. It takes years. We know those companies and organizations working in infectious disease vaccines and microbiology. It's a relatively small group. Last year we invited academics from all round the world who are utilizing STM to join us in London and encouraged them to disclose their research findings.

We can help them in their research work because STM is an incredibly complex process. We have been down that road. We know exactly how to do it! In addition, many academic scientists speak at conferences and publish their results. It is not a question of something slipping through the net.

What happens after the initial stages when costs begin to escalate?

We have a number of options to finance our research – the first is to enter into a partnership deals with pharmaceutical companies who are keen to acquire a vaccine for their pipeline.

In the early stages of biotech development, venture capitalists will generally provide the initial capital. This could then be followed by an IPO. For Microscience we could consider an IPO in early 2003 when several of our vaccines will have proved efficacy.

The third option would be a takeover by a major pharma company?

Yes, this is certainly an option. There are a number of major pharmaceutical companies who have little presence in vaccines today. With the growth potential over the next few years Microscience's strong vaccine portfolio could well be of interest to them. We also consider that the vaccines market will grow considerably in Asia, and in particular Japan; we could well be a target for companies there as well.

We all look at the likely market size before deciding to embark upon the development of a vaccine. The market for a typhoid vaccine, for example, is at least $300 million, probably much greater – unless you have that size of market, it is not worth developing the product; the risks are too great. We estimate that our vaccines will each have markets of between $300 million and $750 million. Vaccines have smaller markets than therapeutic drugs. With market sizes below $500 million the large pharma companies are less interested in developing products and are happy to let the biotechs develop them with a view to licensing later. So we have this window of opportunity to create value for ourselves at this earlier stage.

Our development programme targets a number of products for which there is an unmet medical need. We have identified a number of candidates, for example, ETEC, meningitis B and group B streptococcus which are in early development and for which there is no current vaccine.

There is a great need to develop oral vaccines to treat travellers' diarrhoea and hepatitis B. We are developing a range of vaccines for these markets. These are scheduled to enter clinical development in 2002. Together they represent significant commercial opportunities estimated at $350 million and $700 million respectively.

There is a great deal of interest in meningitis. There is now an effective vaccine for meningitis C, but there is currently no treatment available for meningitis B which is responsible for more than 50 per cent of this severe and sometimes fatal infection. It is also thought likely that the prevalence of meningitis B may well increase as reversion from meningitis C to B. There is no vaccine available for this serious disease. The market opportunity is substantial in a childhood immunization programmes of around half a billion dollars each year.

Our novel group B streptococcus protein vaccine development is very exciting. The disease is one of the largest causes of neonatal deaths in the USA, and is transferred from the mother in pregnancy. A baby born with this would be very sick. Dr Robert Feldman, our Chief Scientific Officer, is one of the world's leading experts.

The market opportunity is very large and the product fits our strategy extremely well. We are one of the world leaders in the development of this vaccine. This product will enter Phase I trials in 2002.

You mention the science and the investment in people. Isn't there is a third critical factor for business success: focus on fundamentals? The bottom line surely is that the business is well run and makes a profit?

Absolutely. Our four executive directors are extremely experienced managers, two of whom are scientists and two, Rod and myself, are commercially experienced, having been in senior management positions in pharmaceutical companies. Rod was Head of Global Business Development at Glaxo. At each meeting within the company we balance the scientific and the commercial.

If Dr Steve Chatfield (the Development Director), who has had 22 years of developing vaccines with Medeva and Wellcome, comes forward with a suggestion for a development in our clinical programme – whether we go to the USA to do a trial, whether we stay in the UK – we will always balance these suggestions with the commercial ramifications.

Robert's background was with academia, but he is a clinician and has the vital experience of knowing the requirements of the doctor in treating disease. Three of the four main directors have come, therefore, from large cap public companies.

Microscience has already created substantial value but we believe that, as five of our vaccines enter clinical trials, our valuation will rapidly grow. As a private company we have a tight focus on expenditure. Budgets are extremely tightly controlled. We have met all of our milestones on time and on budget. That is something of an achievement because it is difficult to predict how something is going to go in the laboratory.

We have met all of our " milestones on time and on budget. That is something of an achievement

We have entered into a couple of deals with animal health companies. If one considers how STM works, it uses animal models to find virulence genes. Animal health is a growing field. These companies are aware that we can use our technology straight in the animal which they want to vaccinate, it is an efficient method for a successful treatment. We have recently signed a major deal with a world leader in animal health. We have received from this company signing fees of millions of dollars and we will receive further milestone fees and future royalties. The significance of this deal is that it endorses our technology but also provides funds which we can invest in our human health vaccine development.

If all goes according to plan we should commence our human health licensing discussions in the latter part of 2002, which should lead to revenues and sustainability for Microscience by 2004.

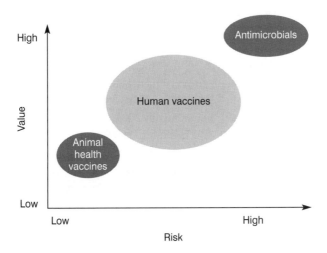

Fig 25.2 Business model

From Fig 25.2 you can see that we are focused on the human vaccine market area because the risks are less but the rewards still great. We have discussed our connections with animal health companies also. We believe that the gene targets we have discovered could make excellent therapeutic drugs but we do not have the finance or the capability to pursue these opportunities. We are therefore planning how to exploit this potential through joint venture or early out-licensing opportunities.

Despite recent income your R&D budget, with five products in the pipeline, is likely to keep on growing?

Yes, our R&D budget in 2000 was only £2.5 million. Our budget is more than £5 million for 2001 because we are moving products into clinical trials and this is where costs escalate. In 2002 our costs will dramatically increase with five products in clinical trials. If we can get five products moving successfully into development with positive trial results, you will see substantial value creation in a short time to match the increase in spending.

You are a private company so you have no market cap. You are owned 40 per cent by venture capitalists Apax Partners who invested £9 million in 1999, and 53 per cent by Merlin Funds who have invested more than £6 million over a number of years. Sir Christopher Evans of Merlin commented that 'Microscience is one of the most successful of our seed investments within the Merlin Fund and we had no hesitation in joining with Apax in committing funds to the company, which has a very exciting future'. So far, so good?

Yes. Our valuation model shows how our valuation as a private company has increased since its formation in 1997 to around £60 million in 2001.

This vindicates our cautious and focused approach. We concentrate on human vaccines, which are less risk-prone. They are quicker to get through Phases I and II. In addition values are higher because we are using the new genomics technologies for the vaccines. and thus will market newer and more efficient vaccines.

We will partner our core vaccines post-efficacy, post Phase II. If they work, fantastic! We haven't spent a fortune to get to that stage. We can drive potential market values of $2 billion from those five products. There will be big milestone payments involved. We could be profitable potentially by 2004.

We have five core vaccines – which is a lot for a company of our size. We have potential to go to 20 products if we want to. At present we cannot afford it. Any non-core genes or vaccine candidates that we find we will partner to share the risk early – obviously pre-Phase I. Bear in mind, though, that million-dollar deals are possible even at that early stage of out-licensing.

The pharma partner would take the process through the clinical trials and we would receive milestone, up-front payments and a royalty on potential product sales. There are many partnering deals in bioscience: biotech-to-biotech; main cap pharma-to-biotech and so on. Microscience is known now by all the largest pharma companies in the world who have any interest in vaccines. Most have been to see us and we are well networked with them.

Your competitors at the moment are mainly much better financed multinationals in the USA and UK, with Germany coming up fast behind.

Competition is a critical issue for any biotech or pharma company. The competition throughout the industry is fierce because of the potentially high rewards. This is a major focus issue for us. We have our eye on the competition every day of the week! That's not an exaggeration. There is a lot of information out there on what others are doing. Even the financial press discusses biotechnology

> **The competition " "
> throughout the industry is
> fierce because of the
> potentially high rewards.**

most days. There's information from patenting activities, papers published in journals and through conferences. You generally get a feel for the competition. We track what phase they are in. There's little point in pursuing an eight-year development programme if you are miles behind the market.

Our competition report goes in the board papers every two months. We analyze by companies, products, and we flag any changes since the last report.

From what you have told me your approach is one of calculated risk. But you do not appear to have a formalized, embedded risk management that 'captures' all of your risks and embeds it within every employee's consciousness?

Perhaps we are too small for that. We make sure that the scientific project staff are aware of their specific risks within the sphere of their own operations – to some extent this should be enough. At the associate and the executive director level we evaluate all the risks in the company all the time. We believe it would be counter-productive to burden all staff with this task as well. To give you an example. We have standard operating procedures, which detail all the elements of all the procedures within the labs. These rules have to be adhered to by all staff at all times – these procedures outline the risks if the procedures are not followed. Our external auditors consider that we have addressed the significant risks but within the corporate governance guidelines we will require, before a public listing, to have in place an embedded risk management approach, which brings together all the controls already in place within the company.

26 Challenging times for large pharmaceutical companies

By Jonathan Symonds, Executive Director and Chief Financial Officer, *AstraZeneca*

I meet Jon Symonds in his office in Mayfair at 8 o'clock in the morning. Although we are a stone's throw from Hyde Park Corner, you can hear a pin drop despite the morning rush hour. I enter the inner sanctum and his bright eyes and alert personality tell me that his brain is already in overdrive. He has recently returned from business trips to China and Paris.

Jon joined the AstraZeneca board and senior executive team from Zeneca, where he had held the position of Finance Director since 1997. He was previously a partner of KPMG, having joined that company in 1980. During his 17 years with KPMG, Jon worked on a number of major flotation and investigation projects, and was seconded to the USA where he gained experience of the US market and Securities and Exchange Commission reporting.

I ask him, how do you manage risk?

There are two ways of approaching risk. You either put in place formal structures that deal with individual aspects of risk. Or you take the approach that management risk is an integral part of what the firm does – you build it into the whole fabric of the organization. If you say to somebody, do you have a risk management process, he'll probably say 'No'. But if you ask him, do you know the risks that you have in your part of the organization and are you managing them effectively, he'll probably say, 'Oh yes. We are doing all these things.'

You are one of the world's leading research-driven organizations, with annual R&D costs north of $2.5 billion. There's a strong research pipeline – more than 150 ongoing projects and 59 new chemical entities; 10,000 research staff mainly in Sweden, the UK and the USA. You're into genomics and proteomics, supported by advanced data management techniques.
   R&D costs are probably one of your major financial risks?

Yes. Risks are probably more sharply identified in the pharmaceutical industry than many other businesses. We are dealing with people's lives. Consequently, the whole fabric of the R&D organization is built around identifying risks. We have to stop projects as quickly as possible if they are not going to be clinically or commercially feasible. In 2000 we stopped development of *Zendra*, a stroke treatment, because clinical trials showed no efficacy benefits for patients suffering from an acute stroke. It's very expensive to keep them running. We need to see some chance of success. The commercial success of products in the pipeline will be particularly important to us because several existing products will lose patent protection in 2001–2002.

You can be talking ten years to bring a product to market and $500 million to $1 billion. So you want to stop projects quickly if they're going nowhere. The kind of reasons you are looking for is if the chemical compound is not

> **You need to have the "manufacturing capacity up five years before the product comes to market."**

active enough. It doesn't produce sufficient clinical benefit. You may have toxicity or it may not be financially viable. Any of these things have to be continually evaluated and judgements made.

All of these things have to be brought together in a pretty comprehensive analysis of whether we should undertake the project. Different parts of the organization come together to make those decisions.

You then have the manufacturing side. You need to have the manufacturing capacity up five years before the product comes to market. How much capacity should we invest in? What is the future potential? Where should it be located? And so on. We have to make the assessments well ahead of the product reaching market. In the context of overall investment in R&D, manufacturing investment is quite small. You're talking $100 million to $200 million for a big purpose-built plant. We also try and make sure that it is multi-purpose so if the product does not come through as expected or it doesn't have the market potential we envisaged, then it can be converted to other products later.

We have a number of supportive policies in place. The overall risk is not necessarily an add-up of all the components of risk. There are correlations. Some off-set one another. Some are additive. If you ask different parts of the business to identify risk, some of the macro risks – economic, health care, global trends in R&D – would not necessarily get picked up. So we have a mechanism whereby several times a year senior management get together to share their risk analysis and identify where individual elements of risks are additive.

Our strategic group spends a lot of time looking at the direction the industry is going in; and what business environment we are planning within. They look at macro-economic factors in general but, more specifically, the effect of macro-economic changes on our performance. There is a significant lag. People currently talk about the current economic downturn in the USA but it would take some time before that downturn turned itself into a reduction in health expenditure.

We're not directly related to economic cycles. What is important is our under-standing of what are the kinds of market situations we will be operating in: trends in healthcare, availability of new medicines, costs of new medicines, ability of governments to fund them. Governments and other bodies are seeking to control spiralling costs. Our strategic planning group is therefore identifying the macro trends and we feed those back into individual risk assessments and say to people over a shorter period – say, three to five years – do you think there will be an impact? If they see a risk, that gets built into their management process.

This is a supportive mechanism to make sure that each part of the organization's management has on its own management agenda not only the business objectives which they need to manage but also the risks that relate to those objectives.

A costly risk for you is the expiry of patents?

" We take legal action if they are judged to infringe our intellectual property.

Certainly drug pricing is a critical macro risk. Patent expiry is not a macro risk. It is a risk which is clear and identifiable. That's a specific business thing that we have to manage. That's the challenge. You have a 17- or 20-year patent.

You're currently facing the biggest patent expiry problem in the industry. Losec, your highly successful ulcer drug, has been the world's biggest selling drug of all time. It accounts for 40 per cent of your group sales. Loss of income when this happens can hit the share price badly.

We have a follow-on product, *Nexium*.

Are 'copy cat' products increasing?

Yes but we take legal action if they are judged to infringe our intellectual property.

Litigation risk appears to be increasing. The notes to the annual report 2000 mention cases associated with Losec, Plendil and Nolvadex. The regularity of patent challenges has also led the increasingly anti-monopolist European Commission to investigate intellectual property rights and associated regulatory and patent and infringement litigation. This is pursuant to Article 82 of the EC Treaty which prohibits abuse of a dominant position.

We look at patent litigation if our patents are challenged. We mount a strong legal challenge to any infringement of our patent rights. What we have to look at is the whole chain of events. Where something starts coming through as 'likely' then we assess what the business impact is. It's not just the product market that you lose but the market implications.

So intellectual property challenge is now a major issue?

Oh yes. In some parts of the world it is.

You can't generalize because health care systems are different: the health care system in Japan, say, and Germany are fundamentally different so we take a country-by-country approach to it, although there are areas of similarity. We organize our business in a way so we have a very separate and identifiable North American business; 50 per cent of our business is done in the USA. We have a clearly identifiable management structure there. Each time we have a senior management meeting there, we examine what are the trends in US health care? The latest pricing negotiations? How are our drugs being affected by current drug pricing?

The key to managing that is to bring through products which have unique medical capabilities. They really identify the value that they are bringing. Pharmaco-economic information is now a pretty important part of positioning products in discussions with organizations so that they understand not just the price they are paying for the drug but also the benefit it has across the health care system. If we're bringing in a new product that, for example, gets to people through a simple tablet and avoids the need for hospitalization or some form of operation then that drug, compared with the costs of hospitalized treatment, is a more valuable proposition. That's how we position products in the USA. I would say the USA is a pretty rational health care market.

In Europe, because there's a complete separation between the cost of drugs and the costs of hospitalization, it means you can't position that. There is a one-dimensional view of the price of the drug. You have nothing with which to compare it. So systems vary and you have to develop strategies that relate to the situation that you find yourselves in.

The group senior executive team has overall responsibility for managing the business and the business risks. It's a board-level responsibility. Our management process is to run the business through a series of inter-locking key performance indicators (KPIs) that comprise financial, shareholder performance measures. The obvious things like shareholder value, sales growth, profit growth, those sort of things. We then break it down because financial indicators are very poor measures for a pharmaceutical business. We break them down into a series of objectives that cover different strategic goals.

We have a short report which is published every quarter which shows how we are performing against those KPIs. We are now seeking to develop that document in a way that, for every business objective, there is a mirror image of it which are the risks associated with meeting that objective.

We are beginning to build that flip side. We will be demonstrating that we understand the risks inherent in the objectives we are setting. That will also link into the macro risks environment to show that we are comfortable with the addition of all the individual risks and that the macro picture still makes sense.

We reassess this all the time. Each part of the business has somebody in the senior management team responsible for advising on risk. We have a risk advisory committee which advises senior management on the emerging risk. There are several people in this process. There's the Head of Internal Audit, who reports to the board. Then we have an insurance group who manage the group's insurance risk. They have become quite sophisticated in their use of risk management techniques – risk definitions and risk mapping. The third person works in the business performance area managing KPI reporting. The three of them have constant dialogue throughout the year with people in other parts of the organization as well as visiting them so that they keep alive the concept of risk management.

So we have specific measures which assess the productivity of R&D; the progress of KPIs; new chemical entities (NCEs) coming through; the speed at which they are being developed; as well as how well our products do on the market.

We get them together two or three times a year. They maintain the risk map for their part of the organization. We share information on new risks. Sometimes the process of talking things through will prompt, say, someone in R&D saying, 'We see this issue emerging.' Somebody else will say, 'Oh yeah, we've got that too.' So you share knowledge. But also you identify where the connections are.

> **Where we've identified a risk, there is a risk owner. We map what the risk is, who owns it, the risk definition.**

Where we've identified a risk, there is a risk owner. We map what the risk is, who owns it, the risk definition, how it ranks in terms of its impact on business, financial figures and on image or business reputation. Then you rank the likelihood of risk, and assess what controls are applicable. What controls and assurances are in place to give us input into how well that risk is being managed. What the performance measures are. How we can improve how it is being managed.

We've tried to say there should be no more than 15 or 20 of these risks – otherwise we're managing the wrong things. Then, for some of them, such as the operational risk and manufacturing risk, you can then take it into some fairly sophisticated analysis which looks at the maximum potential risk profile. We have done this for our plants but we have also been able to get benchmark data. You can rank them in terms of where some of these risks fall: between those which are acceptable to manage in terms of how likely is it against the financial consequence. You rapidly find that we have a fair amount of our manufacturing activity – and not just our activity but also some of the materials that we import – in Japanese earthquake zones, in Puerto Rico and so on. So you stand back and say well, what do we do, because we are carrying this huge risk.

Risk title	Treasury policy
Risk owner	
Risk definition	Two areas of risk: – Executing policy – Breach of control Poor management leads to a material loss not consistent with the impact on other global organizations. Over-exposure to currency, credit, interest rate and cash impacts. Leads to increased volatility.
Ranking *(see note below)*	Impact (I) L(1) Impact (F) M(2) Likelihood L(1)
Risk score	1
Existing controls and assurances	Centralized treasury department with strict Reverse Powers for banking and trading activities. Separate cash management unit for maximizing global bank relationships and cash pooling. – Monthly exposure report to CFO – performance benchmarked. – Annual policy review between Treasury and CFO. – Annual External Audit (with random spot-audits) by KPMG. – Banking commitee reports to board.
Performance measures	Performance against Treasury benchmarks. Comparison against peers. Accuracy of forecasting
Improvement focus	Revised Treasury report to include better trend analysis.

Impact (I) Impact on Image: High (3), Medium (2), Low (1), Impact (F) – Impact on financials

Fig 26.1 AstraZeneca risk execution

Do you have a universe of risk intranet?

No, we don't have an intranet for risk at the moment. It is something that we may move towards. Some of the tools are available on our intranet in terms of risk definition. We find that this organization doesn't respond easily to instruction or process. I am reluctant to push the formality because what I want them to do is manage risk as an integral part of managing the business. Not as something that they're doing because the CEO or the CFO has told them that they've got to do it. That's not going to work. Some people may say that's too informal. But I think we have a very good appreciation of risk across the business and not just a couple of risk experts in the centre saying, 'We understand the risk but we don't understand the business context.'

Everyone is on a learning curve, post-Turnbull. Has Turnbull focused your approach?

Yes. I think we will get more sophisticated with this. We've made a few tweaks. We've formalized the process of reporting risk to the board. We explain at least once a year through the audit committee what we consider the major risks to be. I was determined that, again with Turnbull, we would not add any additional business processes but make sure that the ones that we've got work effectively. Risk factors are fully reported in the annual report. Generally we have had to do very little. What we already had in place was sufficient.

Where is the business going today and tomorrow?

The two important dimensions of the industry will be the capacity of governments to fund pharmaceuticals and health care in an environment where people are living longer, getting more affluent. People have higher expectations of quality of life all the way through to the end of it. In many countries it is becoming increasingly difficult to fund that. One of the biggest trends will be how governments can properly fund expectations. The second big issue is the ability of the pharmaceutical industry to regenerate itself every ten years. It is an intensely competitive industry. The technology platforms are moving continually in terms of genomics, genetics. You need massive computing power to assess results. The main difficulty for us is to maintain our productivity and make sure we maintain a scientific environment where we can generate a supply of new products that will keep AstraZeneca growing in the future.

As of today, we are in a remarkably rich period with a pipeline that is probably one of the best in the industry.

In what way?

In terms of its size, its richness and its depth. In terms of the number of products that are coming through that are seen as the best in their class. We can also extend a product's life cycle by broadening its medical use. We make sure we have good mix in development.

Is the productivity of R&D measured?

You can go to any of our research sites and they will be able to tell you what their key productivity measures are in terms of the number of candidate drugs (CDs) that they are putting into the development process each year. If you talk to a discovery scientist, he or she will know what their objectives are and then as those products move into the development market there will be different objectives but you can identify what they are doing to bring those products to market as quickly and as valuably as possible.

We're trying to identify more clearly the key decision points rather than letting things progress of their own accord. Trying to identify where the critical development and decision points are so we have transparent decisions right then. The consequences of moving a drug into a later stage of development when it hasn't passed all of its milestones is very expensive – and potentially dangerous as well. It may take ten years – although the time is reducing with technology. So we have a clearly identified set of decision points through R&D to make sure we identify and assess the risks at the earliest possible opportunity.

> **We're trying to identify more clearly the key decision points rather than letting things progress of their own accord.**

It is clearly articulated as to which levels of management make the risk-based decisions at different points. When you get to the point when it looks like you've got a product that has market potential, it moves in from, well, we've spent $200 million and now we need to spend another $300 million or $400 million. That decision comes up to the group executive committee.

There we evaluate a number of risks. Does the drug have market potential? Are there competitive products? Is this a product that can position itself? What medical need is it meeting? How well defined is that medical need? What are the current treatments that are available? What are the alternative treatments? Is it something that will have a unique market position?

We have to assess the risks of it failing the next phase of the development cycle. What results have we seen in terms of its clinical effect? How have we designed the trials? What statistical end-points and out-puts do we want in the next stage of trials? What does the toxicity data tell you? Is it safe? Does it look as if it has any long-term carcinogenicity attached to it?

This whole package of information is built up and the decision is based on the relative risks. Very rarely do you get a situation where you get unambiguous ticks in every box.

Do you know what is the drop-off ratio of successful to unsuccessful ideas?

Yes. That's where the productivity tools have come from – trying to improve on the historical rate. If you look at both Astra and Zeneca, together they would be putting about ten new chemical compounds coming from discovery and going into the development process per year. This would produce one or two new drugs out of thousands of compounds that have been screened.

The competitive input is important. We all publish our development pipelines and have access to patent filings so there's good intelligence about what's going on. If you have a new drug coming into an area where your competitors have similar products, you can generally assess quite well what the relative strengths and weaknesses of your own product are. You can stop product development. This is normally based on a package of issues. It might not be potent enough to distinguish from the competition. Or there may be concerns about side effects. You could not produce it in the most convenient way for a patient. For example if it is a drug that's taken three times a day as opposed to once a day.

We're now going for 15 CDs a year because we are looking for productivity improvements.

With the technology improvements that have been made in discovery around bioinformatics, genomics, genes, these will improve productivity. This will increase the probability that something going into development, because of the sophistication of the screening and how it impacts on body metabolism, has a higher certainty, that it will pass through to the market.

It is now understood that many diseases are related to genetics – either inherited or developed during our life. The output from mapping and sequencing the human genome is now a key element in the discovery process. What is your interest in this fast-moving area of discovery?

Our Enabling Science and Technology Group, located in the UK, Sweden and the USA, combines state-of-the-art, high throughput technologies and novel scientific approaches in:

- drug target identification and validation;

- combinatorial and parallel chemical synthesis;

- bioinformatics and cheminformatics;

- mathematical modelling of human physiology and disease.

At Boston, for example, we're leading the search for new antimicrobials by utilizing powerful new technologies, including the rapid sequencing of microbial genomes and gene identification in pathogenic microbes. Major advances in genetics continue to be made. With the full map of human chromosome 22 completed in time for the millennium, the human genome project has made great strides.

When coupled with molecular biology, we can quickly identify the potential drug targets of a micro-organism. We're applying these advances to our pursuit of new classes of antimicrobials that hold promise in combating the growing occurrence of drug-resistant bacterial, fungal and viral organisms.

Our R&D centre at Boston adds dynamic new resources to research efforts in cancer. Leading-edge technologies increase scientific resources, strengthening the contributions to life-enhancing drugs for cancer patients.

I believe you have also established a centre of excellence at your facility in Bangalore for the discovery and development of new medicines of importance to the developing world?

Yes. Bangalore aims to recruit world-class scientists who will focus principally on finding a new treatment for tuberculosis, a disease which affects 2 million people every year in India and 16 million people world-wide, mostly in the developing world (World Health Organisation Report, 2000). AstraZeneca is the only pharmaceutical company to recognize this area of medical need with a research programme in India dedicated to TB.

The investment programme will include $10 million to create new research laboratories in Bangalore, and $5 million in 2001 to support research activities. With no new drugs for TB in the past 40 years, our remit will be to improve understanding of the basic physiology of the TB pathogen so that we can provide both a reliable diagnostic test and a more effective cure for the disease. These new laboratories will form an integral part of our research into infectious diseases and, together with academic collaborations, AstraZeneca in Bangalore will become a leading centre of excellence for TB research. The laboratory has 65 scientists, and plans to recruit more scientists over the next five years from India and overseas.

How important are alliances?

You cannot manufacture human innovation. Just because you are big does not mean that you will get a bigger share of discovery.

I think we are realistic enough to know that there are going to be more discoveries outside AstraZeneca than within it. Biotech companies are usually scientists who have come out of the big pharmaceutical companies, set up on their own and want to pursue a particular field. They are quite likely to come up with some interesting discoveries. We maintain close links with biotech companies to make sure we have the widest possible access to drugs. What's clear is that, because of the hundreds of millions of dollars which are required for development, the small biotechs are not able to take these products all the way to market. They need a relationship with a pharmaceutical company to commercialize it.

> **You cannot manufacture human innovation. Just because you are big does not mean that you will get a bigger share of discovery.**

Merck helped develop Astra's business in the USA in the 1980s. Just before Astra and Zeneca merged, we bought out the Astra part of the relationship. It is now not an alliance, it is a purely financial relationship.

We have more than 300 collaborations with commercial partners, such as small biotech companies, research institutions, universities and the like to give us access to emerging science.

The formation of alliances with universities and other external partners is key to AstraZeneca's research strategy. In particular, we have strong collaborations with leading biotechnology companies world-wide. We are always interested in forming partnerships with start-ups with proven early-stage research, novel compounds or technologies.

Table 26.1 Some of AstraZeneca's 300 collaborations

Partner	Area of collaboration	Partner	Area of collaboration
Affymetrix Inc.	EasyAccess for GeneChips	Griffith University, Brisbane	Natural product screening
Amersham Pharmacia Biotech AB	Proteomics and microarray cDNA hybridization technology	Incyte	Genomics databases
Baylor College of Medicine	Novel drug targets in major disease areas	Isis Pharmaceuticals	Antisense-based drugs
BioChem Pharma	Peptides (analgesia)	Jackson Lab	Mouse genetics
Cambridge Combinatorial	Lead explosion chemistry	Megan Health Inc.	Vaccine development
Centaur	Radical scavengers (CNS)	Oxagen	Genetics (atherosclerosis)
CRL	CRL Microtech programme	Pharmacopeia	Combinatorial chemistry
CSL Limited	Immunotherapy (gastroenterology)	SNP Consortium	SNP discovery
European Bioinformatics Institute	Bioinformatics	University of Dundee	Novel kinases
Genome Therapeutics	Genetics (gastroenterology) Wellcome Trust and Consortium	Oxford University	Human genome research

Strategy for change

- 'We're not looking for magic bullets any more,' **AstraZeneca Chief Executive Tom McKillop** has said. 'Our aims are more modest, but they are also more insightful.'

- In AstraZeneca's annual report and form 20-F 2000, McKillop identified the key to future performance as, 'an effective performance driven culture'. People risk will be managed to measure and reward performance.

Drawing the risk map

'Within the company we have some excellent risk assessment and risk management processes,' says **Neil Campbell, Director, AstraZeneca Risk and Insurance Services**.

'Obviously the healthcare industry is one of the most regulated industries, and the earnings potential of many of our products is vast. The company instinctively understands the need to be able to identify, assess and manage risks at every level.

'As such there is a momentum towards pulling together a framework and some standard methodologies in order that the SET (senior executive team) have an accurate overview of the major risks to the company (in terms of their potential financial or reputational impact and the likelihood of their occurrence) and the means that we use to mitigate such risks.

'Therefore the key elements that we are trying to build into the methodology are:

- a broad understanding of what we mean by 'risk';

- a means of ensuring that every relevant type of risk is considered;

- quantification of the potential impact and likelihood of risks occurring, which requires good technical knowledge of the inherent nature of the risks themselves, the environment and the experiences of the industry;

- an understanding as to what types of risk are 'acceptable' or 'unacceptable' to the company and its stakeholders, and a means of expressing that acceptability level through financial measures;

- a means to look at the consolidated risk profile across all 'risk owners', whether they be functions, businesses, therapy areas or territories.

'I think we are well positioned as a company to put in place the right framework that both gives the SET an accurate picture of the key risks while not imposing a dampener on entrepreneurial activity, as we have been using the process very successfully in some parts of the business for many years.

" I am aware the insurance and reinsurance market reacts very positively to the way AstraZeneca manages its risks.

'From my own point of view I am aware that the insurance and reinsurance market reacts very positively to the way that AstraZeneca understands and manages its risks.'

Macro risks

'Industry growth and the increasing rate of change are reinforcing the importance of brand strength and intellectual property within the healthcare sector,' **Alex Hindson, Technical Adviser, AstraZeneca Risk and Insurance Services**, told a workshop at the annual conference of the Association of Insurance and Risk Managers (AIRMIC) in June 2001.

'Amid the growing consolidation of leading companies in the industry, there is a push to rationalize and improve the effectiveness of the research pipeline.

'Technology changes based on genetics and bioinformatics are causing a step change in productivity,' he said. 'There is a major drive to leverage the sales and marketing effort to launch potential "blockbuster" products to increasingly more sophisticated markets.

'This has driven the organization to focus on strategic marketing and research activities with a drive to outsource support activities, especially in the manufacturing and information systems areas. This increase in growth and the rate of change have reinforced the importance of brand and intellectual property. A growing proportion of the risks facing the organization is now outside its direct control,' said Hindson.

▪ World-wide activities

AstraZeneca was formed in April 1999 with the merger of Astra and Zeneca.

- It is one of the world's top five ethical pharmaceutical companies.

- Sales in 2000 were $15.8 billion, up 8 per cent.

- Operating profit was $4 billion, up 14 per cent.

- US pharmaceutical sales were $8 billion, up 12 per cent.

- Annual investment of more than $2.5 billion was made in pharmaceutical R&D.

- It has operations in more than 100 countries.

- It manufactures in 19 countries, and has six major research centres.

- It has more than 50,000 employees.

- *Losec* sales were $6.3 billion, up 9 per cent.

- Sales exceed $1 billion in each of five therapeutic areas – gastrointestinal, cardiovascular, oncology, respiratory and pain control.

- Sales of seven products exceed $500 million each – *Losec, Zestril, Seloken, Zoladex, Pulmicort, Diprivan* and *Nolvadex*.

- The project pipeline has more than 150 products and 14 chemical entities.

- It is the world number one in gastrointestinal medicines and anaesthesia.

- It is the world number two in anti-cancer medicines.

- It is the world number four in respiratory medicines.

- It is the world number five in cardiovascular medicines.

E-strategy

Interestingly, Jon Symonds is also charged with responsibility for information services. The latter, through its huge contribution to R&D, e-commerce and stakeholder communication, is recognized as a critical business tool and interface. Enhanced capabilities in e-business and R&D informatics, as well as the strategic decision to outsource global IT infrastructure to IBM, are part of IS risk management.

Health care professionals and patients are relying increasingly on the internet for up-to-date information. The challenge is to ensure that that information is up to date. Projects in train that will add value include e-detailing; e-CME (continuing medical education); hand-held physician devices; remote patient monitoring; and online community building.

An upside risk of serious entry into the American market was a steep learning curve on web marketing and internet promotion including use of web tools for clinical study set-up, training and data management. E-procurement, connection to e-marketplaces, followed.

■ Environmental risk

AstraZeneca claims to apply best practice in the environmental and social area and reports on these in brief in its annual report. It continues to reduce emissions of solvents but does not say by how much. Some 60,000 tonnes of waste, half hazardous, is generated, 47 per cent of which is incinerated with energy recovery, 30 per cent without. An annual review of safety, health and environment (SHE) is presented to the board with advice on risk management.

Contaminated land is becoming an increasing and major risk for all companies where remediation legislation has been passed, including the USA, UK and Germany. AstraZeneca has environmental liabilities at some current, formerly-owned, leased and third-party sites in the USA and presumably elsewhere, which are reported in the notes to its annual report. The actual costs are not identified but remediation typically runs into millions of dollars per site. The company says it, 'has provision in respect of such costs' in accordance with normal accounting procedures.

> **" We deal with some very dangerous materials. We're continuing to learn about the impact our manufacturing processes have on the environment.**

The company or its indemnities have been named under US legislation (the Comprehensive Environmental Response, Compensation and Liability Act of 1980 or CERCLA) as potentially responsible parties in respect of 34 sites.

Symonds admits: 'We deal with some very dangerous materials. We're continuing to learn about the impact our manufacturing processes have on the environment. We are dealing with toxic or harmful substances which are raw materials for many of our products. We comply with stringent safety regimes. We adopt, not the requirements of the local market, but the highest standards wherever we manufacture. I was in China last week and saw our plant there. It is state-of-the-art. It has the accumulated knowledge history of all of our experience in pharmaceuticals formulation and processing.'

AstraZeneca's mission is to be first for innovation and value in the provision of products and services to improve human health and quality of life. SHE considerations are core to this and their aim is that all activities should take account of social, environmental and economic factors so as to:

- meet or exceed legal requirements, regulations and international agreements;

- create a culture where SHE considerations are integrated into all activities across the group;

- conduct business as a responsible corporate member of society committed to continual improvement in all aspects of SHE performance;

- provide a safe and healthy work environment for all our employees;

- economize on the use of natural resources and work to minimize the impact on the environment;

- aim to eliminate all injuries and incidents;

- be among the industry leaders in SHE performance;

- provide information on SHE performance and communicate openly with all interested parties.

Throughout all activities – from research and development to manufacturing and marketing – the SHE impact of every aspect is a fundamental company consideration. SHE is integrated into all areas of business activity. All sites and locations establish and maintain a local SHE management system including a SHE policy based on local legislation and AstraZeneca's requirements. In the absence of relevant legislation, AstraZeneca aims to act responsibly and ethically.

R&D and implementation of new or modified processes or systems and the engineering of new or modified facilities, plant and equipment are based on risk management studies which ensure that all hazards have been properly identified. Routines are established to ensure that equipment, processes and systems are maintained and operated safely and without harm to people or the environment. They aim to implement adequate arrangements to ensure that all other risks arising from work-related activities are recognized and action taken to prevent harm. The SHE factors associated with the development of products and their use are required to be managed responsibly and ethically. The nature and scale of potential emergencies is identified and formal plans, that are adequately rehearsed, put in place. In the event of an emergency, protecting people and the environment is regarded as the highest priority. A SHE assessment is part of any proposal for acquisition or divestment.

AstraZeneca aims to economize on the use of natural resources and work to minimize the impact on the environment. All sites and locations shall identify the environmental impacts arising from their activities and have plans to control and reduce them. These should include consideration of the efficient use of materials and energy, the substitution of hazardous materials, management of wastes and emissions and the protection of soil and groundwater. Environmental impacts are considered during the development, acquisition and marketing of new products and services with regular auditing and monitoring to ensure that there are effective arrangements in place for preventing harm to people and the environment.

Analysis

- Reporting risk: AstraZeneca has a good appreciation of business risk and reports fully on risk in the annual report. All the main risks are covered – but not costed.

- Growing business: the upside risks of being in a growth market are evident – people are living longer and expect a high quality of life and health. The global pharmaceutical market grew by 10 per cent in 2000. The company's US market grew by 16 per cent, global sales were up 8 per cent, but profits by 14 per cent. They continued to grow in Japan after a slip-back, and were up 10 per cent in the UK, France, Italy and Spain. In Germany, the leading EU market, they grew only by 4 per cent.

- Market share: since Astra and Zeneca merged, has improved to 4.7 per cent but economies of scale and synergies have yet to emerge.

- Exchange rate fluctuations: the company trades in US dollars so has been protected from the high value of the pound. The USA is expected to remain its largest and potentially fastest-growing market.

- Geographical spread: the group's business is spread, with $3 billion coming in 2000 from the UK market, with $6 billion from continental Europe, $9 billion from the Americas, and $2 billion from elsewhere, with profits in similar proportions ($600 million, $1 billion and $1.7 billion).

- Macro risks: AstraZeneca shows a deep awareness of the macro risk framework – the external influences that could knock them off course.

- Contaminated land: the company rightly states that, in many cases, the liability to clean up contaminated sites is only actionable if the site is sold or if the use of the site changes. However, for a company that purports to adopt best environmental practice, it could be argued that remediation should be done anyway. The company expects to be indemnified by the vendor of eight of its contaminated sites in the USA. Many sites, particularly in the USA, may be covered by past insurance.

  It reports that, 'In future the availability of historical insurance to offset these liabilities will be reduced as a result of certain insurance settlements effected this year (2000) by Stauffer Management Company (SMC), an AstraZeneca group company, as part of closing out our exposure to some material environmental claims'.

- External stakeholder risks are being managed by making more information available, particularly to doctors and increasingly information-demanding consumers via the internet among other media. In the USA, this extends to advertising to the customer.

Analysis

- Growth in genomics offers real breakthroughs in terms of discovery and development time through the advantages of digital technology and the competitive nature of the market. Successes here will improve the return on investment.

- Litigation risk appears to be increasing.

- Pressure on prices: social and political pressures to reduce prices are a growing risk, not only from developing countries unable to pay top buck for drugs but also, increasingly, developed countries where governments are trying to keep health costs under control. The threat from generic drugs is likely to increase. There is currently no direct government control of prices for non-government sales in the USA. But there is pressure for rebates. Pharmaceutical companies will increasingly need to address the ethical issues raised by the high perceived costs of drugs and the related emergence of less expensive 'copycat' versions. The existence of legally enforceable patents will not prevent ethical objections, particularly in Third World countries. There are likely to be significant legal costs involved here. There is also the logistical difficulty of enforcing patent rights.

- The environmental risks which will come increasingly to the fore include:

  - resistance by consumers to the solvents and other hazardous chemicals used in drugs;

  - requirements for integrated pollution prevention and control;

  - product liability claims.

27 Business interruption – our vision is never-fail

By Richard Pursey, Managing Director, *Global Continuity*

I have to hand it to Richard Pursey! He appeared not at all put out when I arrived for our meeting well over an hour late. I had advised him I was running late and then compounded the insult by getting lost in the motorway system round Newbury in Berkshire. I know! I've read the book... Why men don't listen and women can't read maps.

Global Continuity is a world leader in NeverFail™ Systems and Solutions. With offices in Belgium, Germany, Europe, the USA and South Africa, the group provides a range of high-technology continuous business processing solutions to leading organizations from around the world. It is located on an industrial estate somewhere near Newbury.

It runs itcontinuity.com – a high-power portal on IT risk, disaster recovery, cyber terrorism and continuity. It claims to be 'the world's leading online news and service provider for continuous business processing. Focusing on prevention as well as cure, Global Continuity provides technical services, products and solutions that minimize and often eliminate system downtime'. In this it claims to be a world leader.

Such is the new emphasis on avoiding business interruption that, since entering the market in 1994, the company has grown 87 per cent year on year, which, according to Time Magazine, made it Europe's nineth fastest-growing company in 1999.

I asked Richard, what's your track record in continuity management?

I was working in IT on Kleinwort Benson's Forex trading floor. Trading floors are a maximum-up-time environment. Failure is not an option! I was pretty aware of the market: who was doing what to whom in the City. I saw a gap in the market and, in 1986, I set up European Dealing Room Solutions, the UK's first consultancy based purely on dealing room crisis management. This became Adam Associates Limited, which rapidly became known for its expertise in disaster recovery services, particularly for finance houses in the City of London.

In 2000 we reengineered it to take advantage of the emerging continuous business processing market, successfully migrating to a disaster recovery and business continuity company. We rebranded as Global Continuity. Seventy per cent of our business comes out of banking and finance. We are selling fear, uncertainty and doubt.

> **We are selling fear, "uncertainty and doubt.**

We're a typical small company: very innovative, very creative, things change very quickly. In 1999 we had Y2K risks coming our way. We said: 'The Y2K problem is nowhere near as big as people are making out.'

We are an IT business through and through. We are, specifically, a disaster recovery company.

What's your definition of 'disaster recovery'?

One of our customers has a major business interruption, calls us and we replace their IT systems with duplicates. What happened with the so-called 'millennium bug' was that the whole profile of interruption moved out of business housekeeping to board level. Board directors were asking, 'What are the implications for us?' This was brilliant for us because, from the day we started, we've been saying that this is a necessary business discipline.

But it was good news/bad news. They were saying, 'I don't want to buy anything yet. I just want to know what my risks are.' We have lots of risk specialists here who understand the vertical markets. They look at the scale of the threat and, more importantly, they determine the software that is needed. It may be manufacturing, it may be banking and finance, it may be petrochemicals. While the definition of risk is common to everybody it is clearly different depending on the risk environment existing in the particular business. You go into a petrochem company and you find they're more of a finance house than anything else. Marks & Spencer is really a finance company.

So, October 1999, we can see the writing on the wall, but disaster recovery, almost anything to do with risk, is still compared with insurance, or linked to insurance. And insurance is a 'grudge purchase'. What happened was that many businesses woke up to it just about prior to midnight on New Year's Eve. We were swamped beyond belief. We were doing £1 million of consultancy a month for November and December. In January 2000 we did £25 million, which was exactly what we predicted!

The good news was that the 'millennium bug' got people thinking about genuine risk and the impact of interruption. So we had an opportunity. We created a web portal called globalcontinuity.com. The idea of that was to build a membership base on a real-time basis. It would enable us to move quickly and adjust our service offerings to meet the market demand.

It was a phenomenal success and you've probably got 16,000 'members' in 96 countries.

That substantiated our market vision that businesses are becoming less tolerant of any form of interruption – especially because you're in a global market and especially because of the great thing, e-commerce. The world wide web has made customer loyalty non-existent. If the web site is not there, I double-click and go somewhere else, thank you very much. There is no patience in the world any more. I may be competing with some guy in Bogota for all I know. He could be writing software that is 10 per cent better than mine. You've got to be fleet of foot and so on. We call that continuous business processing. So our business went from, one, disaster has happened, now come in and sort us out to, two, business continuity which is an IT risk, to three, business risk, which was the best news of all into, four, continuous business processing, business availability, zero downtime, which is the market we are now in.

How do you define 'customer' and 'member'?

A customer is a fare-paying passenger. They're not all customers who log into our news service. Some are. The reason they get on our site as a member is that every day globalcontinuity.com loads and shows risk news from round the world. They are getting something for free. To get it for free you have to register as a member. Every now and then we poll you and ask, what do you think of this? Or we load a bit of news and ask for some feedback. It's a good site. There's real value in that site. It e-mails you daily with breaking news if you want it; if you don't you switch that option off.

It's good marketing for you?

Also, many people contribute news back so, as long as we can substantiate it and validate it as being correct, it is very productive for everyone else.

This is why I had difficulty with logging on to your website and, also, establishing what kind of company you were: a news agency? A risk consultant? In business interruption logistics?

I'm not surprised you've had difficulty with our website. As the business had migrated we have gone for reengineering because of the changes relating to the millennium bug. Only in the summer of 2001 did we reach the point where Global Continuity had become the brand to replace the other five brands. The corporate website is now gc.plc.com.

What are the logistics of what you do when a client suffers business interruption? Do you duplicate their IT systems?

We have core patented product which is NeverFail™ Server which is the world's first fully automated continuous business processing solution to incorporate real-time, immediate server continuity with data mirroring and post-failure hardware rebuild.

It protects the complete system, from the operating environment (Windows NT®) through to the applications and data. Unscheduled downtime is a thing of the past. The highest value is the premise that no risk is acceptable – and that's NeverFail.

> **The highest value is the premise that no risk is acceptable.**

We say, let's take away all risk. It just won't happen. Your servers will still fail but nobody will notice. Our vision is absolute zero tolerance for any form of interruption. Our business is about ensuring things never fail – whatever they may be – and you define what you want to protect.

Disaster recovery is a physical defence system that remains appropriate but only as a second line of continuity.

Exactly. You want continuous business processing.

Even with that, you remain vulnerable if a source server has failed and the catcher has taken over. What if the catcher fails?

The NeverFail™ Server triggers construction of a perfect replacement server based at an operations recovery centre. The catcher forwards mirrored data to the NeverFail™ IT operations centre. Rapid recovery servers take on the failed server's identity. Within 15 minutes of automatic notification of a source server failure, a rapid recovery server is fully loaded with operating system, applications and data ready to be transported to a recovery site. Alternatively the rapid recovery server could be connected via a WAN link and brought online immediately.

What if a virus infected their system? Surely it would be posted to your mirror system?

Yes. The virus would be transmitted straight through to our 'catcher'. We segment that virus, cut it and put it somewhere else. What happens is that the data mirrors the data twice so that it can delay the mirroring process long enough to 'clean' it of any viruses. We can delay it for one minute, two hours, a day or not at all. We can prepare for it.

We have customers who have used our services because their project time has, typically, been halved. This happens all the time. It's just happened out in South Africa with a customer. That constitutes a disaster.

People are also worried about the risk of physical disasters, like terrorism, fire or flood.

The NeverFail™ SOS tool is used in case of a disaster such as a fire when the building burns down. It allows our clients to contact many people simultaneously by placing just one call to a central database run by Global Continuity; we then instantly distribute the messages electronically by phone, fax and e-mail.

SOS is used to:

- inform employees, management and executives about incidents, emergencies and other urgent situations;

- contact the media and keep them up to date with press releases and bulletins;

- invoke emergency response and disaster recovery teams;

- alert IT staff when critical systems are down;

- notify customers and suppliers about incidents and ongoing progress reports.

NeverFail™ Plan helps you in a very structured way. It talks to your business heads. It gives your business the ability to manage the entire business continuity process, not just the plans. It provides an easy-to-use framework, designed to help the whole organization participate in managing business risk. It's loaded on to the customer's system. They use the software.

The design brings business continuity planning within the reach of all levels of business user. Its user-friendly Windows interface encourages ownership through involvement. The software is quick to learn and helps produce quality plans. The Plan can be tailored to a consistent corporate standard. It gives the business consistency in its risk management, crisis management and contingency planning across the world. This is what multinationals are now demanding. They are protecting their reputation. SMEs are protecting their livelihood. There's a big difference. Disaster recovery never used to be bought by small companies. NeverFail is a software solution they can afford. Hence Global Continuity as a name now.

The elegant structure ensures that valuable management time is not wasted on complex configuration and customization – whatever the size of the organization. Management reports help to keep them on top of plan status, maintenance, testing and training.

There is a major American bank who have their own technology centre. Their London trading floor is one of the biggest. Their telephone system was going up and down like a fidler's elbow. While it wasn't failing, it was creating insecurity for the guys. They didn't know whether they were going to get cut off. They decided to relocate their whole business to their recovery centre because they couldn't handle these unforeseen interruptions. We recovered that whole environment in less than four hours. There was something like 363 computers to set up. They remained on that system for four weeks until there was confidence.

Several customers have suffered computer theft, aimed particularly at the memory chips and the processors. We've recovered organizations who have lost access to their buildings because of terrorist bombs, especially Canary Wharf in 1996. We recovered five companies. In Manchester the customers lost access to their premises. They went to recovery centres. We got their technology up and running for them.

In this building alone we have something like 1,000 separate computers held on stand-by for our customers. They are configured to make them look just like the computers to which they have just lost access. They have a disaster, call us and we load in the client's 'image'. Then we become a logistics company. We deliver that equipment to the customer.

> **In this building alone we have something like 1,000 separate computers held on stand-by for our customers.**

At first, our customers for disaster recovery contracts would accept a 24-hour business interruption. We were given 24 hours to deliver the equipment to their business recovery point. Since 1994, the demand for shorter delivery times has intensified. We are now into continuous business processing: you must not go wrong in the first place. That typically means an organization cannot outsource this service. They have to do it internally. Companies want a suite of services they can use on site.

Demand for zero interruption has been driven by the growth in e-business, globalization, legislative forces and market demand. A lot of companies are concerned about whether their supply chain would survive. The whole concept of protecting operational risk has reached board level.

Many organizations are dependent on third parties. The bigger organizations are focusing hard on the survivability, the resilience of their suppliers. That makes them check on their suppliers. So our market has expanded beyond recognition.

> **The whole concept of protecting operational risk has reached board level.**

Banks and the way they do credit risk rating are only half the story. You may have an AAA rating if you have a very good balance sheet. I believe there should be RRR rating for good management of risk. Why should any investor or lending house invest in a company if their operational risk management is not secure?

Organizations have gone bust because they have suffered interruption as a result of a major disaster. When two organizations merge, the risk profile goes through the roof. The chances of getting it horribly wrong are high: you get disgruntled employees, you get employees that become nervous, overworked, overlooked. They can get angry and do nasty things to you. You miss out on the detail. You forget your customers. Blending systems which may not blend well means that your whole risk profile has changed dramatically. M&A time is when you need to have meticulous contingency plans.

RRR ratings should be an essential part of business life. I would say that, wouldn't I? But I do believe that. When we purchase from companies on which we are dependent for supplies, we look at how they operate their systems. Our reputation as a business is only as good as the last time a customer called on us. If we have to rely on our suppliers to ensure that our business reputation is maintained then they have to be quality suppliers.

Outsourcing is a risky game in itself. M&A, any form of corporate activity on a large scale, is high-risk.

Is business continuity centrally managed?

Some companies do it centrally. Others don't. The problem is that the business at street level isn't understood centrally.

Risk is reviewed by internal audit.

Internal audit is a driving force. They tell business units, 'You cover this because you are exposed.' Then we get called in to cover it. The people who focus on it are finance directors, IT managers, corporate risk managers and compliance officers. Turnbull is a classic driver. So are British Standard 7799 for Information Security; and the Blue Book regulations in the USA which require finance houses to protect client interests. This also drives business for us with the American banks in Frankfurt, Johannesburg and so on.

We often find that, after companies have done their risk analysis, they find they have a department or two that they actually don't need. They close them down because they find that doing so doesn't make any difference to their business whatsoever. Which is a fascinating outcome from a risk analysis. Whole areas have become self-perpetuating with raging self-interest but no business logic.

Call centres are an example of technology – website development – rendering people redundant.

Absolutely. What that means is that the dependency on that technology has got higher and higher. It has led of course to dependency on power supplies. You cannot afford to go down for 24 hours. It focuses the mind on the priorities. Priority management is key.

There's a definition in e-business of a 'sprinter'. It means, 'Must get into that market quickly to stop anyone else getting there!' They cut corners, get there quickly, but then find their systems don't work properly. They spend an absolute fortune getting it right. If they'd got it right first time they wouldn't have the problem.

When companies are investing in new IT systems, we encourage them to invest in their contingency planning at the point of initial procurement. That can save a fortune down the line. Change management is the time to start your risk management.

There's a new determination to be available 24/7. By getting those basics right it sends a signal that they have probably got the other basics in their business right too. They'll do well.

The barriers to entry for dot coms are extremely low. A dot com by definition trades globally so by definition there are tens of millions of others who could compete with your idea. The idea that you load on the web tonight will be cloned tomorrow. You must never forget the needs of the customer. You must make sure that you are getting the customer-driven part of your business right. You must ensure that they never have a reason to double-click and go somewhere else.

Two things they have to do are, one, ensure that when the customer looks for the site it is there and they can get what they want, when they want it and quickly.

And at the right price.

For sure. You always have to get the fundamentals right. For dot coms, you have to ensure that people stick to your site and don't go somewhere else. The servers, the software, the site must always be there. The software that you write is properly stress-tested before you load it because software goes wrong.

The biggest reason for interruption is scheduled down-time, because they've never got it right in the first place. Don't be a sprinter. Get to the market in time but get it right. Build in continuity. There are so many tricks that competitors may play – trying to block your website. You get a message saying the system is unavailable right now.

You're not given a reason.

You don't know whether the site's been brought down deliberately. Whether it's a malicious attack. Or it might be the network provider. The bottom line is that the customer goes somewhere else. All he knows is he can't buy. The whole thing about e-business is you get what you want when you want it 24/7. For every one site that's not available there are ten in the line ready to step in.

On two occasions I purchased stuff online and it took weeks and many phone calls to chase the order before it arrived. In both cases it was the same courier company that fouled up.

What's the point of getting the site right when the delivery is poor? That's the supply chain problem I mentioned earlier. That's a moment of truth. The website's the best in the world but the delivery guy is a sloth. You've lost it!

How many dot coms have business continuity problems?

I'd say at least three quarters of them. Take a simple thing like a power cut. If they don't have stand-by generators, they will go off-line for hours.

> **Take a simple thing like a "power cut. If they don't have stand-by generators, they will go off-line for hours."**

Problems can be self-inflicted.

Many dot coms have only one means of selling – through their website. If that is down, no sale. I also tried to buy something over the web recently. The site was down. But, by persistence, I got hold of a call centre phone number. I said I'd like to order this item. The lady was in Brussels and repeatedly told me I could only buy using the website. She said, 'We do not take orders over the telephone.' I said, 'Your website is down.' She said, 'The only way you can place an order is through the website. I can't do anything about it.' What is the point?

A dot com is particularly exposed if the website is the only means of selling. Again, beware of having your call centre in only one place. Postal strikes, any kind of distribution delay, will leave you vulnerable.

In Japan, our NeverFail systems will be sold by one of the world's biggest IT companies, IBM. The Japanese economy is far more electronic-aware than in the UK. One company alone sells 1.5 million mobile phones a month. They are so technology-dependent.

They are also more risk-aware. They have earthquakes, the volcano is erupting as we speak. They are a culture that is prepared to accept risk. The more technology-dependent the solution, the more they are likely to buy. Great culture. I love it!

Conservative values and biotech gambles

28

By Gareth Hayward, Stockbroker, *Charles Stanley*

I guess Charles Stanley is what you would call a 'niche' stockbroker. It was founded in 1792 as the Walkers, Eyre and Stanley Bank in the then booming steel town of Sheffield. The partners – fellow members of The Monthly Club, a philosophical, literary and scientific gathering – included William Stanley, a businessman described by a contemporary as 'a gentleman well-known and much respected'.

Thanks to prudent management the bank flourished while many others (very nearly the Bank of England among them in 1825) went under; and in 1835 at the age of 21, Charles Stanley succeeded his father as head of the firm.

Charles spent increasing amounts of time in London, supervising the bank's investments and bullion shipments, and by 1852 had become a member of the Stock Exchange, laying the foundations of the firm as it is today. This venture prospered in an unregulated and volatile market where financial catastrophes were common.

In 1886 the firm registered what is said to be the UK's first telegraphic address ('Chastons') – a pioneering step in new technology. In 1995 it scored another 'first' when it became the first UK stockbroker to go online.

Today it serves retail clients whose financial affairs it has managed for generations, some perhaps for 200 years. In an age of tracker funds, risk-based investment and automated investment decisions, Charles Stanley still promotes the idea of close personal attention, coupled with day-to-day contact with the market.

The 'Big Bang' stock market revolution in the 1980s led many stockbrokers to ally themselves with large domestic or international investment banks in the pursuit of institutional business. Again, Charles Stanley refused to follow the herd, maintaining its independence and private-client focus. The technology may have changed since 1792, but its principles haven't!

Which was why I was surprised by the refreshingly candid approach of one Gareth Hayward, when I visited him at Charles Stanley's offices in the City of London. No stiff upper lip here. He says exactly what he thinks.

I am interested in the role of the investment community in general, and how it protects its clients, particularly in growing but high-risk sectors such as biotech, TMT and online trades. Gareth explains his approach:

Risk, in one sense, for us is managed by the compliance department that makes sure that we take on clients properly and that we adhere to money-laundering rules.

If most of your clients are high net worth individuals, perhaps some of them are engaging in a bit of money-laundering?

Well, we try to make sure they are not. If we don't, we are criminally liable! To be fair, if you have a degree of experience, the little hairs on the back of your neck can stand up. You sort of say, well, we simply don't know where this person comes from. You see, most business is referred by a friend. In other words, clients come with provenance. They are a bit like an antique really. I would hope that I know where they've been!

Then of course we have the discretionary management agreement. If you want to become a client of mine, you sign The Schedule which says, under Investment Objectives: 'Unless you indicate otherwise, the firm will manage your portfolio with a view to a combination of capital appreciation, an average level of equity income, and a medium level of risk for the portfolio as a whole, but with the possible inclusion of up to a third of the portfolio in higher risk investments, without other restrictions on the size or type of investment. These may include investments which are not on exchange or which are not readily realizable investments.'

" Different people have completely different attitudes to risk.

Now other firms I have seen, when you sign a discretionary agreement, they say, 'tick the box – high risk (we'll lose all your money very quickly); medium risk (we'll lose it a bit more slowly); or low risk (well, it'll take a while but we'll still get there!)' You know Groucho Marx's definition of a stockbroker, don't you? 'Someone who invests your money for you until it's all gone!'

I'm being facetious! Of course different people have completely different attitudes to risk.

How do you define risk?

I define risk as maintaining people's capital value wherever possible. Because markets are volatile, they go up and down. There are people who can predict. They are very intelligent or they have computer programmes that are incredibly sophisticated, they can spot infinitessimal signals which mean, 'it's about to go up 1 per cent; it's about to go down 1 per cent' but by and large for the average Jo watching the market and investing, it really is difficult. There are people doing things you have no clue about, no understanding of, no insight into, no knowledge of.

There's a company who posted a loss of £7 million just a few months after they floated. Did they issue a warning before they went public?

People tend not to promise things because prospectuses have to be verified by lawyers. So if you say, 'We're going to make a thumping great profit next year,' the lawyers say, 'Prove it.' Of course you can't. So you don't make the statement.

If you buy shares in a business that's losing money, and dot coms were a classic, in the hope and expectation that revenues would rapidly rise, when those revenues don't rapidly rise, the earnings don't come through on the back of revenues and lo and behold the valuation put on it at the outset turns out to have been rather fanciful.

One of the other things I noticed about the dot com scenario was it's all very well for companies to raise money for research, for having a go – how was oil ever found in Iran? Somebody, somewhere raised a lot of money to go and dig a hole to find oil. There was no guarantee that they would find oil but the venture was worth doing. You have to put the money up. As long as it's done on a reasonably sensible basis and there are reasonably sensible people involved, it's got some chance of success. A biotechnology company that's looking for a cure for Alzheimer's disease, a dot com business that's going to sell air tickets online and it's never been done before…there's a high level of risk because they're not generating money, are they? They're spending money initially.

How do you see the biotech sector?

You're buying the future. You're buying the promise. You know, there's gold in them there hills. There's oil in that lake. I've got a cure in this test tube. Frankly no-one knows – least of all the investment professional because by and large he's not a scientist. He doesn't know whether that molecule is any better than that molecule. There's a well-worn path towards assessing biotech companies. There has to be a regulatory approval process for new drugs.

How do you approach biotech shares?

If you come back to discretionary management, someone gives you a lump of money to manage and you say, 'What do you want?' They say, 'I don't want you to lose it.' Fine. We'll buy some very boring shares and we'll hold on to them for a very long time and they'll produce income. No problems. On the other hand, they may say, 'Well, I've got a very good job. I earn sufficient money. I don't mind if there's a little bit of risk in my life. I don't mind if you buy me some biotech or some dot com. Follow your nose. Find something a bit interesting.'

If I'm investing half a million pounds, say, for somebody, I talk to them and say, 'As to 90 per cent, let's be boring, we'll buy some gilts and we'll

Maybe one of them is going "to turn into a very major pharmaceutical company?'

buy some FTSE 100 companies and they'll be volatile and go up and down. But would you like me to put £2,000 or £5,000 in something more speculative that gives you the hope of enormous gains because maybe one of them is going to turn into a very major pharmaceutical company?'

Another way is you go and buy an investment trust or a unit trust that specializes in a sector. There are investment trusts that do nothing but look at biotech companies or emerging health care companies – 3i Bioscience, International Biotechnology run by Schroders, and Finsbury Life Sciences.

This is not to say you don't research genomes and so on?

Sure. You talk to management. You have clients whose day job is working in biotechnology. You talk to them about their industry. It's a feel that you get. Let me give you an analogy.

I have a client who owns racehorses. It's fascinating. You sit down with him and, being an amateur, you haven't got a clue. You just hope they all have four legs and occasionally win a race. I sat with him over lunch before the first race and he said, 'This one can't win. This one won't win. This one won't win.' He's immediately knocked four out in a ten-horse race. They can't possibly win. 'This one's got a chance. This one's got a chance. The best value bet is probably to try and get the first three horses, in no particular order.'

And that's your approach to investing in stocks and shares?

In a sense, why buy something that you know nothing about? Occasionally the outsider comes in – but not often. Lots of people made lots of money in 2000 on dot coms. Lots of people lost it. Some of those investments were akin to the outsider. You reduce the odds of getting it wrong just by paying a bit of attention, reading, visiting management, talking to them, being curious, never letting go. Worry at it. Watch it.

Research is critical to good risk management.

It takes some of the risk out of it. In theory, the more you know about something, the more you remove the risk element of something unexpected happening. It's the unexpected that always trips you up. You didn't foresee the profit warning. You didn't realize how exposed that company was to that particular marketplace or to that currency risk or whatever it happens to be. It's like going to a race course and saying, now which horses don't I even need to be bothered with?

Peter J. Tannous, in the Investment Gurus, makes the point that many fund managers are good for, say, five years but not many are good for decades.

You do find that there are periods when fund managers are out of sorts with the world. An awful lot were in 2000. An awful lot of people sat there scratching their heads, saying, 'I don't understand this.' I was one of those. Clients would ring up and say, 'You're missing it!' You'd say, 'Well, that's because I don't understand it. It's frou frou dust.' Clients feel bad when they haven't got exposure in this sexy stock. It's dinner party conversation. But you have to be true to yourself. I don't believe an investment manager should suspend belief and do something that he is fundamentally concerned about.

> **You do find that there are periods when fund managers are out of sorts with the world. An awful lot were in 2000.**

The fundamentals of corporate survival are that a company is well-run, that it makes a profit and that it is aware of the importance of profit-and-loss and cash flow. Many of the companies that failed in financial terms in 2000–2002 had management weaknesses in these areas.

Take Allan Leighton. You can see the influence of, dare I say it, a 'real businessman' on the business of, say, Lastminute.com. One of the figures that jumped off the FT at me when I was reading it on the train was that the 'burn' rate, the rate at which they are spending cash, is down from 'x' million to less than that. This can only have come about for two reasons. Either revenues have gone up, which they don't appear to have done massively, or they have cut costs. So they have actually cut costs to reduce the burn rate. That's basic business discipline.

I am not disagreeing with the concept of Lastminute.com. It is just the basis on which they were valued. Of course there will be survivors. How many people went looking for oil?

Larger companies face different risks. They tend towards monopoly because it's one of the best ways to grow. They want to grow so that they can name their price. The Competition Commission doesn't like mergers that will give one company, say, 30 per cent of the market for this very reason. GlaxoSmithKline got into arguments with the regulators about brands of toothpaste just so that it would be all right. It slowed the deal down, what, six or nine months.

Smaller companies don't have that risk. It's almost as if they are below the

> **Received wisdom says, 'Large company, less risk; small company, much more volatile, more risk.'**

radar screen of the competition authorities. Received wisdom says, 'Large company, less risk; small company, much more volatile, more risk.' The reverse can actually be true.

I think the reverse is true. Jack Welch of General Electric turned that company from a $12 billion business in 1981 to a $440 billion conglomerate with interests in jet engines, financial services and the NBC TV network. The European Commission vetoed General Electric's $43 billion bid for Honeywell which would have been the world's largest industrial takeover. The giant was slayed by Brussels.

The smaller company is less visible, less obvious, less covered by the press.

I'd like to go back to the biotech sector because I know it is one that you follow. Some of them have incredible lists of eminent scientists who are non-execs or act as an advisory board.

It matters not a jot to me. If they're not doing the job, having ten Nobel prize winners on your advisory board doesn't give you an irrefutable clue that the molecules that you are playing around with are any better than anyone else's molecules. Sorry!

I don't believe that's the case. If they are saying that they will review if the science works and their input is that the experiment should go that way rather than that way, then maybe there is some input. You can't tell.

> **If they're not doing the job, having ten Nobel prize winners on your advisory board doesn't give you an irrefutable clue that the molecules you are playing with are any better than anyone else's.**

It is a bit like a geologist. If you're a geologist you can get turned on by a certain type of rock formation. You can say, 'The last time I saw that rock formation there was oil below it.'

Maybe if you're on an advisory board and you come from Glaxo or Roche or wherever and you see that combination of science, that molecule with those attributes, you may say, 'The last time I saw one of those, with that effect, it turned out to be Viagra or some wizard drug that ended up selling billions of pounds' worth.' Maybe you get some of that from it. But you have to be careful because it's easy to get blinded by the flashy bits – you know, the fancy scientific board. You can't take anything for granted in biotech.

How do you rate its profit potential?

Everybody says demand for health care is elastic. There's as much demand as you could possibly wish for. Therefore there will always be money to support new drugs, new treatments. It's getting increasingly expensive. Clearly, to my mind, there is a social compact between the drug discovery industry and the state – or those who reimburse the cost of paying for the treatment. It strikes me that that is a risk.

Health care is our biggest industry.

Absolutely. It is. I live in Cambridge and I bump into these folk. I've had more than a passing interest in the pharmaceutical industry and health care for many, many years. I think the nature of biotechnology is that it will yield enormous riches for those involved. It will be a rocky road. Some will fail, some will succeed, some will merge. Some will be overtaken. Some will be bought by major pharmaceutical companies whose research pipeline looks dated. Oh, it's going to be a significant industry.

It became deeply unfashionable. When it became clear that British Biotech would not be able to deliver the successful drug they had promised, the whole sector's values were blown wide open.

British Biotech was on the verge of becoming a FTSE 100 company. Index trackers decided that one of the ways that they would take risk out of the whole thing was that they would 'buy' the index. For brief periods they have had to buy shares in Baltimore because they became a FTSE 100 company. Index trackers are forced into buying shares in those companies. When the company drops out of the index, they have to sell because they are no longer part of the index.

People now have a lot more experience of the biotech sector. They know what to look for. They're older and wiser in the ways of biotechnology and the health care industry generally. There's a general acceptance that the mapping of the human genome will transform medicine. Whereas ten years ago people said, 'Genetic engineering? Wazat? What's a gene? You've got Levi's. Wranglers or something.' There's more acceptance now. But as an investment professional, how do you participate in it? How do you reduce the risk? How am I to know? Which is why the collective approach is less risky.

Some people view it as a cop-out. They say, 'You're just passing on the job of investing in biotech to Finsbury Investment Trust.' I talk to a fund manager at Finsbury. I may say, 'What's going on?' He'll say, 'There's a bit of a panic in the USA – there have been a series of failed clinical trials. That always has a bad effect.' A business runs out of money. Aortech tried to raise money, failed, pulled the issue. There are no guarantees in it. The best way to do this is via the collective approach. How do I know that Cambridge Antibodies stands a better chance of discovering the billion dollar drug than does Peptide Therapeutics or Xenova?

Major pharmaceutical companies license technology from biotechs. Presumably that's their way of reducing their own risk of undertaking proprietary research and failing. They have to fill a gap in the pipeline that looks as if it may appear.

The biotech firm needs to ask, do we have enough money to get us where we want to go? Do we have contingency plans in case we run out of

> **The biotech firm needs to ask, do we have contingency plans in case we run out of money?**

money? Do they go cap in hand to the bank? Do they go back to shareholders? Do they have an agreement with shareholders that they can ask for more money if push comes to shove?

29

The risk managers' risk manager

By Philip Thomas, Director of Risk Management, *Bass*

' **B**ass plc is now a substantially different company,' from what it was just two years ago, Chief Executive Tim Clarke commented in December 2000 while presenting the company's results. They showed turnover up 23 per cent to £3.7 billion, operating profit up 25 per cent to £776 million and profit before tax and major exceptional items up 19 per cent to £756 million. Adjusted earnings per share were up 9 per cent to 62 pence. A final dividend of 23 pence was recommended, which with the interim dividend of 10 pence per share amounted to 33 pence per share for the year, an increase of 3 per cent over 1999.

After selling the core brewing business for £2.3 billion in 2000, the company's priority changed to high-growth global hotels and high-return pubs and restaurants. The new aim is to, 'build strong brands, reinforce market-leading positions and aim for above average growth. Our hotels and resorts business has performed strongly across the world and expansion has continued with the number of hotels passing 3,000. Inter-Continental has grown its profits by 69 per cent since acquisition in 1998. We are moving ahead with major modernization projects at ten of the largest hotels,' Clarke added.

'We have moved rapidly on the construction programme for brand conversion of 550 sites, the first 78 to reopen achieving sales uplifts ahead of the 40 per cent level anticipated prior to the acquisition. Britvic had a good performance against a background of a challenging summer for the soft drinks industry. The acquisition of Orchid Drinks was important,' he concluded.

In April 2001 Bass acquired 79 mid-scale Posthouse hotels from Compass. It aims to add value by upgrading them to its international Holiday Inn brand. This will enable it to benefit from brand recognition, global online reservations and a combined salesforce. As a result Bass anticipates substantial outperformance in revenue per room.

How does Bass manage risk in a global Old Economy company with so many changes and constant acquisitions and divestitures? I asked Philip Thomas, Director of Risk Management. He reports directly to Richard Winter, Company Secretary, responsible for legal, secretarial, assurance and audit services and risk management. Winter is a member of the strategic business committee. So risk management at Bass is at the heart of business management.

Thomas is an accountant who has won prizes for devising risk management systems. He is also the 2001/2002 chairman of AIRMIC, the risk managers' association. So I guess he is the risk managers' risk manager.

You manage as near as constantly by reviewing what your risks are. Two years ago we were a hotels, pubs and brewing company, known mostly for being a brewing company. At that point the biggest part of our business became our hotel business. All of a sudden we were much less diversified. The defining moment of selling brewers meant that the focus was now much more on a global, as opposed to a UK, business. We immediately became more exposed to the risks of fewer businesses and the cyclical risks of the hotel business. And on a global basis. That's where the main shift changed.

> We immediately became "more exposed to the risks of fewer businesses and the cyclical risks of the hotel business."

Having said that, a global business by definition is diversified. Problems in one part of the world will be off-set by good things happening elsewhere. So we are globally diversified.

Most well-run companies, of which Bass is one, historically have developed systems which has meant that they have been better at managing risk than other businesses – which is why they are successful. Which is why they are a FTSE 100 company perhaps.

Managing risk means you have to employ good people. You have to have the processes in place.

Strategic planning and financial processes (capital appraisal and expenditure) are the three traditional ways of managing risk. Since 1996, we have developed a fourth plank – our major risks process. This is a specific process which identifies and drives the management of our biggest risks. This is facilitated centrally. It is a top-down process whereby we carry out facilitated interviews with all of our senior managers. A 'senior manager' is one of the members of our executive committees – hotels, retail or our central business committee. These are the top men and women in our company. They are the operating boards of each of our businesses plus the central management board – and any other individuals who, as a result of these sessions, we feel we ought to interview as well. This happens on a six-monthly basis.

So we have a database of information on where the risk areas are, what the key issues are. That's not to say we don't identify new risks because we do. Generally the business has not changed so much in six months that you have wholesale change. What you have is that smaller risks grow to become bigger issues; some shrink. We encourage all individuals to think about their business in the broadest possible sense.

1   What are the biggest issues facing the business?

2   What sort of things keep you awake at night?

3   What sort of things could derail the business as a whole?

4   What could derail our strategic objectives?

A couple of people from group risk management meet with them. We generally involve someone from internal audit so they can get a clear feed as to what should go into their audit plan each year because it is a risk-based audit plan.

We have provided them in the past with simple bubble pictures of their business so they are not just focused on their areas of responsibility.

The first part of the session is broad-based. The second part focuses on those risks which that individual has identified previously, or has just identified, which also fall within their areas of ownership. They are the risk owners. We then score the risks in terms of their gross impact, gross probability, net impact and net probability. We discuss what control framework is in place which enables the gross scores to be brought down to net scores. Then we talk about what further actions need to be taken to further reduce exposure to that risk.

Gross basis?

As if there were no management controls.

Net basis?

"" The process is not limited to downside risks. We encourage people to think of lost opportunities, or potential lost opportunities.

What we think the exposure is, the probability is, given the existing level of control.

Then we talk about what actions might be necessary to reduce the net exposure even further.

While people at these meetings will tend to identify downside risks, the process is not limited to downside risks. We encourage people to think of lost opportunities, or potential lost opportunities, as well. That's a side that we are trying to develop.

You define 'upside risk' in terms of missed opportunities. But what about pro-actively looking for upsides? Wherever there is a risk, there is always an opportunity.

This process does not pro-actively look for upsides. The risks that have been identified so far tend to be the tendency to lose upside risks. We are looking back at opportunities lost.

Having a more formal process for the identification of upside risk opportunities – we probably could do more. Having said that, I have to ask if there are enough downside thinkers in the organization anyway? We have to focus on that first.

I have found with clients that anything that energizes people is good all round. If they think they are making a positive contribution, they 'buy' in actively to what you are trying to do. The fact that they are being asked to be pro-active about identifying issues and identifying the upsides of risk will energize everything you are trying to do.

Yes. What we are doing has evolved cumulatively over five years. The overall impact is that the issues that are identified are firmly put back into the executive committees within our organization. Risk management issues are firmly on the agenda.

It throws up few surprises. What it does is throw up the issues which you get to hear about around the organization but sometimes such issues don't always find their way into the boardroom.

They would otherwise fall through the management net?

Yes. For example, everyone knows that the talent of your people is key. You may have a strategic plan, but if you don't have good people to implement that plan then it's not worth much. This is a process that puts people risk firmly into the boardroom. You say, 'You must come up with a plan to improve the quality of your staff.'

We haven't eliminated any of the risks. Prior to the process senior management's day-to-day radar screen would have had a number of risks on it. They would have been actively managing those risks as far as they could. What this formal process has done is to give them a far broader radar screen. There would have been risks missing from their radar screen. This puts the full range on there. They have a more balanced, quantified and broader view. The risks that come from left field include the 'softer' issues, the business continuity issues and other things they would not have flagged up before. Not things which are surprising in themselves but just getting enough air time with senior management.

There are issues associated with mergers and acquisitions, branding, reputation which, in the past, may not have been seen as risks. Then there are totally new risks associated with the New Economy.

You've taken the words out of my mouth. What might happen to your reputation if you had a crisis management failure? Crisis management regularly appears on

> **There are totally new risks associated with the New Economy.**

our reports. There are people issues, quality of people is firmly on the agenda. IT risks. One thing the process has done is bring together a number of smaller IT risks, accumulated them and come up with something that is bigger than the sum of the parts.

E-procurement and e-sales are a growing proportion of our bookings.

Are you monitoring the growth, monitoring the risk? Is it flagged up as a risk?

It is flagged up as a risk and an opportunity. It is a matter of having the best websites. We can get it right or wrong.

Once a year the risk register and, more importantly, an executive summary of the top 15 to 20 risks is passed to our strategic business committee, our board and our audit committee. They get an update on our risk management framework and all the evidence that our directors need in terms of our compliance with corporate governance requirements.

> **What Turnbull did internally was to 'sell' the message about the importance of formalized risk management.**

The major risks process is one of four or five planks of our internal control framework. Interestingly, prior to Turnbull we had a rather bureaucratic process in place for signing off high-level financial controls which was a requirement under Cadbury. When Turnbull fell into place, the major risks process replaced the bureaucratic financial controls process. What Turnbull did internally was to 'sell' the message about the importance of formalized risk management.

The art and the science of risk management. The science is tied up with the history of risk management which has its feet in the insurance world. There is a lot of risk management science in how insurance is priced. What we are trying to develop is a more scientific method of managing risk on a corporate basis. Efforts are being made to make it more scientific against a much broader range of risks rather than just insurable risks.

One of the keys to successful corporate risk management particularly is the art – and that is simply the ability to communicate risk management at a senior level. The board needs a balanced view of risk – not just financial risk and return on capital but operational risk, reputation risk, business continuity risk and so on – across the whole range both graphically and in words.

Complacency kills 30

By Allan Leighton, Chairman, *bhs*

I met Allan Leighton in the reception area of bhs, of which he is Chairman. No plush chairman's office, no ghostly calm meeting room. Allan has brought the ASDA style to bhs headquarters in London's Marylebone Road. Both organizations have armchairs and low tables for meetings in reception. And that goes for meetings right up to chairman level. He placed himself in a low armchair in a position where he could see everything that was going on in reception.

He was looking bronzed from a week in Sardinia; he told me that no alcohol had passed his lips while on holiday – and he felt much better for it. He raced through our meeting. Blasted through is a more accurate description. He'd had my questions a week in advance and fired the answers back like gunshot. Like all smart directors he doesn't use a thousand words where three will do. And he always calls a spade a spade.

He is best known for having been Chief Executive of ASDA and jointly responsible with Archie Norman (the then Chairman) for turning that 25p-a-share group round into a highly profitable, low-cost supermarket. Following ASDA's takeover by Wal-Mart for £6 billion, he was made President and Chief Executive Officer of Wal-Mart Europe. In 2000 he left to launch Going Plural, a vehicle to allow him to pursue directorships in a basket of companies that he fancied.

I asked him, how do you define 'business risk'?

My definition of 'business risk' is some activity you're prepared to take to propel the business forward with a pretty good chance of success. I don't think risk-taking should carry little chance of success. That would be stupid.

There's risk in everything – it's just to what degree. Half the risk is in the execution. Generally, the biggest risk is in the idea.

That's right. There are ideas people, but they may have only one good, commercial idea in 1,000. Then there are people who are more calculating, who focus their energies. Most of their ideas will succeed. It's a question of judgement, isn't it?

There are two important things in business: strategy and execution – 30 per cent is strategy and 70 per cent is execution. You can have a great strategy and lousy execution. Forget it! You can have not such a good strategy and good execution and it's probably slightly better. So if you run a business, you've got to run at the top and bottom of the pyramid. You've got to be absolutely, fundamentally focused and sound about the strategy. Absolutely down at grass roots level to make sure that it happens. That's the way that good leaders as opposed to good managers spend their time.

Is your strategy high, medium or low risk?

My style is probably high risk. But under my criteria I have always approached it as a calculated gamble. It's not an off-the-cuff gamble.

The most important thing is that businesses won't grow without taking risks. But you can really mitigate that risk. That's in the planning and the execution. And that's not always to do with time. It's to do with the quality of the planning and the quality of the execution.

> **" The most important thing is that businesses won't grow without taking risks. But you can really mitigate that risk.**

Exposure in all the organizations of which anyone's a director is to do with complacency. What kills business is complacency. Complacency is always the greatest exposure. That's why people get it wrong. What happens with complacency is, one, you get further away from the customer; the other is you get further away from your people. That is it. There are only two things in business.

How do you avoid complacency?

You have to stay very close to the customer and your people. The people who tell you it first are the customers…If you listen to the customer, you'll see if you are getting complacent or not. You've got to find ways of doing that.

What I insist on in all the businesses where I am chairman is, if anybody writes in to me, I want to see the letter and I want to sign it. You just have to find ways of always being close to the customer. It's very easy to do

It's rare.

> **" What good leaders do is they create very good middle management.**

It is. That's part of the problem. It's becoming more common. When I say I sign every single letter I mean every single customer complaint that lets down the business and is addressed to me, I sign. You have to put checks and balances in the business. What good leaders do is they create very good middle management.

When Leighton was Chief Executive at ASDA – a client of mine – I always got the impression that much of middle management were managing, not just working for the company. They were focused and working flat out to deliver. I remember the same restless energy at Shanks when they were a client. It stems from a management with vision. A management which inspires and empowers people.

Let the middle management handle the glue – because that's what they do. How do you get from the strategy to the execution? Well, it's managing all that glue. So if you get very good people, you don't have a problem about that. The problem is if you are not very careful, people spend all the time in that bit. Well, that's not it. Get good people. Let them manage the glue. You focus on the strategy – and then get out, whatever 'get out' means.

More importantly, when things change and you get feedback, make sure you adjust to it. There are lots of different ways you can do that. The most important is that you have to see that as being the most important thing. People don't.

You know, I see the most important thing in bhs is visiting the stores.

You met 156 bhs managers within four days of starting as chairman of the company?

I am going to do them again next month – 156 in three days! I see them all every three months. I take the plane and see them in groups of 20. I go to a store to see them. I just go on my own. I don't want anybody else.

What feedback do you get?

They tell you what's going right, what's going wrong, what morale's like. All sorts of things: whether a product's selling particularly well, if it's not; what the communication is; what are the issues they are finding; why is the turnover going up or going down? Then, you know, I probably go to half a dozen stores a week. When I'm in the stores I talk to staff, customers.

At Wilson Connolly Holdings, the house-building company where you are Deputy Chairman, you do the same?

Yes. I'll probably go to ten sites this week. I'll talk to the people. I'll try and talk to somebody who has moved into a house on that site. People say, 'Ah! God! It takes so long!' It does take a lot of time. But I'm not managing the middle bit. I'm not worried about the gubbings.

What about the personal risks that you take (financial, reputation)?

> **" Personal risks that you take are largely reputational because if you do many things then your reputation is on the line quite a lot.**

Personal risks that you take are largely reputational because if you do many things then your reputation is on the line quite a lot.

How do you decide which companies Going Plural advises?

My criterion for Going Plural was three-fold. One is I was only going to work with people I like. Two, I was only going to work in businesses that could grow because I think that that's the idea of business. Third, where there was some degree of innovation, invention or reinvention required in the business actually taking place. They're the things that turn me on.

To what extent do they want you for your body, ie a 'safe pair of hands' that will impress the City? And to what extent are you taking a hands-on role in managing the businesses and their risks?

I don't know whether it's a safe pair of hands! It's probably a useful pair of hands. The City is largely impressed by performance over a period of time. In terms of managing the business, it depends which business it is. If it's a business which I am chairman of, clearly I'm more hands-on than the businesses where I am just a non-exec director. But I try to be involved in whichever way I can. I prefer to be involved, not just someone who turns up for a meeting once a month. I'm not very good at that.

You already have quite a portfolio. I wonder if you are now an embryo management consulting company?

I don't think I am a management consultant company because I deal in execution as well as strategy and for me that's the big difference. Most consultants I know deal in strategy. They're not very good at execution. As far as what would happen if I took on so many responsibilities that I was employing people to deliver, well, if the business performs, that's the only thing that counts. That's the whole thing to me. It doesn't matter who delivers. If everybody in the business contributes, that's much better than any one person. It means there's longevity. There's something that will stand the test of time.

Some of the businesses I have equity, some I have an investment in, others just pay me a salary. I buy shares in a lot of the businesses that I am involved in as well. If I haven't got shares, it's largely because whenever I've wanted to buy it's not been the right time. It's not a question of the share price, it's because there's activity going on which doesn't allow that to happen.

What's your approach to growing the companies in a dynamic, fast-changing business environment?

My approach is always the same. You know, I've got a bit of knowledge now about how things can work.

How many years' experience have you got?

I've been in industry for 25 years. But I don't think about it like that. I think that's the danger. People think about knowledge in years. It's to do with experience.

> **People think about "knowledge in years. It's to do with experience."**

That's true. In one respect, I learned more in two years at Andersen than in the last I don't know how many years.

Yes. You can have a tremendous amount of knowledge and only having been doing something for two years. You can have absolutely no knowledge and have been doing it for 25 years.

Some people have loads of ideas but only one in 100 might be a good one. Others have 100 ideas and 95 are good ones.

Definitely. It's all about experiences, not experience. Which is why companies can be run by much younger managers than used to be the case.

> **Companies can be run by "much younger managers than used to be the case."**

And the big experience today is IT…

It is. It's a pseudo-science. A lot of companies have spent a lot of money in the past ten years on IT which has probably been a complete waste of time. The thing about IT is that it gives you the capability if you use it. Where most IT falls down is in a complete disconnect between the technology and the end user. So the only way to approach IT is it's got to improve the business in some way, shape or form – not as a smart new system we can buy off the shelf with lots of gizmos.

How do you assess the risks and opportunities presented by the 'New Economy'?

I don't think there is a 'New Economy' and 'Old Economy'. Basically businesses in the 'New Economy' have to be run in exactly the same way as businesses in the 'Old Economy'. Probably the experience is that where they haven't, it hasn't worked. Where they have, it begins to work. The thing that the 'New Economy' brings is this technology. It's the next generation of technology.

When I think about lastminute.com, this stuff is being invented as we speak. It's being developed by some very bright people in the business there and then. It's not something you buy off the shelf. You can't go and buy a piece of software to do some of this stuff. You have got to make it, invent it, design the thing, create the architecture for it. And then make it happen. This is technology at the bleeding edge.

> **" This is technology at the bleeding edge.**

If you're very, very good at it, you get it 80 per cent right. So that means you're going live with stuff which you know is not quite right. You've got to improve it on the run. It's been going in for 18 months. Some of it has to be written in days, some of it takes months, sometimes it's only when you get it live that you realize that the bit that you need to work on is this bit. Therefore you've got to go and invent something pretty quickly to get that bit to work. Or to give you the interface that you need. Or to speed it up or make it personalized. That's how fast it is.

I say to everybody that one year today is ten years. When you've done two years, you've got 20 years' of experience! That's the good thing and the bad thing about it. It's very quick! Sometimes you don't know if it's going to be all right or not. Until you try it you don't know.

How many times has the system at lastmin gone down?

This time round we've had a real focus on downtime and reduced it by half in the last quarter. It's not that it goes down. We've never lost it for more than two or three minutes. The problem may be it doesn't go as fast as we'd like. Or that piece of customization isn't there or that piece of the site doesn't work as well as it should.

Lastmin's a retail site. It's like a shop. If the shop's not open, no-one can shop in it. The first thing is you've got to get in. The second is you've got to shop it easily. The third thing is you've got a great product. You can have great products but if you're not easy to shop or you can't get in, you're not that great!

How do you address the fundamental management issue of where the business is going: yesterday, today and tomorrow? How far ahead can you predict?

I always try and keep at the very top line a three-year view of what the businesses are trying to do. There are three horizons of growth. You have years one, two, three and you are always updating years one, two, three. It doesn't have to be at detail level but at the vision and framework level. You just keep moving.

As a consultant I have always found that I learn mountains from clients as well as having the satisfaction of helping their people. How steep has your learning curve with the Going Plural portfolio been? What did you learn previously from the Wal-Mart experience?

I find exactly the same thing. I now know more about power, vacuum cleaners and so on. Business is always done in the same way. What is different is the environment – that's basically customers and people.

You are Non-Executive Deputy Chairman of Leeds Sporting plc. Do you believe that a football club needs to manage risk in the same way as a plc? How do you think it's managing its people risk and reputational risks right now?

Yes they do. The biggest risk there is in the stadium: things like safety which is fundamental. That's why a huge amount of money now goes into making it safe.

There is a potential that people get killed – as we have seen in the UK, the rest of the EU and West Africa. What makes it worse is that the average age of the spectator is low.

I would say not. It is probably in the mid-30s. The other big risk we have is our players, who can get serious injury. What has become very important in football clubs is getting the physios, doctors, consultants. The people who can get the players back on the park become very important.

> **The other big risk we have is our players, who can get serious injury.**

The British construction industry is extremely slow to adopt environmentally friendly building materials and renewable energy. In Amsterdam, in 1997, the local electricity utility ENW led a partnership with the construction company who built the New Sloten housing estate to install a roof of photo-voltaic modules, instead of conventional roof tiles and cladding. The system is connected to the electricity grid. The houses were sold to individual owners but the utility company runs and maintains the system, selling solar energy to householders and any surplus goes to the grid. This kind of thing isn't happening in the UK, is it?

In board meetings the whole energy and environment thing is a big deal. This triple bottom line idea which is about profitability, the community and your people is the way to think about it. If you don't protect the environment, that affects the bottom line eventually.

At Wilson Connolly Holdings, the house building company where you are Deputy Chairman, do you see scope for a 'greener' approach to construction?

On house building we are getting 'greener' by design. It's harder. The planning is more difficult. There's much more inner city than greenfield land. We use a lot of timber frame – probably half our construction will be timber frame. It's much more efficient. I think it's something people have been dragged screaming towards.

Unless you can take this 'greener' approach, it will just be harder and harder to build and get planning. The regulations are getting tougher and tougher and tougher. We've got a very good guy, John Weir. He goes round and looks at everywhere in the world looking for ideas.

> **Unless you can take this 'greener' approach, it will just be harder and harder to build and get planning.**

In 1999, you were appointed a Non-Executive Director of British Sky Broadcasting (BSkyB), who had launched the UK's first digital television service, Sky Digital, the previous year. This was a new departure in British TV. What do you bring to the party?

I don't know what I bring to Sky. I've been on the Sky board a long time now! I guess there are two or three of us who are not involved in the industry in some way or shape or form. First of all, I try and be very supportive of Tony Ball (Chief Executive and Managing Director). He's a first class CEO and he has done a fantastic job. We chat.

BSkyB is on track to return to profit by the end of 2001 after meeting revenue and subscriber targets. In the first quarter of 2001, the company reported a rise in annual pre-tax losses to £514.5 million from £262.7 million in the previous 12 months. The losses include the cost of providing the set-top boxes required by digital subscribers. But it reported a 21 per cent rise in digital satellite subscribers to a total of 5.5 million in the year to June 2001. In the third year of digital services there is no sign of a slowing down in subscriber growth. The churn rate, which measures the rate at which subscribers leave the service, was flat at 10 per cent. Operating profits, which exclude costs associated with the digital service, rose by 88 per cent to £160 million.
    Why did they want you?

I just try and think, back to customer, back to strategy. I try and be very supportive of the CEO. The other advantage is that, when I was on a board, I was a CEO. Those of us who are or were CEOs talk the same language.

You were recently appointed a director of George Weston. When I think of George Weston, I think of Wagon Wheels (the biscuit), one of the wealthiest companies, and some of the wealthiest directors around. George Weston has been run by the same family since 1882. It operates two distinct business segments – Food Processing, which encompasses fresh and frozen bakeries, biscuit and dairy operations, as well as fish processing; and Food Distribution, operated by Loblaw Companies Limited, the largest food distributor in Canada.
    In 2000 it had sales of $22 billion, exceeding 1999 sales by more than $1 billion. Net earnings per common share, including unusual items, net of tax, were $3.66, 37 per cent or 99 cents above the $2.67 earned in 1999. In 2001 Weston entered into an agreement to acquire Bestfoods Baking Company in the United States, from Unilever, at a price of US $1.765 billion or approximately C $2.7 billion in cash. That's quite a track record, isn't it?

Weston is just fantastic. Because of its scale in Canada it has to be very much of the community. It is a caring company. It is committed to creating value for its shareholders and to the belief that it should participate along with its more than 126,000 employees throughout its businesses in supporting the communities in which it operates.

Its support is shared across Canada and is directed mainly towards medical research, education, conservation and community projects. George Weston is one of many Canadian corporations that recognize and support the goals of the 'Imagine' caring company campaign. As a member of the 'Imagine' programme, George Weston commits to contributing a minimum of 1 per cent of pre-tax profits (cash and in-kind) to charitable organizations in Canada and encouraging employee volunteerism.

Then the Canadian Merit Scholarship Foundation, in partnership with the W. Garfield Weston Foundation and other supporters, grants scholarships to outstanding students entering university and community college who show promise of leadership and a strong commitment to service in the community.

I've known Galen (Weston, 60, and for 29 years Chairman of the Board) for a long time. I just thought it was the best supermarket business in the world. It has the best own-brand business in the world. I love going there. The great thing about having Scottish Power as a directorship too is that I still go out to the USA and to Canada. Over the years I was a hell of a lot in those markets. It's not just in retail that America is great. Sure, the own-brands, the freshness of the food at Westons…

Is it the quality of the goods?

Yes. And the packaging and just the thinking process. But generally, when I am out there, I go and look everywhere, every shop, everything I can look at. It's a great place for innovation.

> **I go and look everywhere, "every shop, everything I can look at.**

It's very different from Europe.

It's very different. They are nationalities where they are encouraged to try things.

Your track record is impressive in shaving operating costs to start restoring companies such as ASDA and bhs to profit. Your appointment to lastminute.com steadied City nerves for this reason alone. But there appear to be various non-financial risks there that are threatening survival: people risk; competitor risk; and credibility to name just three.

Lastminute is a fantastic business. The fact that they started it from scratch! It's a great brand name. I love the brands that do exactly what they say. 'In the can' as they say, and this one does.

Customers cannot buy by phone, can they? One of the things people dislike about internet shopping is that they can't get a more personal service.

We've tried voice recognition which will be the next big thing on a trial basis. People will be able to order on the phone.

A lot of people browse on the net but seal the deal, and most importantly the details of the deal, by phone or by enjoying the 'retail experience'. If you don't offer that facility, you are missing out?

Clearly the route for lastminute is to increase our points of distribution. At the moment you can only use the internet so you have to be at home or in the office. You will be able to use voice via 3G and Reality; then interactive TV will be a route for us. So you get the brand going, you get the product going and then you crunch your way through. You use the same database. The thing for us at lastminute is I've said that we'll get there. We'll be one of the few that do but it's tough.

> **We've spent the past 20 years getting some of the best managers in the world in England. But we've lost a few of the leaders...**

People give me a load of stick about it. But for me the riches are in the learning. I've learned so much in a relatively short period of time. I think the other thing is that it just demonstrates what I've always believed, that we've spent the past 20 years getting some of the best managers in the world in England. But we've lost a few of the leaders...

Leaders?

Yes. There are not so many leaders. Lots of good managers but not that many good leaders.

Entrepreneurs?

No. They don't have to be entrepreneurs...

People managers?

No. What I mean is...leaders do the right things. Managers do things right. Doing the right things as opposed to doing things right.

There's a lot of gut feeling, instinct in good management...

There's quite a lot of instinct in it but it is this 'this is the right thing to do'. And then managers go and do it the right way. I think what the internet has spawned for the country, we won't really see the benefit for another five or ten years. At a very early age it has given lots of people lots of experiences in which they have acquired great leadership skills. You couldn't create a university to do that. In a strange way that's what we did.

What's the difference between lastmin when you joined and lastmin now?

One thing we've always done is hit all the numbers. Cash burn has probably gone down 35 to 40 per cent. A bit's probably come out of the costs. It's not to do with me. They are just outstanding. And not just Martha and Brent, it's a group of people there. They just needed a bit of air cover. I take the flak. Plus I've been in retail a long time. I gave them a bit of experience.

That's what I meant by 'credibility'. There was incredible envy that a couple of guys straight out of university were suddenly worth millions. They lost goodwill. It was straight envy. There is also this feeling, rightly or wrongly, that they are taking their cut. They are not offering the lowest deal.

I hope they succeed. They deserve it.

You're also a non-executive director of Dyson, Scottish Power and Consignia.

James Dyson is just a creative genius! He's a pleasure to work with.

ScottishPower is managing its growth risk by transforming itself. The group supplies energy to millions of business and domestic customers across the UK and the western United States, with combined sales of £6.5 billion. ScottishPower's ten-year record since privatization has included significant organic growth. It owns ManWeb, the Merseyside, Cheshire and north and mid-Wales electricity distribution and supply company; Southern Water; ScottishTelecom, offering internet and interactive services, data and telecommunication services, and call centre services. In the USA it owns PacifiCorp, the electricity supply company for Oregon, Utah, Wyoming, Washington, Idaho and California which has one of the most extensive transmission systems in the USA, and serves electricity customers in the Australian states of Victoria, New South Wales and Queensland.

It was judged the UK's top utility in an annual survey of environmental performance. It promotes energy efficiency to help businesses and to fight fuel poverty, enabling disadvantaged customers to benefit from the competitive energy market.

It is one of Europe's biggest windfarmer developers. It is managing environmental risks through measures at conventional power stations, such as the introduction of clean coal technology, and investment in new gas-fired generation. This will help meet our targets on emissions.

Local businesses can now plug in to green energy generated in Wales with the launch of Welsh Green Source. This is the first time wind energy has been directed specifically at the Welsh business community. More than 2,000 sites operated by the nine public sector member organizations of North Wales Energy Partnership (NWEP – an energy-buying group) will now have a large proportion of their electricity supply matched to small-scale hydro, on-shore wind sources of generation and landfill gas.

Consignia changed its corporate name from the Post Office in 2001. It aims to be a big player in the global distribution market. It now offers e-commerce fulfilment, billing and customer management, as well as logistics and warehousing. ParcelForce Worldwide is hugely important. We now have agreement with 11 major financial bodies enabling us to provide universal banking services at Post Office branches.

bhs is in a sector needing some retail therapy itself! Again, the company has impressively cut the costs of sales and simplified the supply chain. Tell me more. And how will you address stuff like:

- *decline in the retail sector;*

- *the need to modernize brand;*

- *the risk of misreading 'lifestyle' aspirations;*

- *M&A risk: growth in competition from French, Spanish, German and American retailers;*

- *risks inherent in overseas expansion, which have slashed profits of Body Shop, Laura Ashley, Sock Shop, Sainsbury, M&S?*

bhs needs a bit of retail therapy. Retail sales in the UK are not declining. They are probably the best they have been in years at the moment. There are always casualties.

Do you not think that brands today have a limited life? New brands such as Gap emerge and steal sales from those that are 30 or 50 years old.

They are not so hot. Gap have had four profit warnings on the trot! Actually it is very interesting that bhs and M&S are institutions. This whole thing about brands...I mean. I don't think there are many 'brands'. Okay. There are lots of things that people advertise. You can get the two things confused. To me a brand has been around for at least 10 or 15 years. It has proved its staying power over that time. bhs is a real brand. M&S is a brand. Woolworth is a brand. It's like where people know the name.

> **The Mars brothers told me years ago – and I've never forgotten it – that brands don't die. People kill brands. That's what happens.**

You know, if you look after brands and keep improving them then they can go on for ever. The Mars brothers told me years ago – and I've never forgotten it – that brands don't die. People kill brands. That's what happens.

What tends to happen is that somebody comes along and changes something and it doesn't work. When a brand has been around for 10, 15, 20 years, it stands for something. I remember a guy who told me years ago, 'If you see a dip in performance, just ask: what's changed?'

Because there's always something that's changed. If something changes it doesn't just suddenly go.

Not just how has the product or service changed but also what's the new competition? Something is bound to have changed there.

Yeaaagh. But generally it's not to do with competition. It's to do with an implosion, not an explosion.

Coke sales are going down. People in the west are into natural drinks without additives or preservatives. No marketing people foresaw the exponential rise in fruit juices and bottled water. Coke and catering firms like Bass are now selling juice and purified water.

It depends how you look at it. Coke have always said, it depends how much fluid you can drink. The aim is everybody drinks it with their breakfast. In the USA they do! I think the modernity thing becomes important. You have to keep brands current and modern. That doesn't mean you have to change them drastically. The same values rule.

What's the difference?

Modernity means this 'touch of the tiller' stuff. You adjust. The Mars bar had been going for a long time so they made a Mars ice cream. Tasted just like a Mars bar, looked like a Mars bar, shape of a Mars bar but it was an enhancement of that product.

bhs is a great brand, very high recognition, huge customer base, long footage. Very badly managed for ten years. The Big Idea of this business is bhs. We have to target 40- to 50-year-old housewives. We are now selling products that appeal to them at the right price and we are selling lots of products. When we weren't selling products to 40- to 50-year-old housewives we didn't sell very much. That's where we are very focused. It's a great brand! That's why it's been around for 80 years. It's very simple. Know your customer. Get the right products. Keep improving!

> **Know your customer. Get the right products. Keep improving!**

Do you?

Absolutely! Every single way. Every single day!

Analysis ■

There are two things lastminute could do to boost sales. The first is, they have all this original experience in setting up an e-commerce site, they could sell that experience to other companies on a consultancy basis. Second, there is clearly resistance to them as young upstarts turned instant millionaires. Coupled with a sneaking suspicion that they are taking their 'cut' from great last-minute deals. They can overcome this by adopting the John Lewis strategy of 'Never knowingly undersold'. If they guarantee a partial refund if anyone finds a better deal elsewhere, people will not need to search elsewhere. The business goes to lastminute. Margins may fall, but the greater volume of business may more than compensate. Worth a try!

Some of Allan's potted wisdom from his website.

It's tough to tell what will jell.

He who listens well, hears well.

Effective change is not something you do to people – it's something you do with people.

Never believe your own hype – or what the press say about you.

Listen to the river.

Always search for the jewel in the toad's head.

Confidence is driven by a will and a rhythm.

A leader is a dealer in hope.

Lead customers to where they want to go…but don't yet know it.

Don't just do something – sit there!

Virtual music **31**

By Sir Peter Michael,
Chairman and founder of *Classic FM*
and Adam Turner, Managing Director, *VMS*

I pitch up to Virtual Music Stores' offices just off London's Regent Street. I'm early. Sir Peter Michael, the founder of Classic FM, the world's first commercial classical music station, has not yet arrived. Having lunch in Newbury. No matter. We know each other well.

I start playing with a 6-ft high blue machine that looks like a New Economy version of a 1950s juke box. This is his latest venture. 'You make your own CD,' says the receptionist. 'Can I make one while I wait?' I ask. 'Of course.' She gives me a quick run-through. You sort of scroll through using various options, such as artist, find the track you want, and put it into your virtual shopping basket. I look for Tina Turner and Maxim Vengerov but can't find them.

(I later learn that VMS, which started only in the summer of 2000, has not yet signed up all the music labels. And the whole system is still being trialed. There are some tracks that I won't find. 'Pamela's right,' says Sir Peter later. 'We need to tell customers what they won't find on the system, not just what's there.' There's a risk customers will get frustrated otherwise, I point out.)

I find that my mind goes blank. I can't think of all the music tracks that I'd like to have on my very own CD. I land up with a mixture of Enigma Variations, The Chieftains, Toni Braxton's The Art of Love and Dionne Warwick walking on by into my virtual shopping basket. By this time a secretary is telling me that Sir Peter has arrived. To her astonishment, I tell her, 'hang on a minute,' because I can't drag myself away from the machine.

I go upstairs and Peter introduces me to VMS Managing Director Adam Turner. Grey hair, matching grey shirt, 30-something. Turner was formerly Managing Director of Music and Events at EMAP Performance, the music titles and radio stations. He ran the commercial side of Kiss. He's been in music, advertising and media – at EMI and Sony Music in marketing and management.

The place has a buzz about it. The guys are all young enough to know what yoof culture wants. But experienced enough to have held senior positions in mainstream music.

I ask Adam about the Virtual Music technology and how the trials are going.

We use our own patented audio compression (AC) technology with simultaneous decryption/encryption which was originally developed by Ricky Adar. His background is in fibre optics and satellite transmission research. In 1992 he founded CCL, now fully owned by VMS. He developed an effective AC format, probably initially based on MP3, but re-designed and rebuilt. What he had the foresight to do was encode it; make it secure.

It is the first 3D digital distribution system and 3D internet audio player. Spray technology enables recording at maximum speed. Artificial intelligence includes accidental key press and phonetic-based algorithm searches. The sound is up to the Red Book standard for manufactured CDs.

A 40-minute album could be recorded in three minutes. Because it is a digital system, it can access any music which it has licensed. As well as CDs it can record on to minidisks, Sony's memory stick system or WAP phones. Customers can access CD-Roms, DVDs and video games. Retailers no longer have to carry the full range in-store. Customers do their own mixing.

We are now building relationships with music companies to license their music and with retailers to put the machines for making CDs in their stores. The Nexus server records every transaction including tracks, CDs, time, place and price. With licensing information held on our database, it provides full royalties accounting to record company and music publisher.

It's been called a nickel and dime business: every time the music is sold everybody gets a nickel – the writer, the artist, the publisher, the retailer…Now what we're introducing is a technology system which also has unique intellectual properties involved in the distribution of it. Increasingly, the way our world is going is about legal permissions to conduct that process. We have managed a lot of that risk.

This is a highly specialized enterprise – with all sorts of operational, intellectual property, commercial and people risks. How did you put your team together?

The guys are all experienced: half in technology, half in music. They are knowledgeable on the copyright, retail and marketing aspects. Technology and music are totally different! They manage risk in totally different ways.

"" This is a highly specialized enterprise – with all sorts of operational, intellectual property, commercial and people risks.

Technology people manage risk through discipline, procedure, debugging, process, etc. Music people manage by being wily, by deal-making, gut feel, thinking on their feet. This living by the seat of your pants does not sit well with technical people. Trying to create a culture which is accountable to the music people but a little bit more risk-taking for the technology people is challenging.

Andrew Bruce, Operations Director, helped develop NCR's cash point machines. Clive Leonard, Technology Director, is another 'leading edge' player, having worked for IBM, Sony Broadcast and in digital TV and interactive services.

Michael Rowlands, our Commercial Director, was General Manager of Rondor Music and Managing Director of Hit and Run Music responsible for administering the music publishing catalogues of Genesis, Phil Collins and Peter Gabriel.

Randall Harper, our Director, Finance and Corporate Affairs, was Head of Business Affairs with EMI in Australia. In private law practice he represented and advised EMI, BMG, Polygram, Sony, Warner Bros Pictures and Walt Disney.

GWR, another major shareholder, of which Peter is a director, is represented on the board by Roger Lewis, an Executive Director of ING and former Managing Director at EMI and President of the Decca record company. There are no free-loaders.

It is founded on the intellectual capital of its directors. The music industry today offers a phenomenal choice of music. This represents a huge risk to the retail market-place: they have to choose which stock they buy. They started focusing more and more on chart material. So if you want something else you have to go to a megastore.

This is why, when I go to the biggest music store, I don't always find what I'm looking for?

Right. Because it's also a very fickle item, sometimes with a short shelf life, it is difficult for them to choose what to stock, what range to carry. If they get it wrong, it goes back as a return to the record company and they put it into a landfill site. It's a huge waste which goes straight to the bottom line.

When the internet was born, the record companies thought they could use the digital format. They wouldn't have to make CDs. They could release direct to people's homes. Then they hit this wall of risk: MP3 and Napster came on the scene. Suddenly they could not control their copyright. The whole global industry was at risk!

> **It's a huge waste which goes straight to the bottom line.**

What we have that is different is the technology to compress music and to offer music companies the opportunity they need. We are a solution that has a lot of security at its core. You compress the product that travels down the telephone line. You can send it round the world, and to every corner of the world, in microseconds.

This is a big opportunity. But unless you can move with it or have an attitude that feels secure with moving with things that fast, all you see is the tail end which is the risk. You are always trying to follow up and keep up behind it. You see nothing but the risk. Actually the opportunity is steaming up front. You have to get up in front of it. You have to celebrate change. Change is what it's all about.

If you want to generate the levels of growth we are aiming at in a very short time you have to be focused.

There are three routes. One, you grow organically, which is a slow process because the world communicates so fast. That puts you at a disadvantage in allowing a lot of people to come up behind you and copy what you're doing. So that's not really an option. Second, you can do it all yourself like Amazon but you need a different culture – the ability and finance to develop distribution centres. My view is that people will come unstuck doing things that are not their skill set. They stretch themselves too thin, and come up against competition. If you want to expand really quickly you secure your core competency, what you're best at. You lock that down and control that. All the non-core functions, you put out to partners. If you manage to protect what is unique to you, you will have a robust, flexible company of relatively few people working virtually. It will make you resilient to change.

> " " **If you want to generate the levels of growth we are aiming at in a very short time you have to be focused.**

We can adapt our model to any territory: if they sell a lot of pop in Germany, we can make it a very pop-dominant partnership. If in Italy, it's going to be an opera thing, we will adjust your model to fit. Other things, such as the manufacturing, will be consistent globally which may require a strategic global partnership.

Business is all about trying to find a position to stop and put down roots: have stability, plateaux of profit. This is what the financial sector expects. They want five years of steady growth. They don't want five years of steady growth and then a complete upheaval and then another period of steady growth – even though that is the reality of what actually happens.

I'm sure if you were to say to a chief executive in any business, 'Okay, do you want five years of steady growth and then turn your business on its head and then go back to another five years of steady growth?' I'm sure they would say, 'Oh no. I don't want that.' In reality that's what happens.

You have to manage the culture in your organization and resist all the demands for security and stability and all that. Accept that the faster technology gets, the more you have to create an environment and a culture that gets used to change, that is comfortable with change.

What is key is that, while I can tell you about the opportunity and show it's all full of risks, if I was to identify the half dozen most risky things in my business, you'd see all the usual things like raising cash and securing content deals and winning over record companies that are reticent because they are worried about Napster, right up among them you would see – trying to manage a team of people that are highly experienced and therefore not very young.

I'm the youngest at 38; they go up to 57. Experienced people are difficult to manage because they are set in their ways. How do you manage experience which in reality is baggage? When you start a new project you start all over again. When you take people out of secure environments and put them in high-risk environments, that exposure becomes a lot more acute unless you train that out. I'm not talking about the cream. I'm talking about the mass of middle management who turn over economies and all the rest of it.

It's all about culture. It's nothing to do with your company or opportunity. It's down to personal need. To effect change. Most people like to live in the comfort zone. If you are growing a company you have to accept that your comfort zone is your risk zone. You're constantly working at risk. Instead of working in the comfort zone, then risk and perhaps a very rare period of panic, you learn to work in the risk zone. When things are comfortable I start worrying that I am missing something. My comfort zone, by definition, becomes the risk zone. I need that sense that I am being hit with problems that I am resolving and containing. You need to pace yourself, have a rhythm. It's like a long-distance race.

> **Your comfort zone is your risk zone.**

What's your strategy?

You have to be clear on vision: what your opportunities are.

What are your vision and opportunities?

My vision is to provide this market solution. To understand my customer, the retailers. The advantage we are giving them is that they do not have to hold the stock. With VMS the stock is 'held' in a virtual environment until one of their customers wants it. Ultimately my customer is the consumer. I need to be very customer-focused. That's not typical of technology companies. They tend to be technology focused.

The team must understand that their technology isn't important unless it provides a consumer experience. Our culture has shifted. It's no longer job satisfaction. It's target achievement satisfaction. Achieving goals and objectives. We all have to share those objectives. It's about managing culture. We have to agree targets. It may not be what everybody round the table would like themselves but we have to have consensus on the overall goal.

It's about honesty. It's about accepting that work is not just something you do and then you go and have lunch. Work is your life as much as anything else. You have to be transparent if you are going to survive the personal exposure: the ability to change, take feedback and all the things that are really important. These are all things I have done before.

If you go to somebody who is pure technology and invention, you're not really going to get their heart if you set them performance targets. You identify those targets in a way that's relevant to them. We don't have any job specs. They are out the window. If you need me to tell you what to do, you're in the wrong place. We have personal job agreements. We say, because we're different we are going to fight a lot and so we have to acknowledge that from the beginning. You celebrate the differences. They make the vision twice as big. You have to build in form and process to dissipate that negative energy. You negotiate who's doing what. That way, nobody undermines anyone else.

This is like Ricardo Semler's 'natural business' approach, explained in his book Maverick. *This was basically: power to the workers and who needs rules? The standard policy of Semco, the company he inherited, was no policy. They picked the best from many systems. From capitalism, personal freedom, individualism and competition. From socialism, to control greed and share information and power. From the Japanese, flexibility.*

> **People perform well because they feel good about themselves. Things have got to buzz.**

It's my personal approach. I am a bit of a hippy. You've got to get something out of life. People perform well because they feel good about themselves. You have to make money. You have to find that thing that makes them all buzz. Things have got to buzz.

I would measure performance targets against a whole range of criteria, some of which would be shared goals and profitability of the company. If you accept that culture is essential, communication is essential, people development is essential to achieve change. If you accept that those are as critical as designing and manufacturing the product to so many pence, then you reward people for those skills too. So you say, 'Your bonus is based on profitability but I will also reward you for winning and keeping three critical middle managers and we'll agree that between ourselves.' But we write it down. When you're into these 'softer' KPIs, you have to ensure that they're not soft. And you get appraised by the people who work for you.

What happens if they score badly? Do they get sacked?

No. That was not the criteria against which that performance target was set. But it would affect their bonus or whatever the criteria was. It stops someone thinking they are always right and everyone else is wrong.

Does VMS have competitors?

We did but I think we're the only ones who have made the technology work and be commercially viable. Market risk is critical. The high street retail environment is very hard at the moment. There's no point in going to the marketplace unless you have something that is going to scale out. Retailers are not interested in trials for the sake of it. They don't want to be sexy. They want turnover. The public's fickleness in demand for entertainment products is challenging. They have to keep rebranding, repositioning, updating, restocking. It is a short shelf-life, margin-sensitive environment. Promotional discounting has become a daily part of stock management.

One media company is interested in doing something similar but they haven't got a system that works and they would only sell their own catalogue. There may be competition from the digital TV world.

Then there's Liquid Audio who did not own a format so they couldn't distribute music. I think they had to license a format from Dolby. So they were always beholden to Dolby and Dolby's agenda. Whenever you don't own the proprietary technology, that adds risk. We have the technology. Sony owns more of the 'food chain'. They will be a serious competitor or partner for us in the future.

What you offer is a product people mix themselves then play in their homes or their cars?

Yes. By the summer of 2001 we had trials going at various HMV stores in London's Oxford Street, Covent Garden; in Newbury, Reading and Bracknell; and at Sainsburys in Bagshott.

The machines could go in hotels or leisure centres?

Eventually they could go into airports, motorway service stations, hospital waiting areas, anywhere where people are hanging out and likely to buy music for themselves or as a gift.

Our research shows that the high street retail experience will continue to dominate sales for at least another ten years. After that, people will still want 'hard' copies to play in their cars. But, according to a record industry executive, 'The high street will have to be as compelling as PCs.'

Are you aiming at the British market or the world market?

The world market. This is the way we manage the risk. We've looked at all the internet companies trying to do world-wide deals. They are trying to do copyright deals when there is no world-wide copyright standard. You can't get a one-size-fits-all agreement. They haven't been able to commercialize it. Apart from those who have done it illegally, nobody has managed it. Our approach is to go to the territory where we want to start and know the contractual and copyright obligations and do deals in line with local copyright law. We'll get the content because our system's secure. We're biting it off territory-by-territory.

Will you manufacture the kiosks or buy them in?

Manufacturing cost will be a big financial risk. We will spec up our own equipment so if push comes to shove we can manufacture ourselves. Because we are not manufacturers, it's risky for us to do that. But it would add 40 or 50 per cent on to our financial risk. If I can find something of value I can trade with a manufacturing company, something of strategic value to them, ie our technology, that will reduce our costs.

Sony, Hewlett-Packard, Compaq, Xerox, ICL are all possible manufacturing partners. Another possible strategic partner may be a database organization such as Oracle because there will be huge data storage capacity needs. Nobody else in the world has resolved this problem. There is going to be a huge commercial advantage to somebody to own the technology to devise and manufacture this system.

It's not in our business plan to be into data storage. So if we create the initial marketplace, that would be a benefit for a data storage company. What we want back is for someone to help us reduce the costs of these mega-databases.

So do we have what they want? We understand customers, content, value, copyright, the emotional needs of artists. Maybe our new technology patents. For example, we have the only compression audio format that has instantaneous compression/decompression. Many people can do compression technology. It is how well you can do it. We were the first to do encrypted, compressed music files; the first to do media players with a level of encryption; the first to devise a server to drive this process.

> **Many people can do compression technology. It is how well you can do it.**

Normally that process takes a long time. You have to take the encryption jacket off it, change from digital to analogue, from analogue to wave file, to record it. Our system does that instantaneously so that you are only limited by the hardware capability. So a 40-minute album takes three and a half minutes to record. That's about six times quicker than any other system. There's something which has widespread potential application: for example for audio players in computers. It would be valuable for someone to have, say, a two-year window where they get first rights to exploit that technology.

We're talking in mid-2001 and you're still in the middle of trials but when do you think you will be profitable?

Perhaps at the end of 2002 or 2003.

Sir Peter Michael has been popping in and out during our conversation. He now takes over:

Pamela, I don't know how you're seeing this business. First of all you have the big five music companies, although they are trying to make it four. The second group are the retailers. They say, 'Ah! Is this friendly to us?' Well, I think they like the idea of a new digital delivery system. But the risk is that you land up with something like the train station where you have half a dozen unused ticket machines because most people prefer to queue up to buy tickets.

The key to making that a virtuous circle is the marketing. There are a number of different aspects. The first is, how do you market this to the retailer? More important, how do you market it to the consumer in the street? In our case, we have chosen the perfect medium for marketing the whole concept of VMS: music radio. Capital FM in London and my personal connections with GWR. The role of radio stations is to tell the consumer what is happening and where they can find the music in the high street.

Binding those three fundamental requirements together is the technology. That technology has to address all of those. Starting out three years ago, one could see that there was going to be a need to – chicken and egg – get the music companies interested, get the retailers interested, get the radio companies interested and develop the technology. It was a challenge.

> **This is a very interesting, "high-risk venture. This could be a £1 billion company.**

It has taken us quite a lot of time, quite a lot of money to get to where we have got to and we still have some way to go. We now can see how to resolve all the different bits and pieces.

To pull this together we needed a unique group of people and the vision of someone that believed that this is possible. There are very few people who have interests in all the parts of the jigsaw. It so happens that I'm one of them.

This is a very interesting, high-risk venture with, potentially, in the future, very high returns. This could be a £1 billion company. It could easily become much more.

You could lose money?

We could. It's unlikely.

How much have you invested?

We're probably looking at about £10 million over three and a half years.

The dinosaur companies (in New Economy terms) are looking for strategic alliances.

I'm sensitive about that. What they would do is challenge our opportunity

Peter, I noted your use of the word 'challenge'. You don't make life easy for yourself, do you? I remember your telling me, a few years ago, that there were several projects you had your eye on but you plumped for Classic FM because it was the most challenging – to make money out of classical radio!

You need a bit of agro to keep yourself going, probably! We have plenty of agro on our latest venture, VMS.

Certainly one makes estimates of what the chances are of trying to do something which is difficult. The outcome isn't always going to be as you predicted. As far as I'm concerned, I like doing things that are very, very intriguing. I love the whole challenge of it.

If there is an intellectual challenge involved in it then it comes down to the people. Time and time again you can have a wonderful idea but you have the wrong people. Then it won't work.

Some executives say they like risk-taking. But they have researched and measured the risks in such fine detail that they have almost designed risk out.

I'd like to think that it was calculated. It is very, very difficult to get that right. Financial risk is paramount. Also how long it is going to take. It normally takes three times as long as you think it will. Once you commit to something, you have to be prepared to have deep pockets. What that means is that, in making an investment, pretty roughly you need to think in terms of putting in one third at the start; and have a balance of two thirds left for later.

This is venturing, adventuring! The venturing community up until about 1990 didn't do terribly well. They didn't do what I have just suggested. They allocated funds and then, when the company, to their surprise, came back and said, 'We need some more,' they didn't have any capacity left to do that. So a huge number of good ideas went down the drain because there wasn't sufficient money to take them through difficulties which they had not anticipated up front. Since then venture capital has been a quite different business.

How do you calculate risk?

As far as I am concerned, there are a number of formal tools that you can use to attempt to work out what is going to be the risk. But the reality of it as far as my personal situation is concerned is that it is gut feel.

> **There are tools that you can use to work out the risk. But the reality is that it is gut feel.**

You have to be able to take some sort of view of it from, maybe, what is experience. I am old enough now to have succeeded and failed lots of times. From those inbuilt lessons, the blood that has been spilled, the lashes across my back, I hope that I can make an assessment of the chances of getting through the main hurdles. They are very often completely different from the hurdles you think they are at the beginning.

A current situation is that everything is going into silicon, integrated circuits, the microchip. The design is, first of all, done theoretically, on paper, mathematically. Then it's transferred into a series of many, many patterns that are etched into the microelectronic circuit and then eventually down the track, that goes to a silicon foundry. That silicon foundry produces a piece of silicon which is then connected and encapsulated. Then it will or will not function.

In the things that I am currently involved in there are maybe six different companies out there, each of which is working on some sort of silicon chip design which is quite unique. It may vary – anything from a telecommunications chip, networking chip, digital radio chip, very high-speed, high-powered computer chip, and so on. I don't think I know at the moment any way in which I can estimate the chances of success of that – looking from the beginning end of the telescope. But what I can do is to say that we have a portfolio of those and, if half of them fail, provided the other half are successful, it won't matter.

Some of them do fail. They fail because the first design of the chip doesn't work so they decide to give it another re-spin. That puts nine months into the cycle and by then it is too late because the market has moved on or the company has run out of money or whatever it may be.

Adam: It's not just about your endeavours. You can work as hard as you possibly can. You can be the best in the business and still fail. You have to be big enough to take that on. It's almost like we're on a Ferris wheel. It's not just about being the best. It's about trying to stay at the top of that wheel for the longest possible time. Luck and timing are as much part of it as anything. When you look at successful companies, you never see the also-rans – only the winners.

I guess that to be successful repeatedly, not at my level, clearly, but at Sir Peter's level, you have to have that sense of perspective. You've got to have that sense that, okay, you've got to sometimes take it on the chin. There's a proverb about how success is not about never falling down. It's about being able to get up again. To be successful, sometimes you have to have been knocked down.

> **To be successful, "**
> **sometimes you have to**
> **have been knocked down.**

It's past seven o'clock in the evening when I leave – but some of the guys are sitting around waiting for a meeting with Adam. They've finished off the process of making my CD for me. It's just like a normal CD except it has VMS on the front of the case. On the back it lists the tracks I've chosen, their playing time and the artist(s). Nowhere else will you find Dionne Warwick and Elgar on the same CD! 'We'll try and make sure Tina Turner is on the machine next time you try it!' says one of the guys – which I think is pretty neat since I'd never seen him before!

I get home with the CD which my 19-year-old picks up a few days later. 'Hey Mum! Did you make this CD?' he asks. 'I didn't think you were into that sort of thing!'

Analysis

Upside risks

It is difficult to assess this business from the risk management point of view because, at the time of writing, it was not yet seriously trading. But, with Sir Peter Michael at the helm, I reckon it stands a good chance. Success will depend on how successful management is at signing up the music companies so that it can offer the widest range of music, interviews and promotional materials.

Looking at the upside, the secure compression technology with simultaneous decryption/encryption potentially has a much wider application than in the VMS kiosks. VMS therefore has a potentially marketable intellectual property quite apart from its audio kiosk products. This could help defray the R&D costs of the start-up business. An alliance or contractual agreement with a mega-partner may have other advantages in terms of growing the company. This side may even come to dominate the company's balance sheet. If it remains independent, this could be a very different-looking media company in five years' time.

The concept is infinitely adaptable. From retail music stores, it would be rolled out to any retail or leisure environment including internet cafes, hotels, hospitals, prisons, etc.

The 'super-juke box' format could make it a prestige must-have for wealthy individuals, particularly those with their own recording studio.

Apart from the fundamental financial and survival risks, the downside risks are as follows:

Product risk

This is a major risk which needs to be managed. There are many risks here because the concept is new and untried. They include:

- The manufacturers fail to meet their delivery deadlines and VMS fails to supply its music retail customers as agreed.
- The equipment is not robust enough for 24x7 use and abuse.
- The equipment breaks down in the shops so retailers cannot rely on it.
- The system is not completely up to date with all new music issues.
- Customers become disaffected for various reasons including inability to find what they want on the system.
- Production of the discs is subject to supply-chain delays.

Analysis ■

Commercial risks

- The major risk is that the major music companies do not sign up.

- The sales message is strong but VMS management need to win over store managers as well as retail bosses.

Footnote: After our meeting I discovered that one of the VMS kiosks had been out of operation. I relayed the news to Adam and he informed me that, 'The systems are fine, however we are having a running battle between the store manager who was not properly consulted by head office and who does not support the system. He keeps switching them off. We go in everyday to switch them back on, he turns them off again...solution – we are moving them to another store.

'We have learned from that experience that however many assurances a head office gives you, you still need local buy-in so we will adapt accordingly before we scale up.

'The systems now have 99 per cent reliability; further experience will get it even better. The answer then is to test. First behind closed doors, but there comes a point when you have to expose your product to the scrutiny of the customer. The more money and time you have, the more you can do behind closed doors, so you do increase your risk in your early years.

'Yes, we will one day sell it to home users and probably give it away free. The interface can be loaded on to a CD-Rom and put on the front of a magazine and then loaded into your set-top box for your TV or PC. Alternatively, when we are all broadband enabled, we can squirt it down the line to people. They will need a CD recorder, currently widely available for around £80.'

If record retailers are smart, they will use the VMS experience to turn their stores into the musical equivalent of an internet café – a place where people spend a lot of time.

It shows that the unexpected always happens! Classic risk management theory!

If you look at high cap risks you invariably find that the cause is subcontractor failure (BP fire at Grangemouth in Scotland, aluminium in water turning people's hair blue in Cornwall). This may be the result of low-quality management; absence of quality management systems; poor training; corner-cutting, etc. Supervision of suppliers is therefore essential to managing the risk.

Failure to engage in dialogue (one-to-one or run workshops where staff and suppliers can learn and raise problems) is also a false economy. Perhaps the manager fears a slump in sales of traditional CDs. Perhaps he is on a bonus related to this? Is he on a bonus for what he sells through VMS? If so you'll have the same trouble with all store

Analysis

managers. I know the managers at a retail client of mine are only interested in one thing – total sales at the end of the week.

Everyone is on performance-related (as a component of pay) these days. Perhaps VMS will operate their own performance-related bonus for store managers.

Update: As this book went to press we learned from managing director Adam Turner that: 'VMS have fully signed EMI/Virgin, Beggers Banquet and Mushroom among others. Things are moving forward on all fronts'.

In 2010, according to John Kennedy, CEO of UMG, the world music business will be worth $75 billion:

- $40 billion through shops, 50 per cent of which will be kiosks, and 50 per cent through manufactured product (CDs and DVDs).

- $25 billion via labels' direct dealings with music fans, 50 per cent in the form of CDs and 50 per cent as downloads.

- $10 billion from public-performance licensing and sources of revenue that do not yet exist.

Seven easy steps to making your own VMS CD:

1 Select track from the CBR format music library at the VMS kiosk.

2 Listen to 30 seconds of the track (music, interview, promotional video).

3 Put it in your virtual shopping basket.

4 Repeat for other tracks required up to 74 minutes.

5 Arrange running order for tracks chosen.

6 Hit record button to create personal CD.

7 After three minutes, collect and pay.

Sir Peter Michael

Sir Peter Michael's guiding hand and experience in the electronic and media business shines through. Peter has founded and run a number of well known technology companies over the past 30 years.

He founded Micro Consultants in 1967 to market high-tech electronics for avionics, computing and medicine, and created the first digital devices for drawing television graphics by computer. In the 1970s he set up Quantel whose Paintbox was one of several commercial applications his company introduced in its 20 years of operation. He went public by merging the company with United Engineering Industries, owners of Cosworth Engineering, which he sold in 1989, merging with Carlton Communications in a £500 million deal.

In 1989 he stepped in as CEO of Cray Electronics and turned the company round from a £45 million loss to a profit of £30 million by 1992.

> **The intelligent but irreverent style rapidly took off with 8 million listeners, Classic FM has become the largest commercial FM station in the world.**

In 1993 he invested £2 million in Classic FM, which he later merged with Great Western Radio. This was the first national commercial radio station in the UK with a potential audience of 50 million listeners. With a lifetime love of classical music, he nurtured the idea of developing a popular format that used classical pieces as entertainment rather than worship. The intelligent but irreverent style rapidly took off and, with 8 million listeners, Classic FM has become the largest commercial FM station in the world. In March 1995, with Sony as a partner, Classic FM US began broadcasting in several locations in the USA.

Bibliography

Books

Bill Gates, *Business @ the Speed of Thought*, Warner Books, 1999

John Harvey-Jones, *Making it Happen – Reflections on Leadership*, Collins, 1988

Mark H. McCormack, *What You'll Never Learn on the Internet*, HarperBusiness, 2000

Allan and Barbara Pease, *Why Men Don't Listen & Women Can't Read Maps*, Pease Training International, 1998

Michael Porter, *The Competitive Advantage of Nations*

Ricardo Semler, *Maverick*, Tableturn Inc, 1993

Other publications

Basel Committee on Banking Supervision, *Principles for the Management of Credit Risk*, September 2000; and other papers on interest rate risk (1997), operational risk (1998) and liquidity risk (2000)

ECOSOC Opinion, *Employment, Economic Reform and Social Cohesion – Towards a Europe of Innovation and Knowledge* (CES 244/000 E/o, March 2000)

Federal Reserve Bank of New York Reserve's March 2001 Economic Policy Review Volume 7, Number 1, *The Challenges of Risk Management in Diversified Financial Companies* by Christine M. Cumming and Beverly J. Hirtle

National Energy Policy – Report of the National Energy Policy Development Group, May 2001, US Government Printing Office. Internet: bookstore.gpo.gov

The President's 2001 US Energy Blueprint – What Does it Mean for the Utility Industry? PA Consulting Group, 25 May 2001

Proposed 'Green Screen' Approach for National Wildlife Federation Equity Investments: Goals, Methodology and Implementation, Report to the NWF Board of Directors Finance Committee, 18 January 1999